PICTURE BOOK OF LIVING CREATURES
(...OR APPEARING CHARACTERS)

TATSUMI

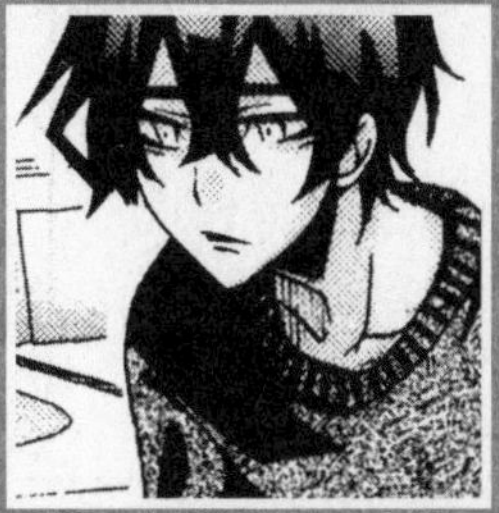

The owner of the house. High school boy. He's good at cooking and household chores.

KASUMI

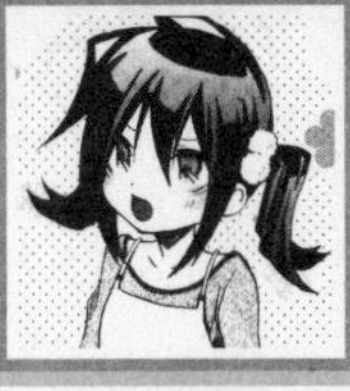

Tatsumi's little sister. Loves her big brother very much. Her rival is Wakasa.

UNCLE HISATORA

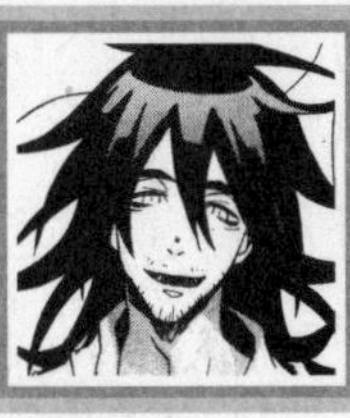

Tatsumi's uncle. He develops suspicious medicines and has Tatsumi test them out.

SOUSUKE

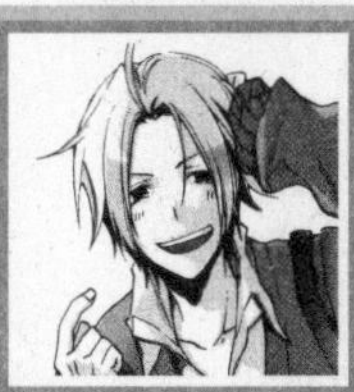

Tatsumi's friend. He has two older sisters.

MAKI

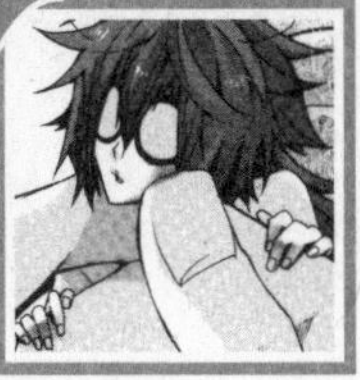

A snail that appears quietly at the bath. Super nearsighted and has a negative personality.

WAKASA

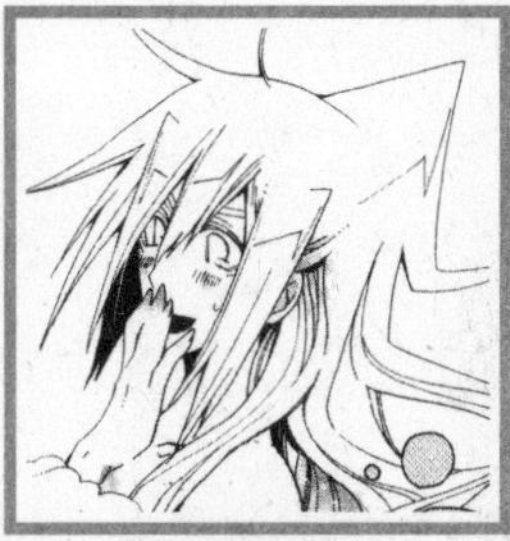

The freeloading fish of Tatsumi's house. His age... don't ask.

MIKUNI

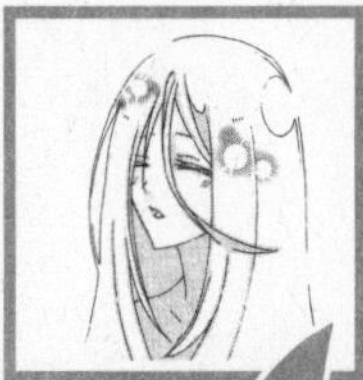

A jellyfish that wanders into the bath. His body is ninety-nine percent water. He loves A*uarius.

TAKASU

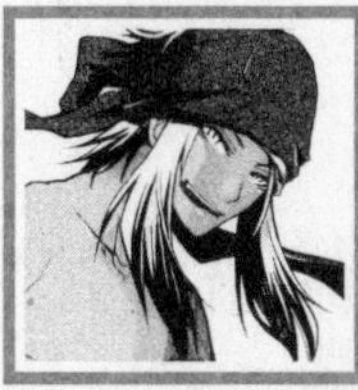

An octopus that sometimes appears in the bath. Seems to be long-time friends with Wakasa. He's good at massages.

AGARI

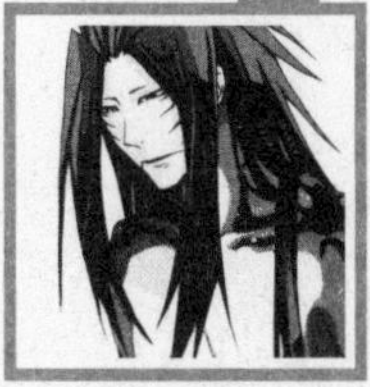

A shark that suddenly appears in the bath. It seems he is Wakasa's senpai.

GOROMARU

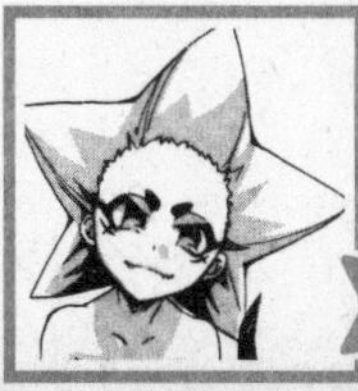

A starfish that appears in the house and often goes unnoticed. He is skilled at clinging.

ECHIZEN

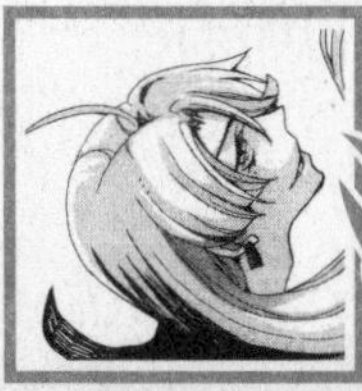

A super-sadistic crab that suddenly appeared. He is trying to take Wakasa back to the water.

SEVEN SEAS ENTERTAINMENT PRESENTS

Merman in My Tub.

story and art by ITOKICHI   volume 7

TRANSLATION
Angela Liu

ADAPTATION
T Campbell

LETTERING
Laura Heo

LOGO DESIGN
Meaghan Tucker

COVER DESIGN
Nicky Lim

PROOFREADER
Danielle King
Cae Hawksmoor

EDITOR
Jenn Grunigen

PRODUCTION ASSISTANT
CK Russell

PRODUCTION MANAGER
Lissa Pattillo

EDITOR-IN-CHIEF
Adam Arnold

PUBLISHER
Jason DeAngelis

MERMAN IN MY TUB VOL. 7
© Itokichi 2017
First published in Japan in 2017 by KADOKAWA CORPORATION, Tokyo.
English translation rights reserved by Seven Seas Entertainment, LLC.
under the license from KADOKAWA CORPORATION, Tokyo.

Seven Seas books may be purchased in bulk for promotional, educational, or
business use. Please contact your local bookseller or the Macmillan Corporate
and Premium Sales Department at 1-800-221-7945, extension 5442, or by
e-mail at MacmillanSpecialMarkets@macmillan.com.

ISBN: 978-1-626925-02-1

Printed in Canada

First Printing: May 2018

10 9 8 7 6 5 4 3 2 1

FOLLOW US ONLINE: *www.sevenseasentertainment.com*

READING DIRECTIONS

This book reads from *right to left*, Japanese style.
If this is your first time reading manga, you start
reading from the top right panel on each page and
take it from there. If you get lost, just follow the
numbered diagram here. It may seem backwards at
first, but you'll get the hang of it! Have fun!!

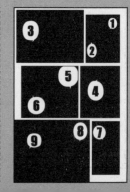

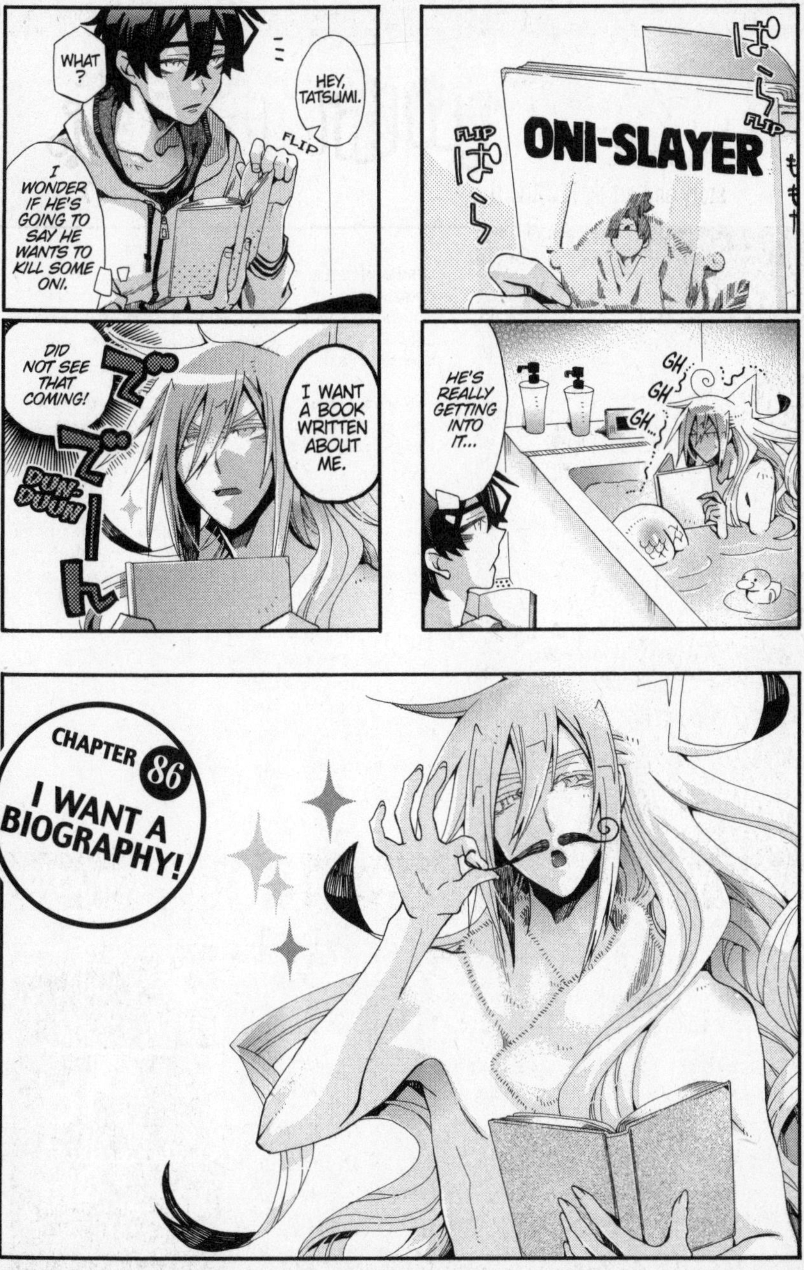
ぱら
FLIP
ONI-SLAYER
FLIP
ぱら
HEY, TATSUMI.
FLIP
WHAT?
I WONDER IF HE'S GOING TO SAY HE WANTS TO KILL SOME ONI.
GH GH GH...
HE'S REALLY GETTING INTO IT...
I WANT A BOOK WRITTEN ABOUT ME.
DID NOT SEE THAT COMING!
どどーん
DUN-DUUN
CHAPTER 86
I WANT A BIOGRAPHY!

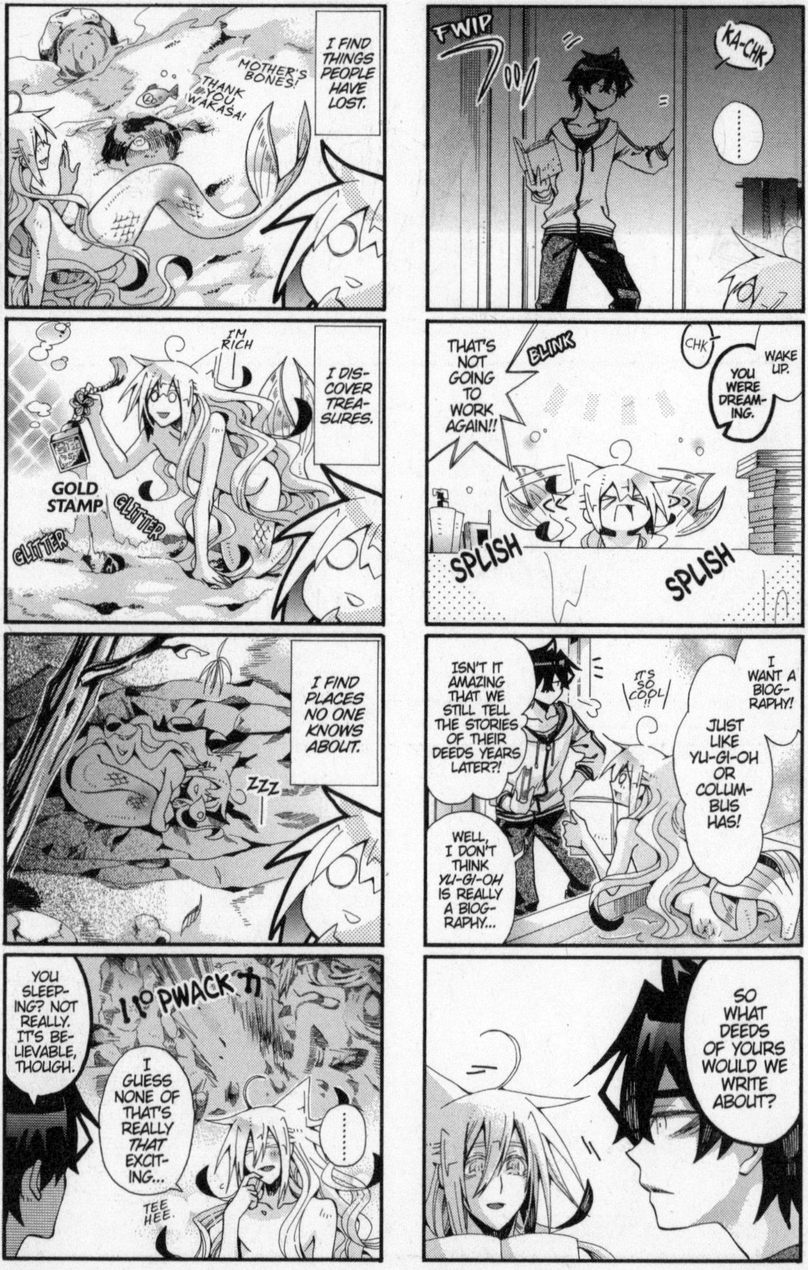
FWIP
KA-CHK
......
CHK
WAKE UP.
YOU WERE DREAMING.
BLINK
THAT'S NOT GOING TO WORK AGAIN!!
SPLISH
SPLISH
I WANT A BIOGRAPHY!
JUST LIKE YU-GI-OH OR COLUMBUS HAS!
IT'S SO COOL!!
ISN'T IT AMAZING THAT WE STILL TELL THE STORIES OF THEIR DEEDS YEARS LATER?!
WELL, I DON'T THINK *YU-GI-OH* IS REALLY A BIOGRAPHY...
SO WHAT DEEDS OF YOURS WOULD WE WRITE ABOUT?
I FIND THINGS PEOPLE HAVE LOST.
MOTHER'S BONES!
THANK YOU, WAKASA!
I DISCOVER TREASURES.
I'M RICH
GOLD STAMP
GLITTER
GLITTER
I FIND PLACES NO ONE KNOWS ABOUT.
ZZZ
PWACK
......
I GUESS NONE OF THAT'S REALLY *THAT* EXCITING...
TEE HEE.
YOU SLEEPING? NOT REALLY. IT'S BELIEVABLE, THOUGH.

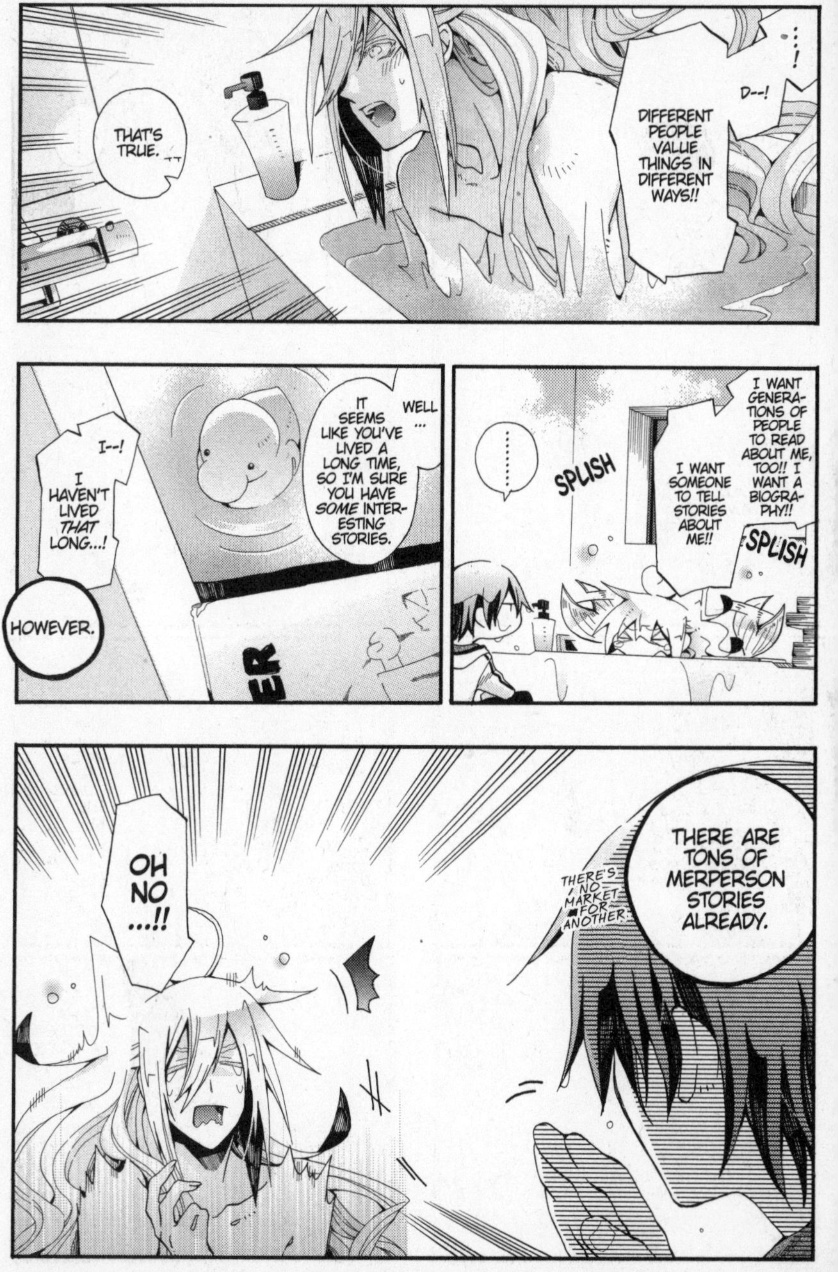
...!
D--!
DIFFERENT PEOPLE VALUE THINGS IN DIFFERENT WAYS!!
THAT'S TRUE.
I WANT GENERATIONS OF PEOPLE TO READ ABOUT ME, TOO!! I WANT A BIOGRAPHY!!
I WANT SOMEONE TO TELL STORIES ABOUT ME!!
SPLISH
SPLISH
......
WELL ...
IT SEEMS LIKE YOU'VE LIVED A LONG TIME, SO I'M SURE YOU HAVE *SOME* INTERESTING STORIES.
I--!
I HAVEN'T LIVED *THAT* LONG...!
HOWEVER.
THERE ARE TONS OF MERPERSON STORIES ALREADY.
THERE'S NO MARKET FOR ANOTHER.
OH NO ...!!

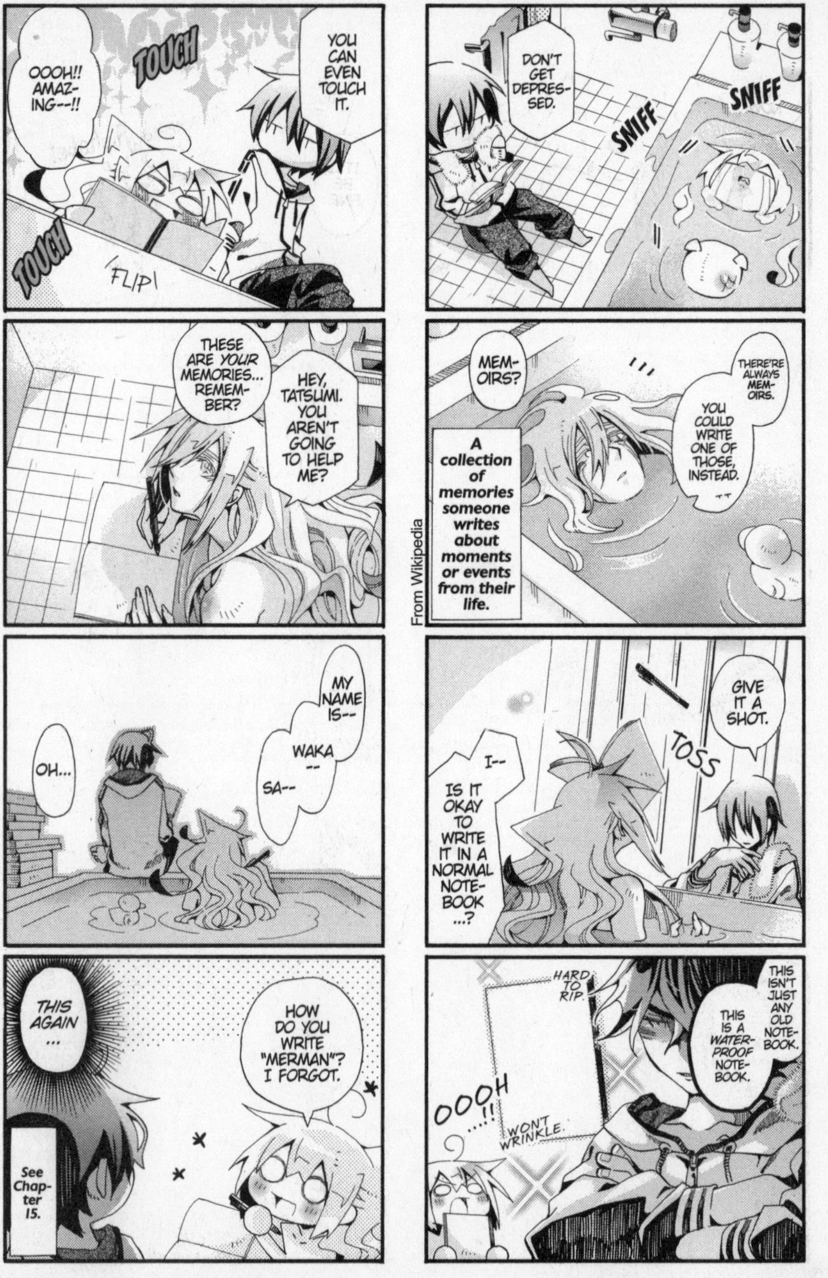
DON'T GET DEPRES-SED.
SNIFF
SNIFF
THERE'RE ALWAYS MEM-OIRS.
YOU COULD WRITE ONE OF THOSE, INSTEAD.
MEM-OIRS?
A collection of memories someone writes about moments or events from their life.
From Wikipedia
GIVE IT A SHOT.
TOSS
I--
IS IT OKAY TO WRITE IT IN A NORMAL NOTE-BOOK ...?
THIS ISN'T JUST ANY OLD NOTE-BOOK.
THIS IS A WATER-PROOF NOTE-BOOK.
HARD TO RIP.
OOOH ...!!
WON'T WRINKLE.
YOU CAN EVEN TOUCH IT.
TOUCH
OOOH!! AMAZ-ING--!!
TOUCH
FLIP
HEY, TATSUMI. YOU AREN'T GOING TO HELP ME?
THESE ARE YOUR MEMORIES... REMEM-BER?
MY NAME IS--
WAKA --
SA--
OH...
HOW DO YOU WRITE "MERMAN"? I FORGOT.
THIS AGAIN ...
See Chapter 15.

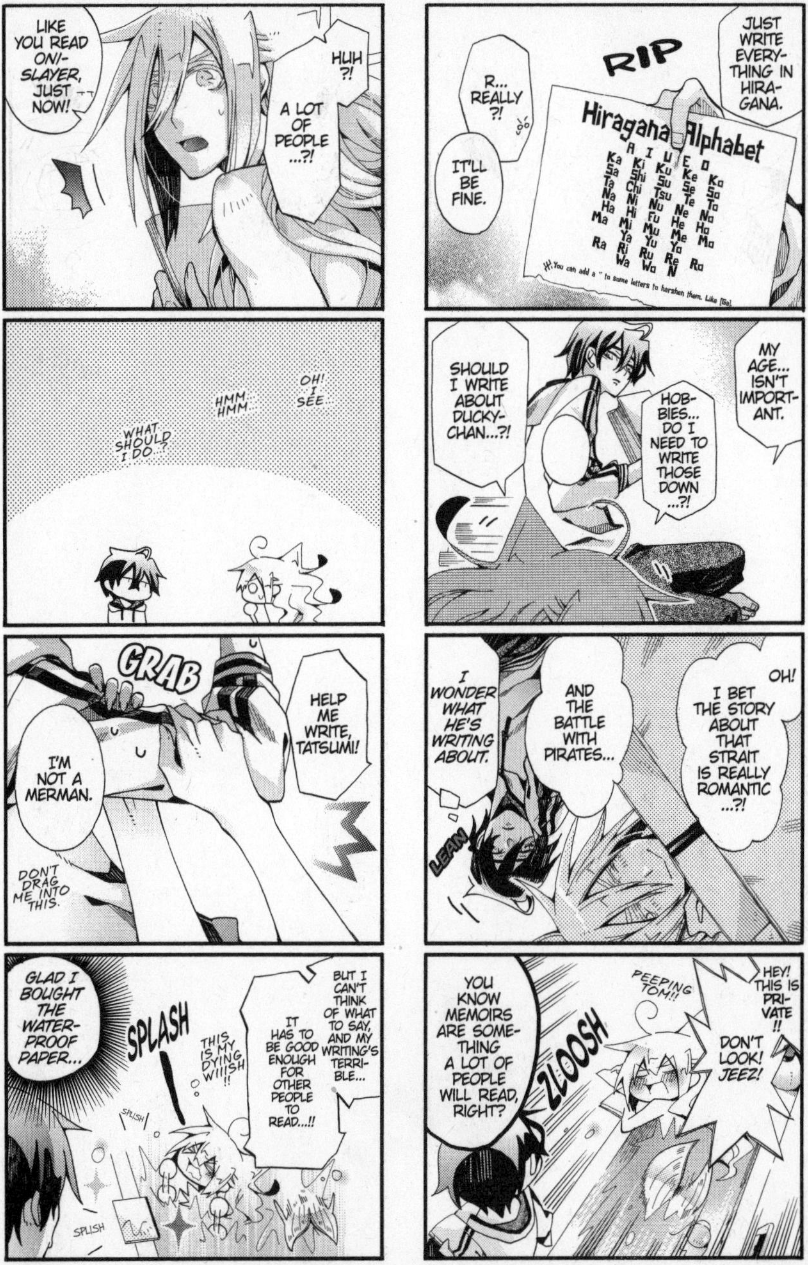
JUST WRITE EVERYTHING IN HIRAGANA.
RIP
Hiragana Alphabet
A I U E O
Ka Ki Ku Ke Ko
Sa Shi Su Se So
Ta Chi Tsu Te To
Na Ni Nu Ne No
Ha Hi Fu He Ho
Ma Mi Mu Me Mo
Ya Yu Yo
Ra Ri Ru Re Ro
Wa Wo N
You can add a " to some letters to harshen them. Like [Ga].
R... REALLY ?!
IT'LL BE FINE.
HUH ?!
A LOT OF PEOPLE ...?!
LIKE YOU READ ONI-SLAYER, JUST NOW!
MY AGE... ISN'T IMPORTANT.
HOBBIES... DO I NEED TO WRITE THOSE DOWN ...?!
SHOULD I WRITE ABOUT DUCKY-CHAN...?!
OH! I SEE...
HMM HMM...
WHAT SHOULD I DO...?
OH!
I BET THE STORY ABOUT THAT STRAIT IS REALLY ROMANTIC ...?!
AND THE BATTLE WITH PIRATES...
I WONDER WHAT HE'S WRITING ABOUT.
LEAN
HELP ME WRITE, TATSUMI!
GRAB
I'M NOT A MERMAN.
DON'T DRAG ME INTO THIS.
HEY! THIS IS PRIVATE !!
DON'T LOOK! JEEZ!
PEEPING TOM!!
YOU KNOW MEMOIRS ARE SOMETHING A LOT OF PEOPLE WILL READ, RIGHT?
ZLOOSH
BUT I CAN'T THINK OF WHAT TO SAY, AND MY WRITING'S TERRIBLE...
IT HAS TO BE GOOD ENOUGH FOR OTHER PEOPLE TO READ...!!
THIS IS MY DYING WIIISH !!
SPLASH
GLAD I BOUGHT THE WATERPROOF PAPER...
SPLISH
SPLISH

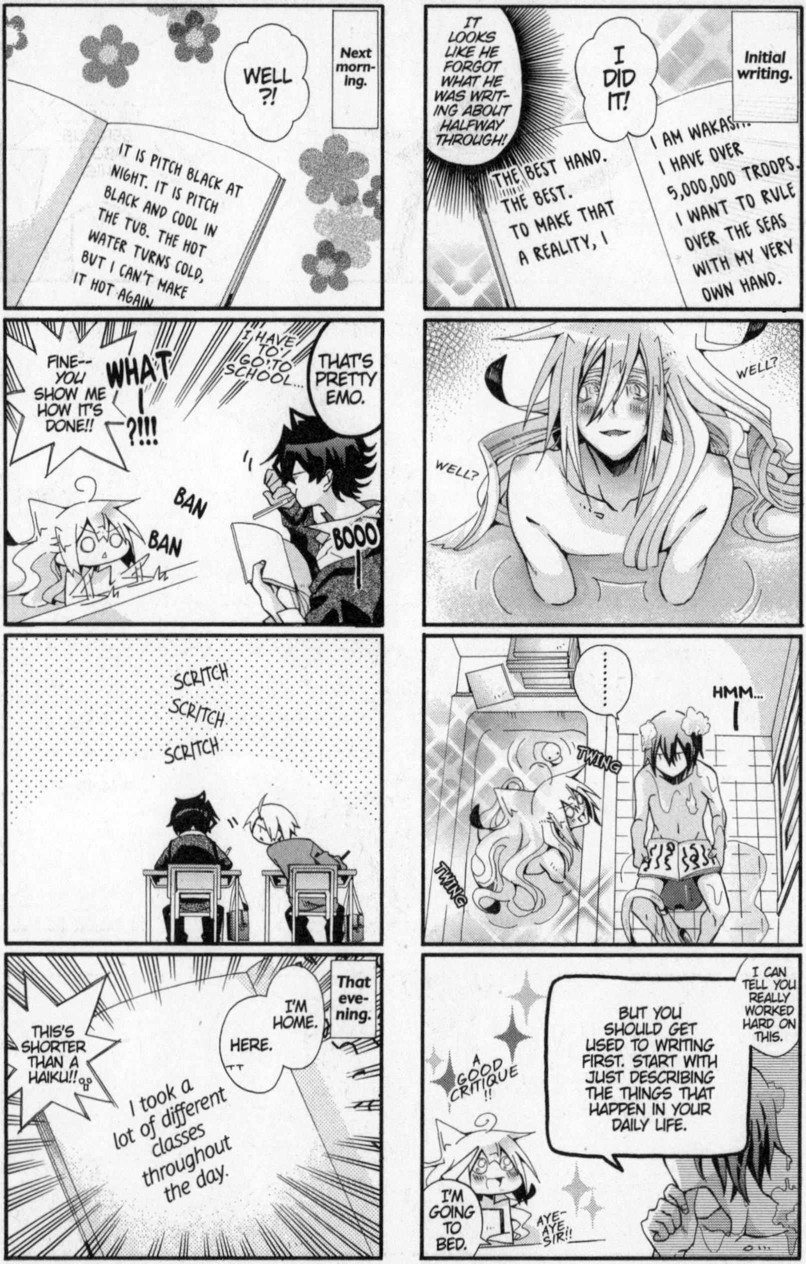

Initial writing.
I DID IT!
IT LOOKS LIKE HE FORGOT WHAT HE WAS WRITING ABOUT HALFWAY THROUGH!
I AM WAKASH... I HAVE OVER 5,000,000 TROOPS. I WANT TO RULE OVER THE SEAS WITH MY VERY OWN HAND.
THE BEST HAND. THE BEST. TO MAKE THAT A REALITY, I
Next morning.
WELL ?!
IT IS PITCH BLACK AT NIGHT. IT IS PITCH BLACK AND COOL IN THE TUB. THE HOT WATER TURNS COLD, BUT I CAN'T MAKE IT HOT AGAIN.
WELL?
WELL?
THAT'S PRETTY EMO.
I HAVE TO GO TO SCHOOL...
WHAT I ?!!!
FINE-- YOU SHOW ME HOW IT'S DONE!!
BAN
BAN
BOOO
HMM... I
......
TWING
TWING
SCRITCH
SCRITCH
SCRITCH
I CAN TELL YOU REALLY WORKED HARD ON THIS.
BUT YOU SHOULD GET USED TO WRITING FIRST. START WITH JUST DESCRIBING THE THINGS THAT HAPPEN IN YOUR DAILY LIFE.
A GOOD CRITIQUE!!
AYE-AYE, SIR!!
I'M GOING TO BED.
That evening.
I'M HOME.
HERE.
THIS'S SHORTER THAN A HAIKU!!
I took a lot of different classes throughout the day.

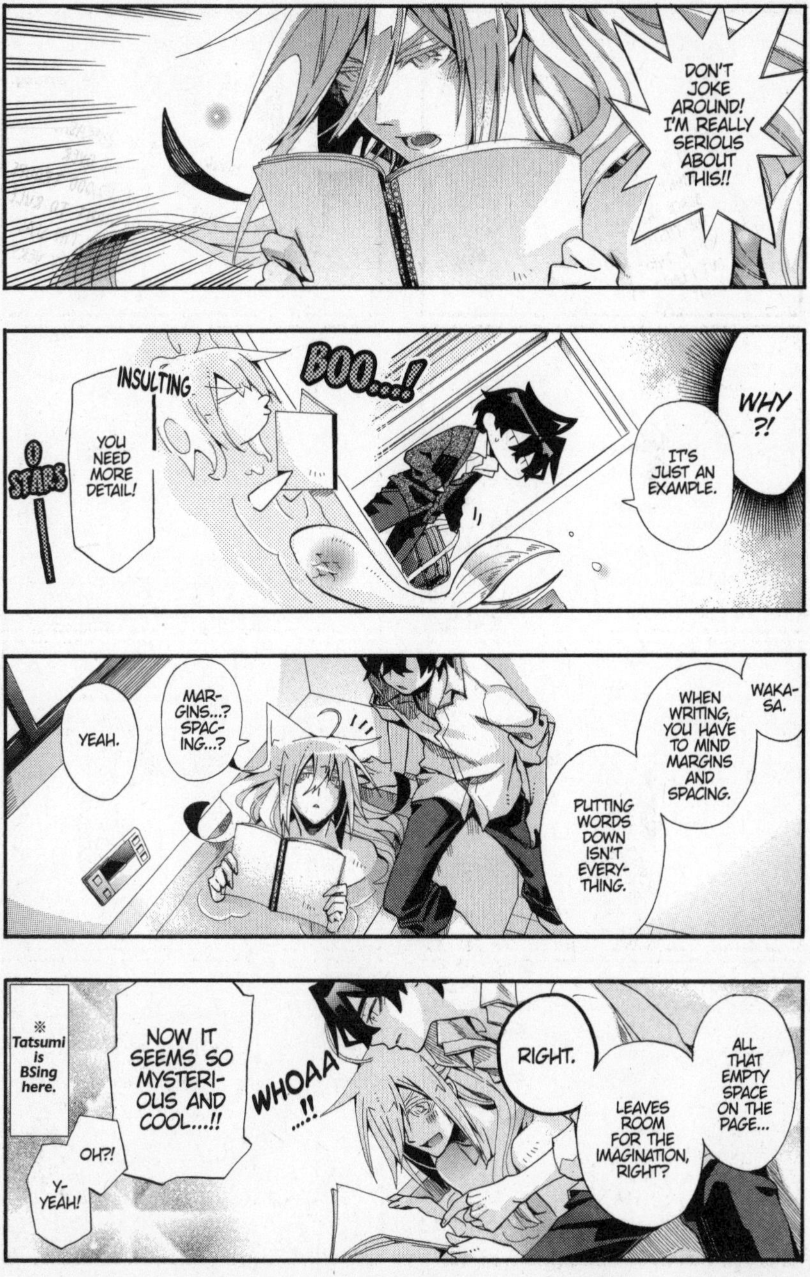
DON'T JOKE AROUND! I'M REALLY SERIOUS ABOUT THIS!!
WHY ?!
IT'S JUST AN EXAMPLE.
BOO...!
INSULTING
YOU NEED MORE DETAIL!
0 STARS
WAKA-SA.
WHEN WRITING, YOU HAVE TO MIND MARGINS AND SPACING.
PUTTING WORDS DOWN ISN'T EVERY-THING.
MAR-GINS...? SPAC-ING...?
YEAH.
ALL THAT EMPTY SPACE ON THE PAGE...
LEAVES ROOM FOR THE IMAGINATION, RIGHT?
RIGHT.
WHOAA...!!
NOW IT SEEMS SO MYSTERI-OUS AND COOL...!!
OH?!
Y-YEAH!
※ Tatsumi is BSing here.

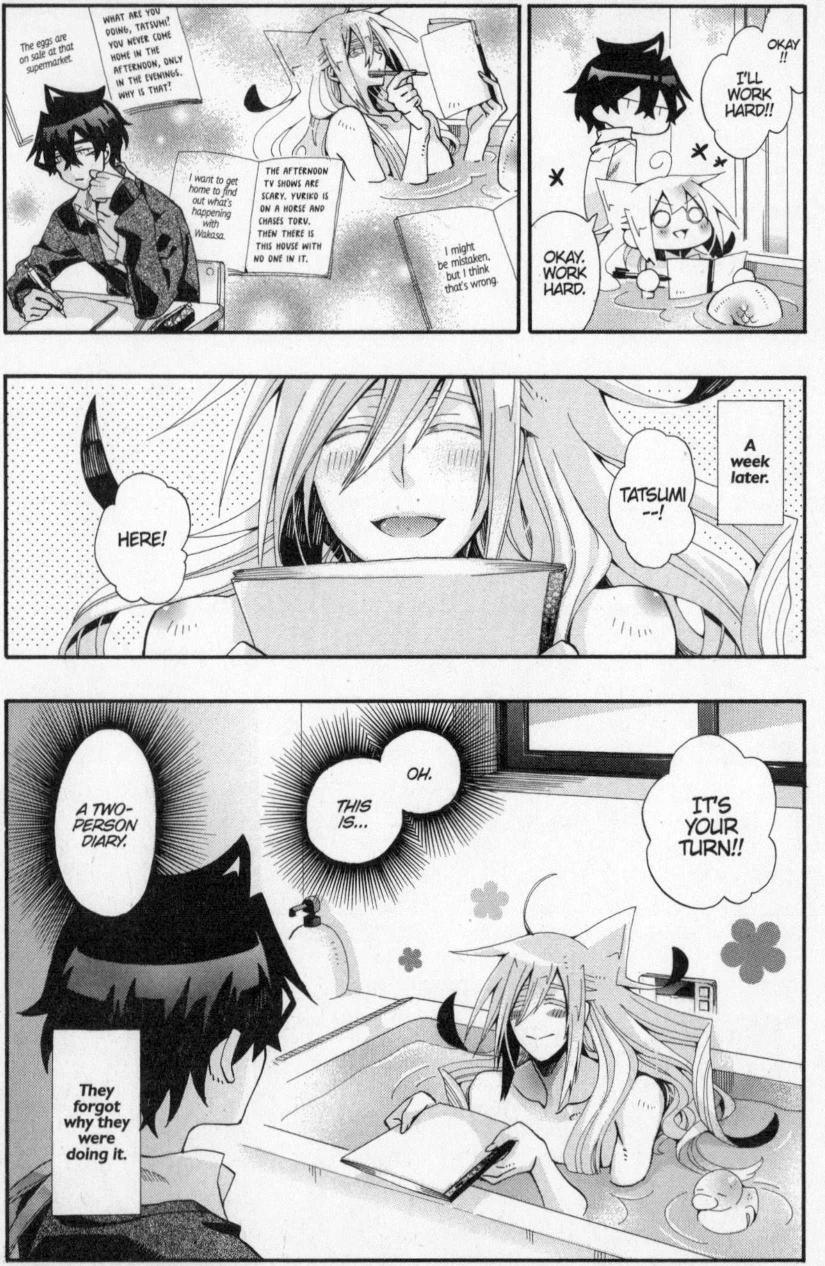
OKAY!!
I'LL WORK HARD!!
OKAY. WORK HARD.
WHAT ARE YOU DOING, TATSUMI? YOU NEVER COME HOME IN THE AFTERNOON, ONLY IN THE EVENINGS. WHY IS THAT?
The eggs are on sale at that supermarket.
THE AFTERNOON TV SHOWS ARE SCARY. YURIKO IS ON A HORSE AND CHASES TORU. THEN THERE IS THIS HOUSE WITH NO ONE IN IT.
I want to get home to find out what's happening with Wakasa.
I might be mistaken, but I think that's wrong.
A week later.
TATSUMI--!
HERE!
IT'S YOUR TURN!!
OH.
THIS IS...
A TWO-PERSON DIARY.
They forgot why they were doing it.

Merman in My Tub

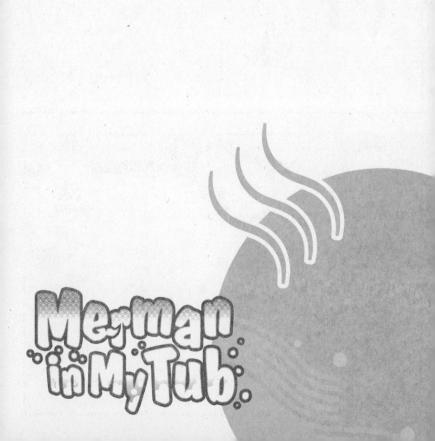

オレん家のフロ事情

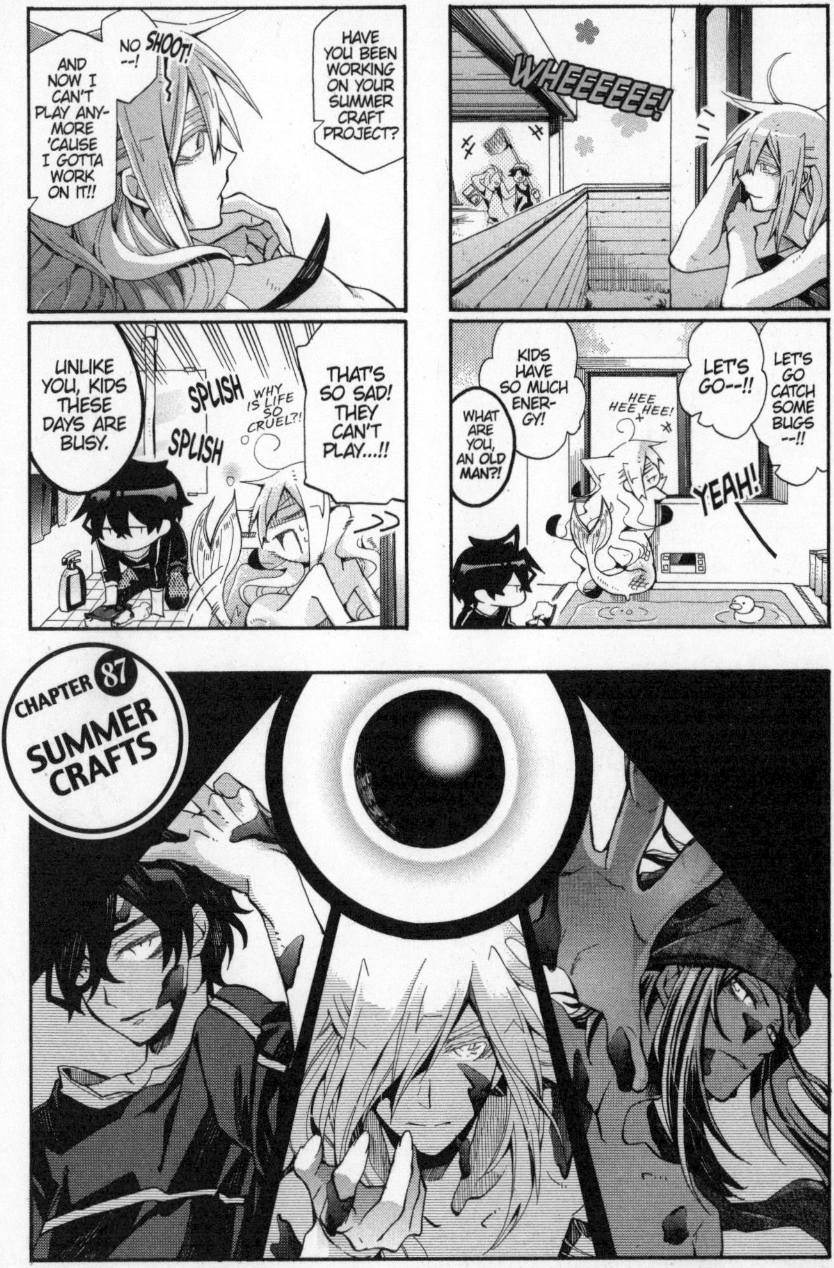
WHEEEEEEE!
HAVE YOU BEEN WORKING ON YOUR SUMMER CRAFT PROJECT?
SHOOT!
NO --!
AND NOW I CAN'T PLAY ANYMORE 'CAUSE I GOTTA WORK ON IT!!
LET'S GO CATCH SOME BUGS --!!
LET'S GO--!!
YEAH!
KIDS HAVE SO MUCH ENERGY!
HEE HEE HEE!
WHAT ARE YOU, AN OLD MAN?!
THAT'S SO SAD! THEY CAN'T PLAY...!!
WHY IS LIFE SO CRUEL?!
SPLISH
SPLISH
UNLIKE YOU, KIDS THESE DAYS ARE BUSY.
CHAPTER 87
SUMMER CRAFTS

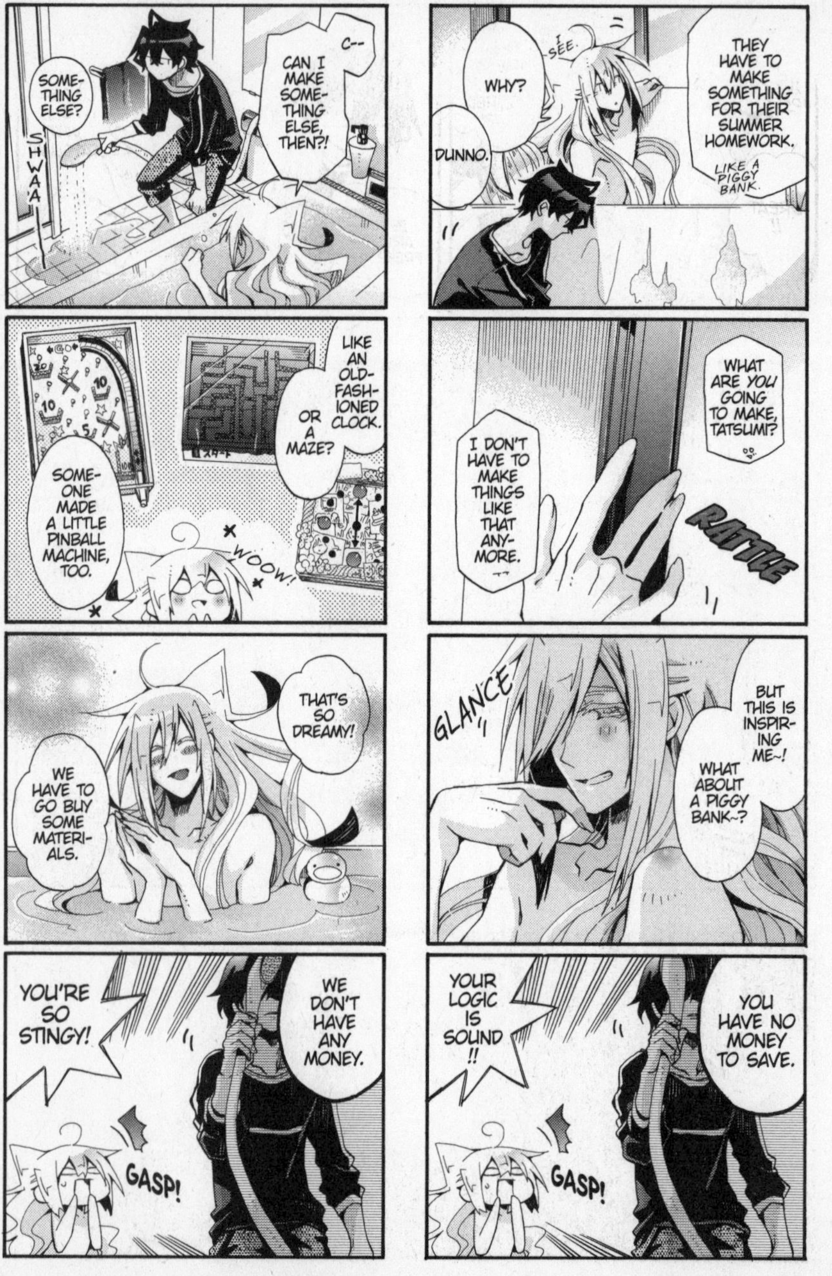
THEY HAVE TO MAKE SOMETHING FOR THEIR SUMMER HOMEWORK.
LIKE A PIGGY BANK.
I SEE.
WHY?
DUNNO.
C--
CAN I MAKE SOMETHING ELSE, THEN?!
SOMETHING ELSE?
SHWAA
WHAT ARE YOU GOING TO MAKE, TATSUMI?
RATTLE
I DON'T HAVE TO MAKE THINGS LIKE THAT ANYMORE.
LIKE AN OLD-FASHIONED CLOCK.
OR A MAZE?
SOMEONE MADE A LITTLE PINBALL MACHINE, TOO.
WOOW!
BUT THIS IS INSPIRING ME~!
WHAT ABOUT A PIGGY BANK~?
GLANCE
THAT'S SO DREAMY!
WE HAVE TO GO BUY SOME MATERIALS.
YOU HAVE NO MONEY TO SAVE.
YOUR LOGIC IS SOUND!!
GASP!
WE DON'T HAVE ANY MONEY.
YOU'RE SO STINGY!
GASP!

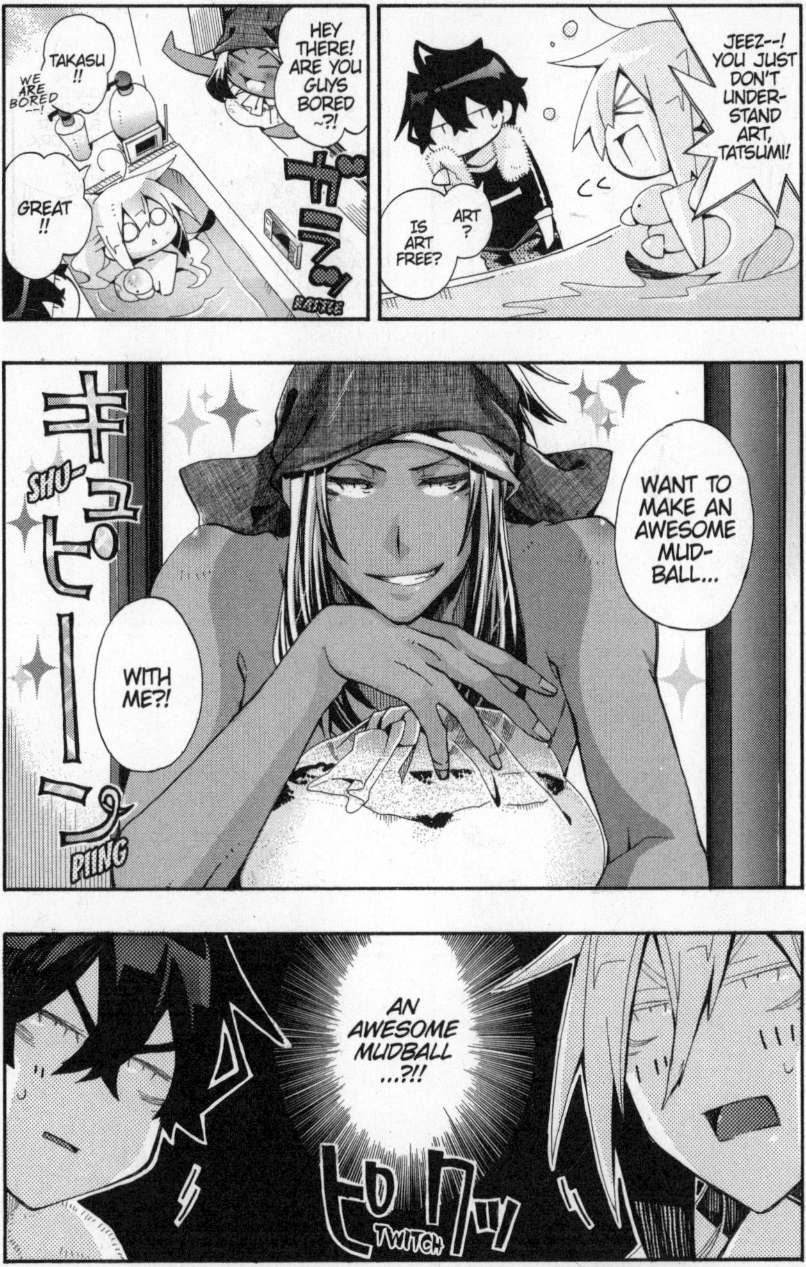
JEEZ--! YOU JUST DON'T UNDER-STAND ART, TATSUMI!
ART?
IS ART FREE?
HEY THERE! ARE YOU GUYS BORED ~?!
RATTLE
TAKASU!!
WE ARE BORED --!
GREAT!!
WANT TO MAKE AN AWESOME MUD-BALL...
SHU-
WITH ME?!
PIING
AN AWESOME MUDBALL ...?!!
TWITCH

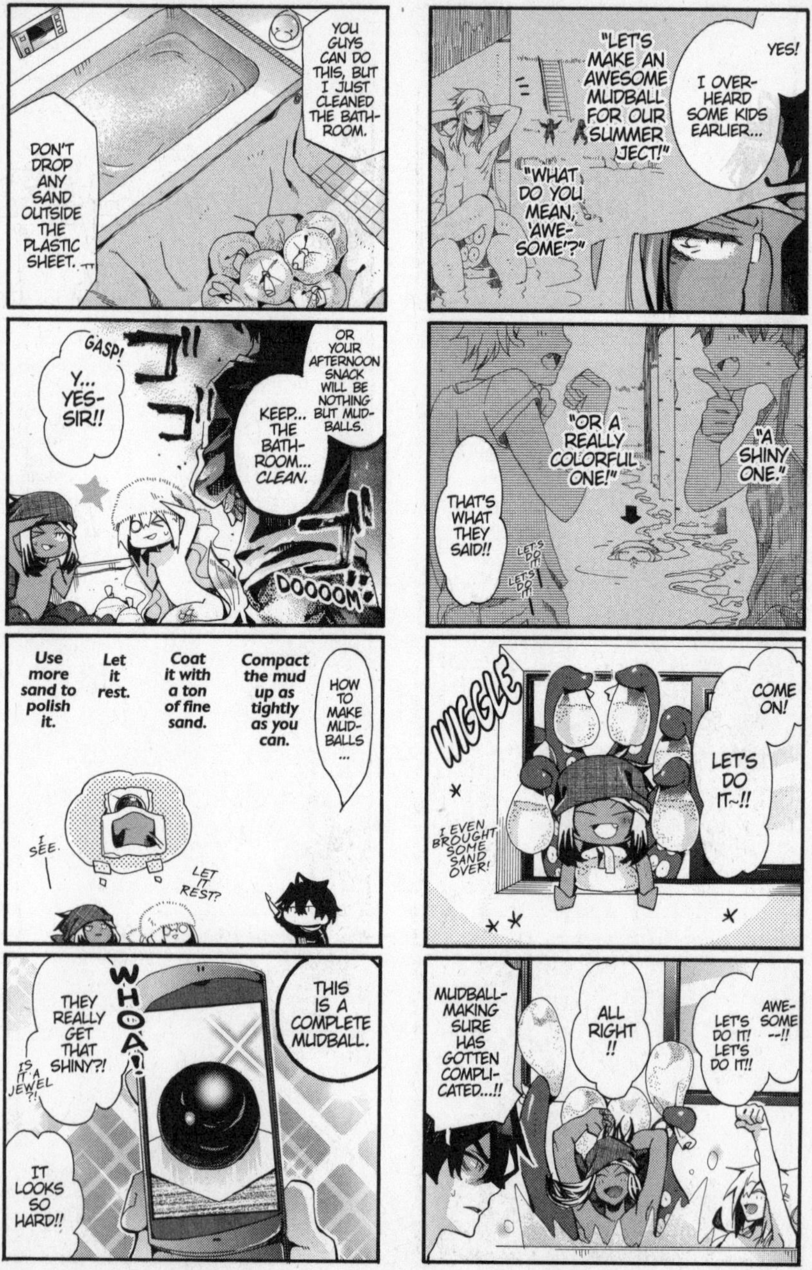
YES!
I OVERHEARD SOME KIDS EARLIER...
"LET'S MAKE AN AWESOME MUDBALL FOR OUR SUMMER ...JECT!"
"WHAT DO YOU MEAN, 'AWESOME'?"
YOU GUYS CAN DO THIS, BUT I JUST CLEANED THE BATHROOM.
DON'T DROP ANY SAND OUTSIDE THE PLASTIC SHEET.
"A SHINY ONE."
"OR A REALLY COLORFUL ONE!"
THAT'S WHAT THEY SAID!!
LET'S DO IT! LET'S DO IT!
OR YOUR AFTERNOON SNACK WILL BE NOTHING BUT MUDBALLS.
KEEP... THE BATHROOM... CLEAN.
GASP!
Y... YES-SIR!!
DOOOOM
COME ON!
LET'S DO IT~!!
WIGGLE
I EVEN BROUGHT SOME SAND OVER!
HOW TO MAKE MUDBALLS...
Compact the mud up as tightly as you can.
Coat it with a ton of fine sand.
Let it rest.
Use more sand to polish it.
LET IT REST?
I SEE.
AWESOME--!!
LET'S DO IT! LET'S DO IT!!
ALL RIGHT!!
MUDBALL-MAKING SURE HAS GOTTEN COMPLICATED...!!
THIS IS A COMPLETE MUDBALL.
WHOA!
THEY REALLY GET THAT SHINY?!
IS IT A JEWEL?!
IT LOOKS SO HARD!!

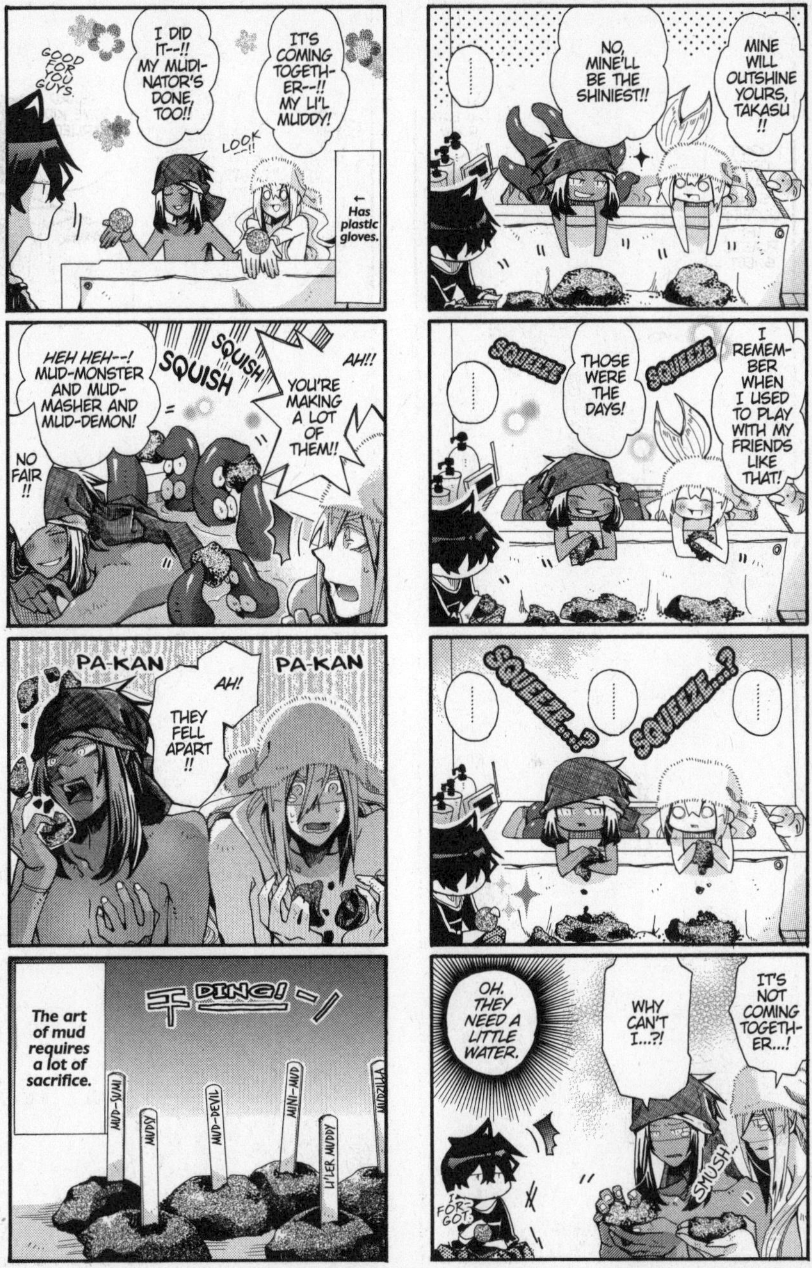

MINE WILL OUTSHINE YOURS, TAKASU!!
NO, MINE'LL BE THE SHINIEST!!
......
I REMEMBER WHEN I USED TO PLAY WITH MY FRIENDS LIKE THAT!
SQUEEZE
THOSE WERE THE DAYS!
SQUEEZE
......
......
SQUEEZE...?
......
SQUEEZE...?
......
IT'S NOT COMING TOGETHER...!
WHY CAN'T I...?!
SMUSH...
OH. THEY NEED A LITTLE WATER.
I FORGOT.
IT'S COMING TOGETHER--!! MY LI'L MUDDY!
LOOK--!!
I DID IT--!! MY MUDINATOR'S DONE, TOO!!
GOOD FOR YOU GUYS.
← Has plastic gloves.
AH!!
YOU'RE MAKING A LOT OF THEM!!
SQUISH
SQUISH
HEH HEH--! MUD-MONSTER AND MUD-MASHER AND MUD-DEMON!
NO FAIR!!
PA-KAN
AH!
THEY FELL APART!!
PA-KAN
DING!
The art of mud requires a lot of sacrifice.
MUDZILLA
MINI-MUD
LI'LER MUDDY
MUD-DEVIL
MUDSY
MUD-SUMI

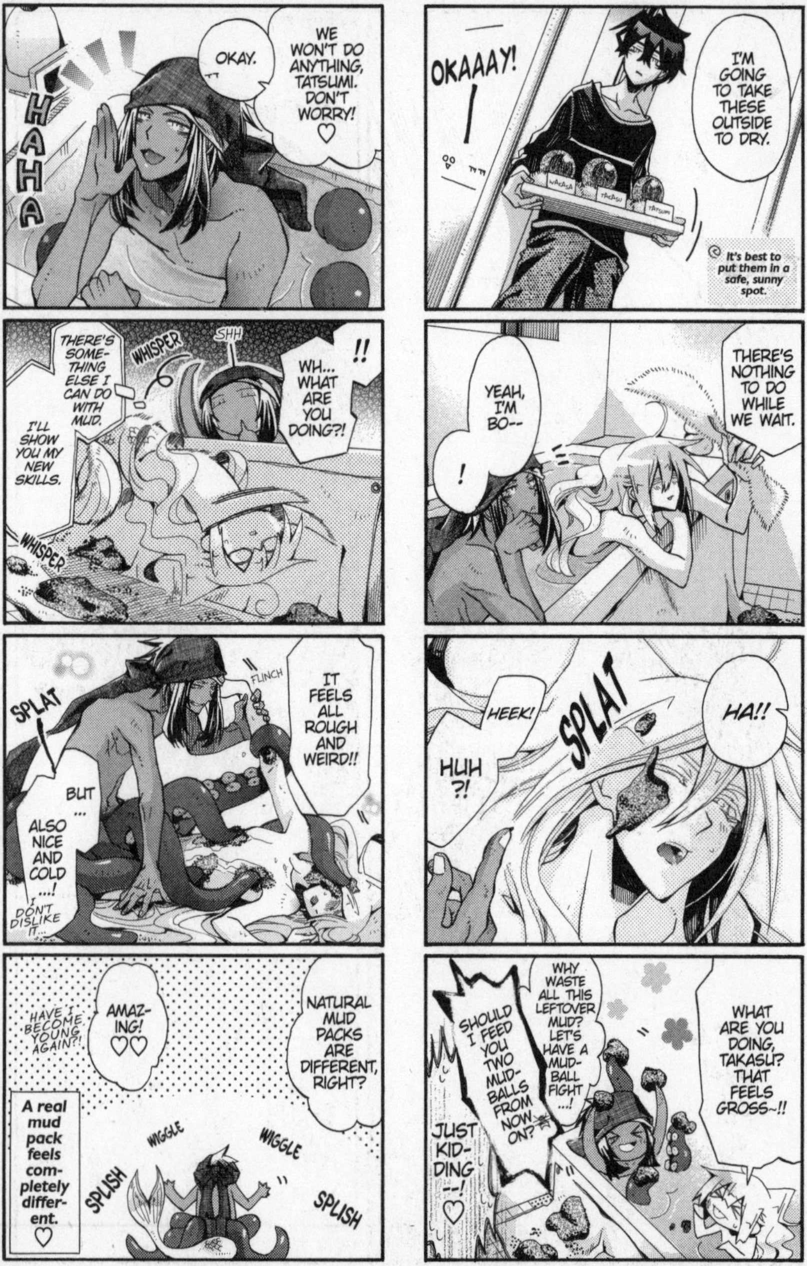
I'M GOING TO TAKE THESE OUTSIDE TO DRY.
OKAAAY!
WAKASA
TAKASU
TATSUMI
It's best to put them in a safe, sunny spot.
THERE'S NOTHING TO DO WHILE WE WAIT.
YEAH, I'M BO--
!
HA!!
SPLAT
HEEK!
HUH ?!
WHAT ARE YOU DOING, TAKASU? THAT FEELS GROSS~!!
WHY WASTE ALL THIS LEFTOVER MUD? LET'S HAVE A MUD-BALL FIGHT ...!
SHOULD I FEED YOU TWO MUD-BALLS FROM NOW ON?
JUST KID-DING --! ♡
OKAY.
WE WON'T DO ANYTHING, TATSUMI. DON'T WORRY! ♡
HAHAHA
!!
WH... WHAT ARE YOU DOING?!
SHH
WHISPER
THERE'S SOME-THING ELSE I CAN DO WITH MUD.
I'LL SHOW YOU MY NEW SKILLS.
WHISPER
IT FEELS ALL ROUGH AND WEIRD!!
FLINCH
SPLAT
BUT ...
ALSO NICE AND COLD ...!
I DON'T DISLIKE IT...
NATURAL MUD PACKS ARE DIFFERENT, RIGHT?
AMAZ-ING! ♡♡
HAVE I BECOME YOUNG AGAIN?!
WIGGLE
WIGGLE
SPLISH
SPLISH
A real mud pack feels com-pletely differ-ent. ♡

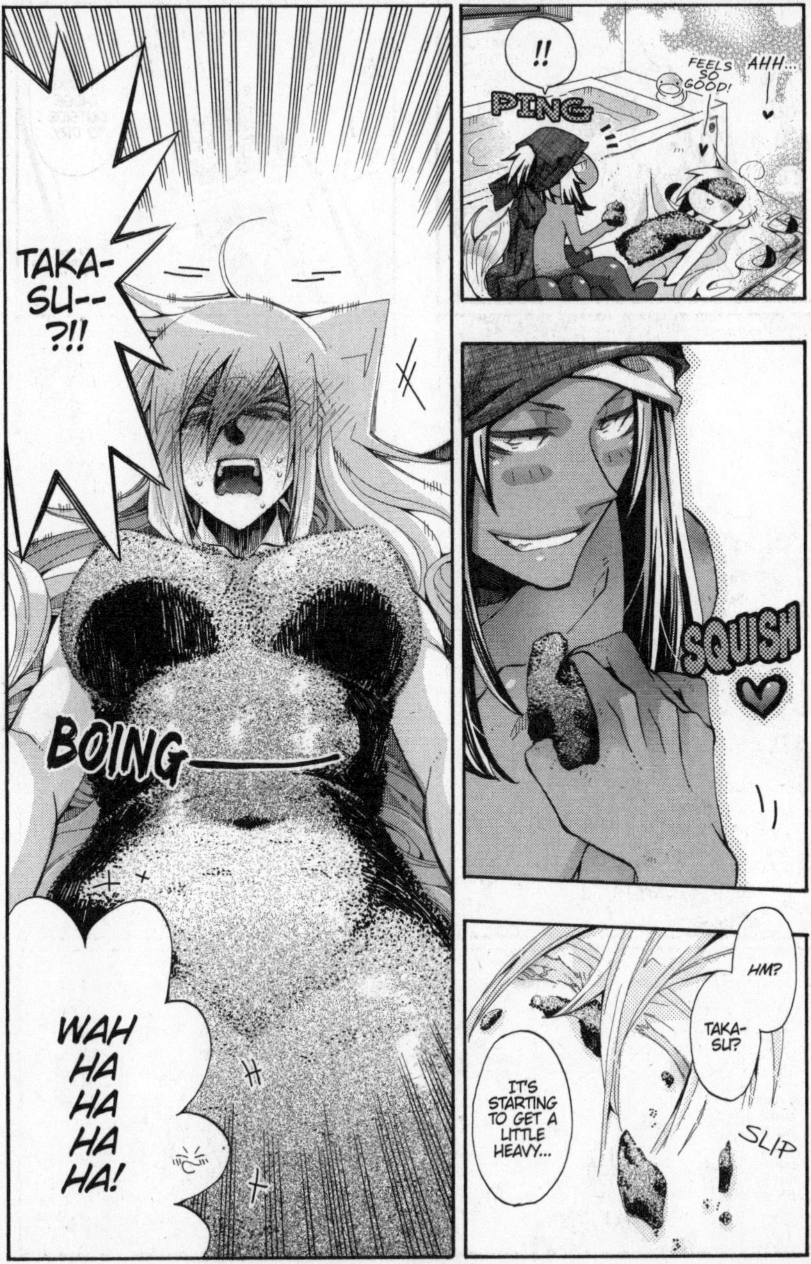
AHH...
FEELS SO GOOD!
!!
PING
SQUISH
HM?
TAKA-SU?
SLIP
IT'S STARTING TO GET A LITTLE HEAVY...
TAKA-SU--?!!
BOING
WAH HA HA HA HA HA!

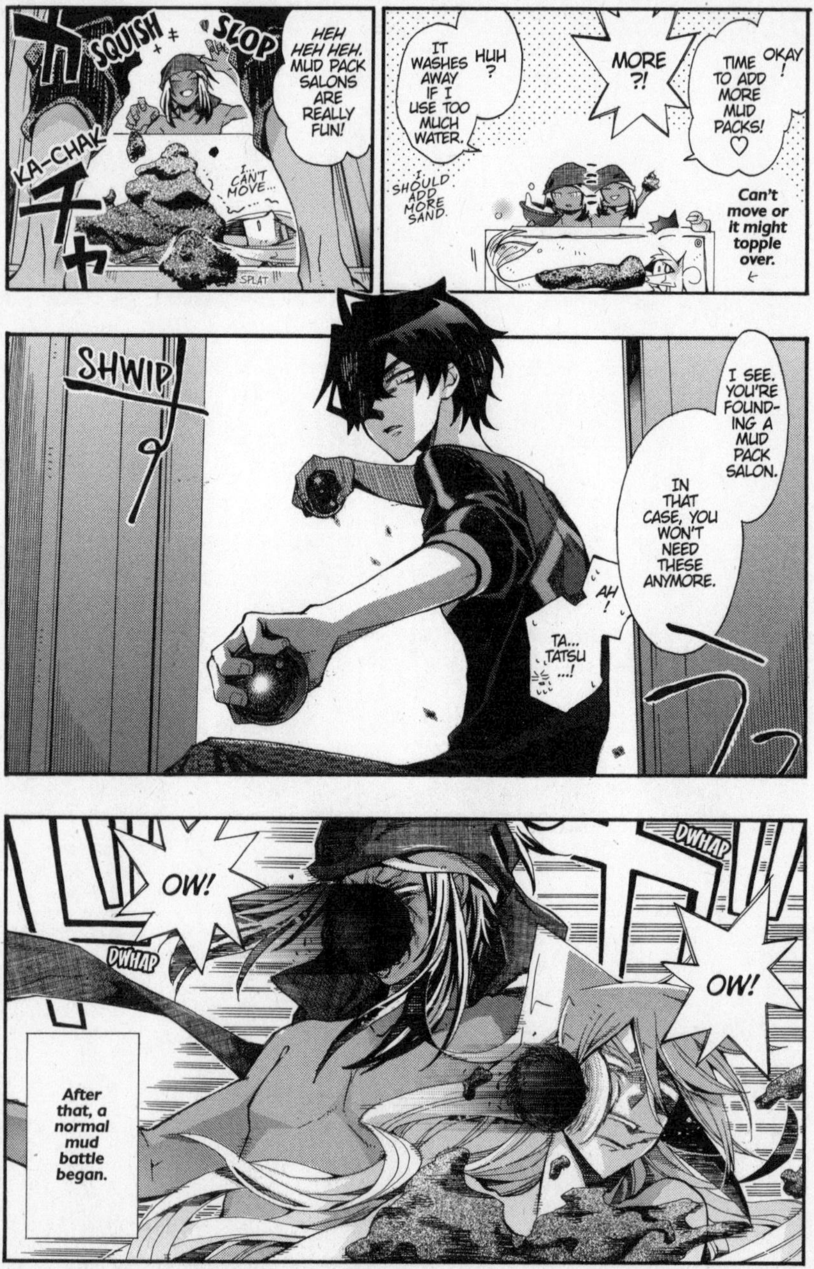
OKAY! TIME TO ADD MORE MUD PACKS! ♡
MORE?!
HUH?
IT WASHES AWAY IF I USE TOO MUCH WATER.
I SHOULD ADD MORE SAND.
Can't move or it might topple over.
HEH HEH HEH. MUD PACK SALONS ARE REALLY FUN!
SLOP
SQUISH
KA-CHAK
I... CAN'T MOVE...
SPLAT
I SEE. YOU'RE FOUND-ING A MUD PACK SALON.
IN THAT CASE, YOU WON'T NEED THESE ANYMORE.
AH!
TA... TATSU...!
SHWIP
DWHAP
OW!
OW!
DWHAP
After that, a normal mud battle began.

Merman in My Tub

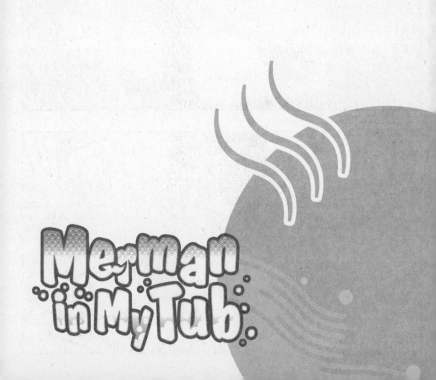

オレん家のフロ事情

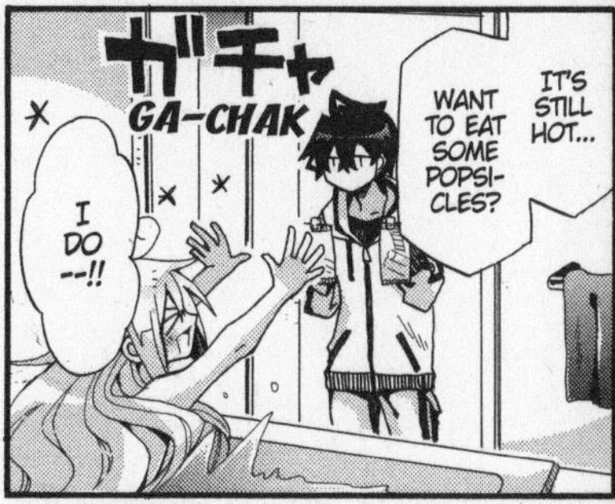
IT'S STILL HOT...
WANT TO EAT SOME POPSICLES?
ガチャ
GA-CHAK
I DO--!!

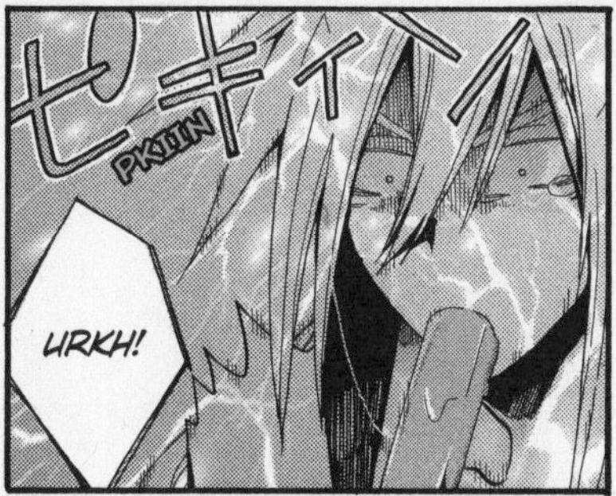
ピキィィ
PKIIN
URKH!

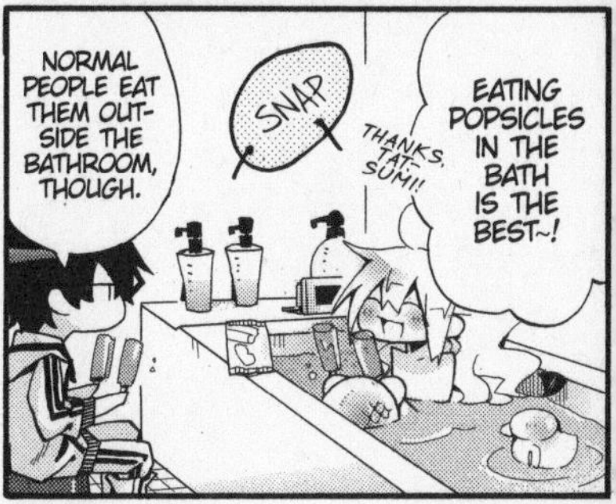
EATING POPSICLES IN THE BATH IS THE BEST~!
THANKS, TATSUMI!!
SNAP
NORMAL PEOPLE EAT THEM OUTSIDE THE BATHROOM, THOUGH.

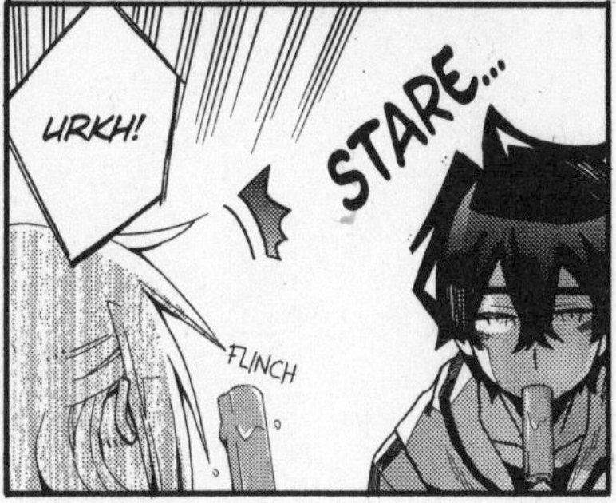
STARE...
URKH!
FLINCH

CHAPTER 88

AGARI-SAN'S CAVITY

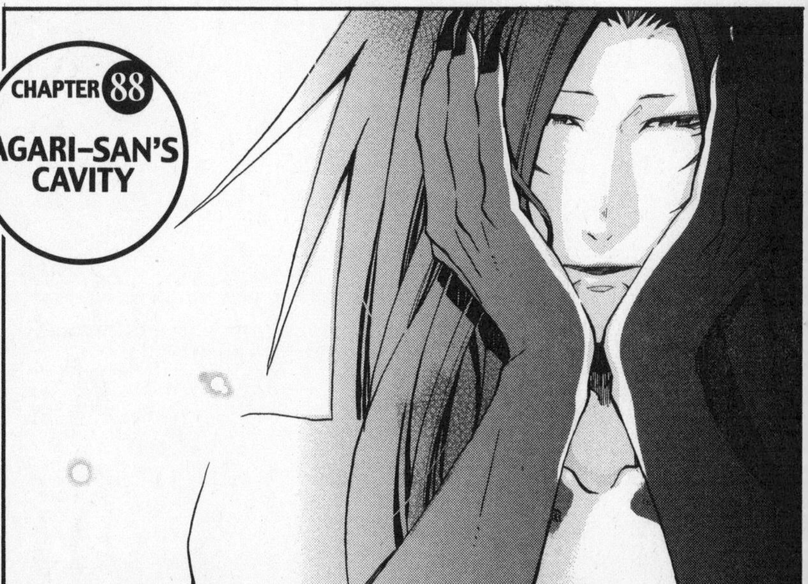

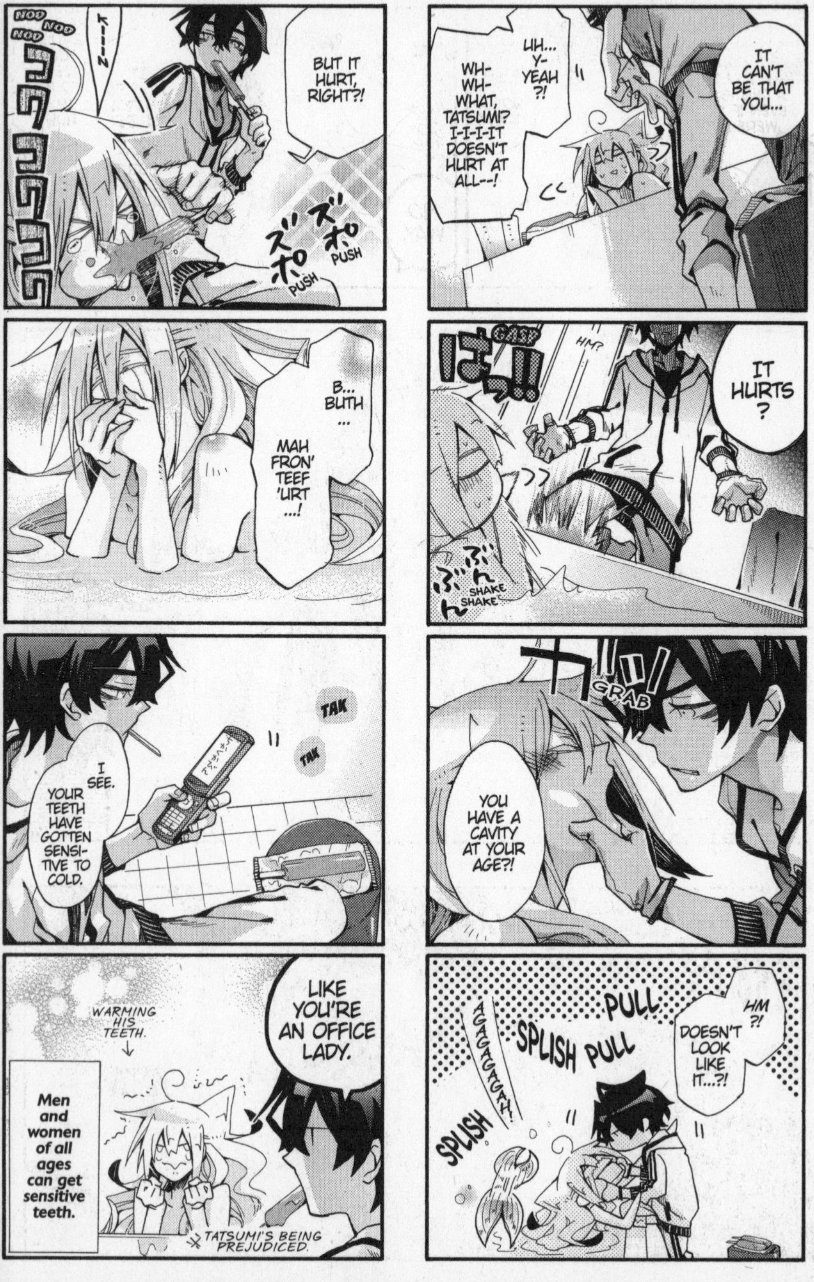
IT CAN'T BE THAT YOU...
UH... Y-YEAH?!
WH-WH-WHAT, TATSUMI? I-I-I-IT DOESN'T HURT AT ALL--!
BUT IT HURT, RIGHT?!
KIIIN
NOD NOD NOD
PUSH
PUSH
IT HURTS?
HM?
GASP
SHAKE SHAKE
B... BUTH...
MAH FRON' TEEF 'URT...!
GRAB
YOU HAVE A CAVITY AT YOUR AGE?!
TAK
TAK
I SEE. YOUR TEETH HAVE GOTTEN SENSI-TIVE TO COLD.
HM?!
PULL
DOESN'T LOOK LIKE IT...?!
SPLISH PULL
AGAGAGAGAH!
SPLISH
LIKE YOU'RE AN OFFICE LADY.
WARMING HIS TEETH.
Men and women of all ages can get sensitive teeth.
※TATSUMI'S BEING PREJUDICED.

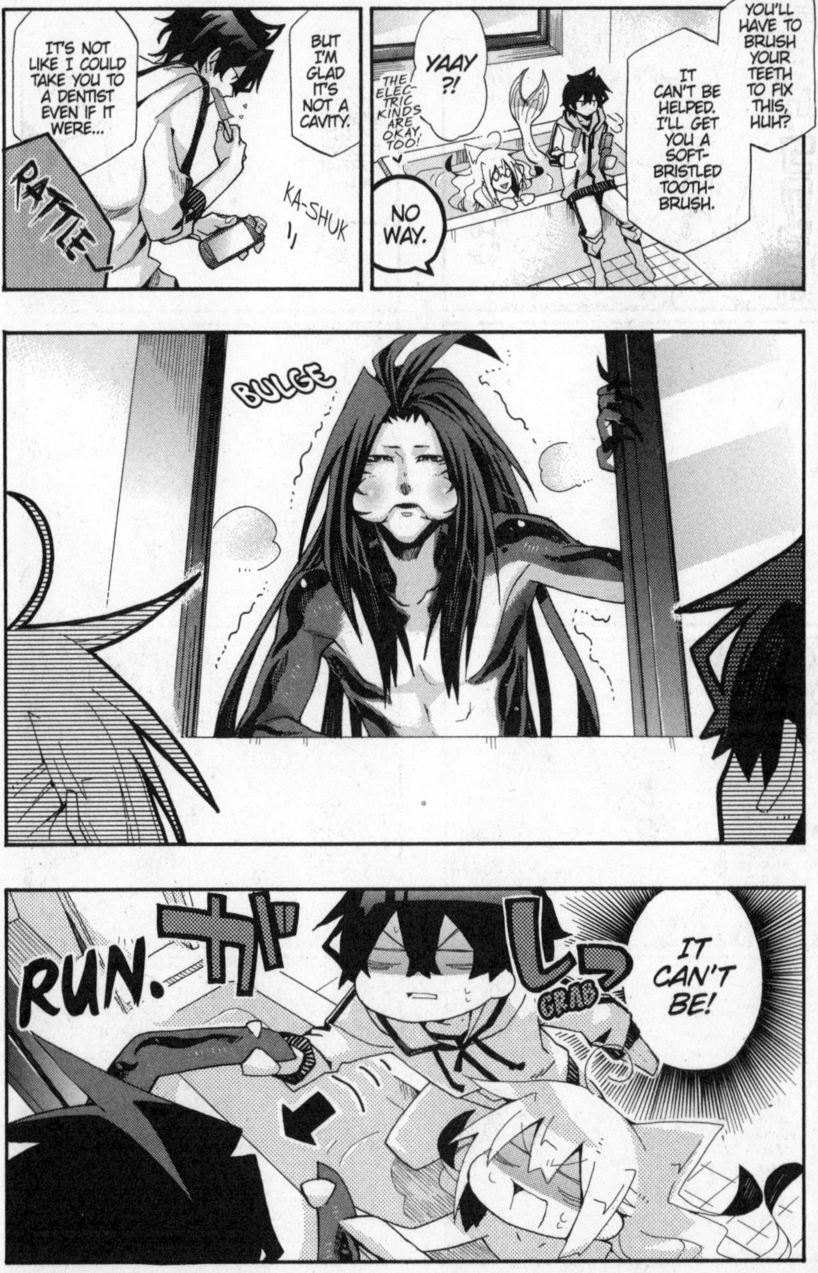
YOU'LL HAVE TO BRUSH YOUR TEETH TO FIX THIS, HUH?
IT CAN'T BE HELPED. I'LL GET YOU A SOFT-BRISTLED TOOTH-BRUSH.
YAAY ?!
THE ELEC-TRIC KINDS ARE OKAY, TOO!
NO WAY.
BUT I'M GLAD IT'S NOT A CAVITY.
IT'S NOT LIKE I COULD TAKE YOU TO A DENTIST EVEN IF IT WERE...
KA-SHUK
RATTLE
BULGE
IT CAN'T BE!
ガしっ
GRAB
RUN.

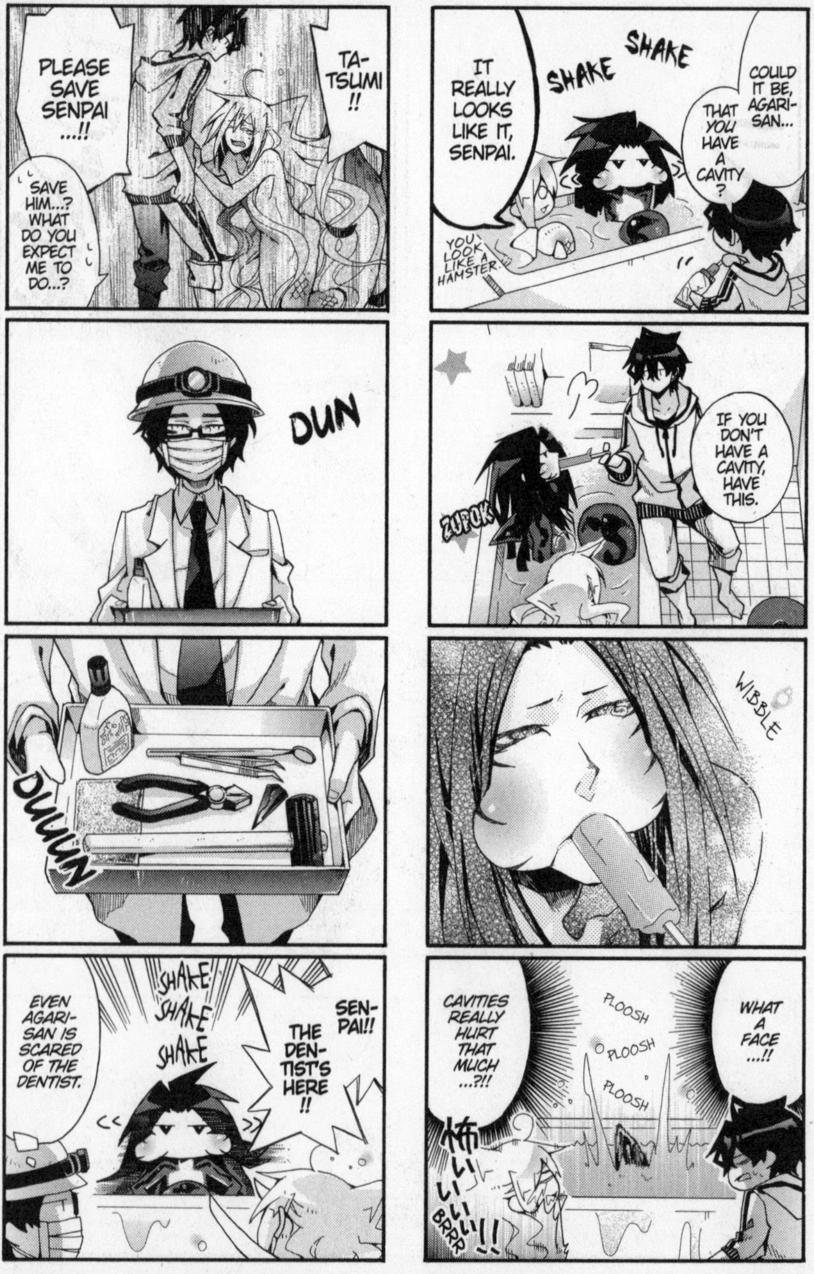
COULD IT BE, AGARI-SAN... THAT YOU HAVE A CAVITY?
SHAKE SHAKE
IT REALLY LOOKS LIKE IT, SENPAI.
YOU LOOK LIKE A HAMSTER.
TA-TSUMI!!
PLEASE SAVE SENPAI ...!!
SAVE HIM...? WHAT DO YOU EXPECT ME TO DO...?
IF YOU DON'T HAVE A CAVITY, HAVE THIS.
ZUPOK
DUN
WIBBLE
DUUUUN
WHAT A FACE ...!!
CAVITIES REALLY HURT THAT MUCH ...?!!
PLOOSH
PLOOSH
PLOOSH
怖いいいいいい!!
BRRR
SEN-PAI!!
THE DEN-TIST'S HERE!!
SHAKE SHAKE SHAKE
EVEN AGARI-SAN IS SCARED OF THE DENTIST.

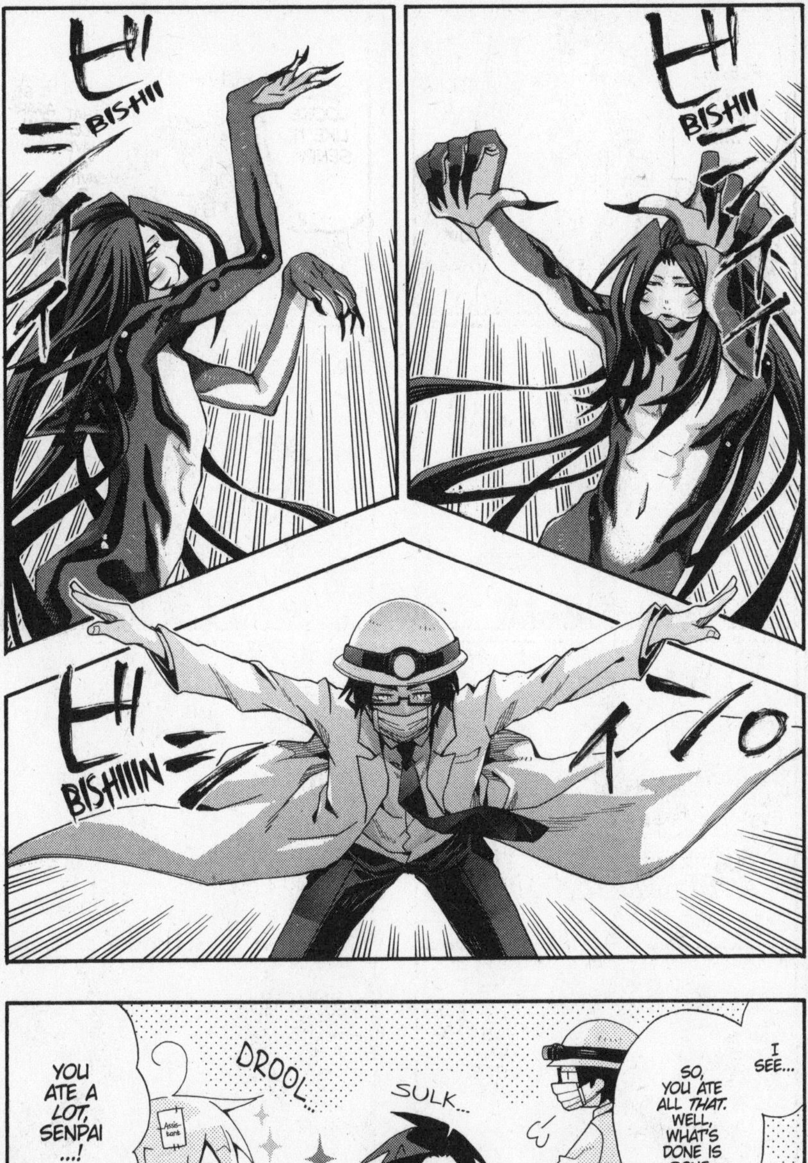
BISH!!
BISH!!
BISH!!!N
I SEE...
SO, YOU ATE ALL THAT. WELL, WHAT'S DONE IS DONE.
SULK...
DROOL...
Medical Interview
Things eaten today
Cake-Bread
Chocolate
Chicken
Assis-tant
YOU ATE A LOT, SENPAI...!

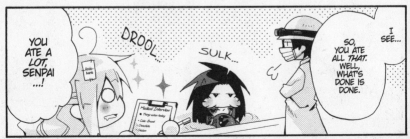

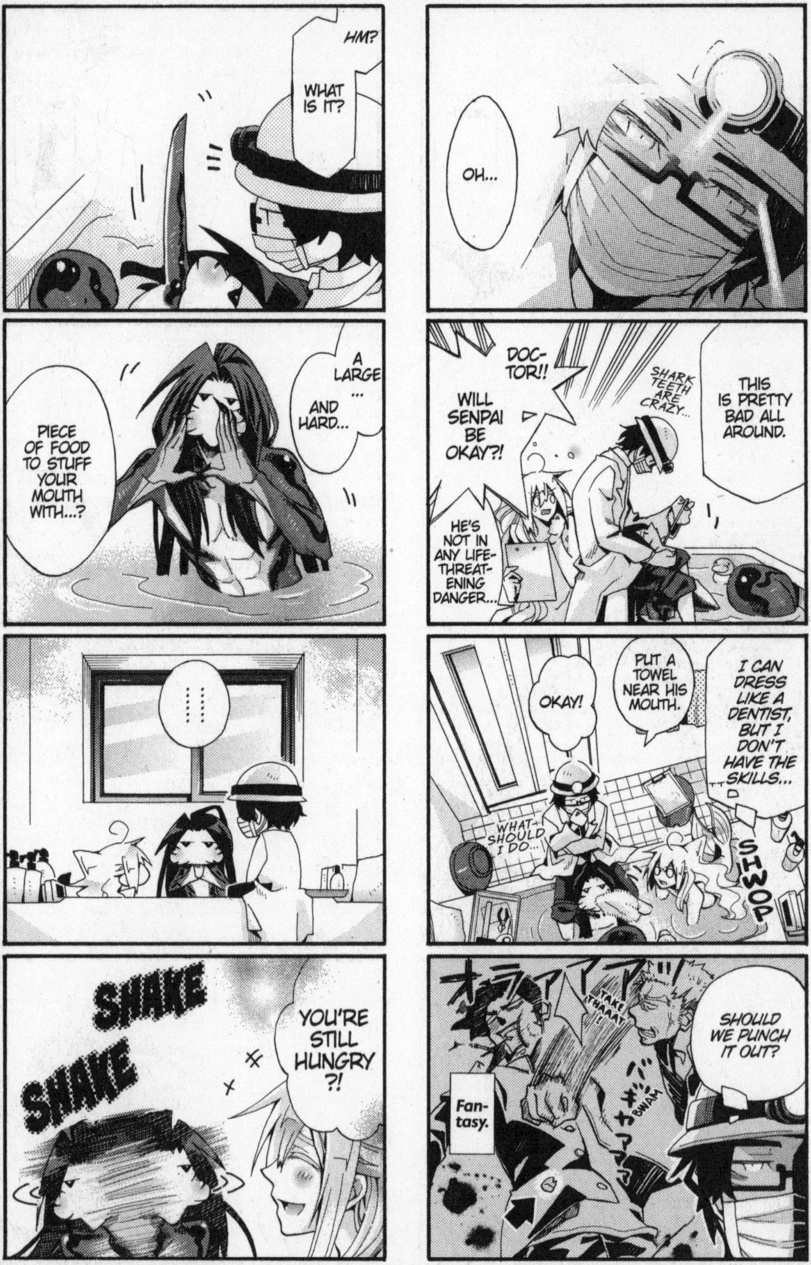
OH...
HM?
WHAT IS IT?
THIS IS PRETTY BAD ALL AROUND.
SHARK TEETH ARE CRAZY...
DOC-TOR!!
WILL SENPAI BE OKAY?!
HE'S NOT IN ANY LIFE-THREAT-ENING DANGER...
A LARGE...
AND HARD...
PIECE OF FOOD TO STUFF YOUR MOUTH WITH...?
I CAN DRESS LIKE A DENTIST, BUT I DON'T HAVE THE SKILLS...
PUT A TOWEL NEAR HIS MOUTH.
OKAY!
WHAT SHOULD I DO...
SHWOP
......
SHOULD WE PUNCH IT OUT?
TAKE THAAAT!
BWAM
Fan-tasy.
YOU'RE STILL HUNGRY?!
SHAKE
SHAKE

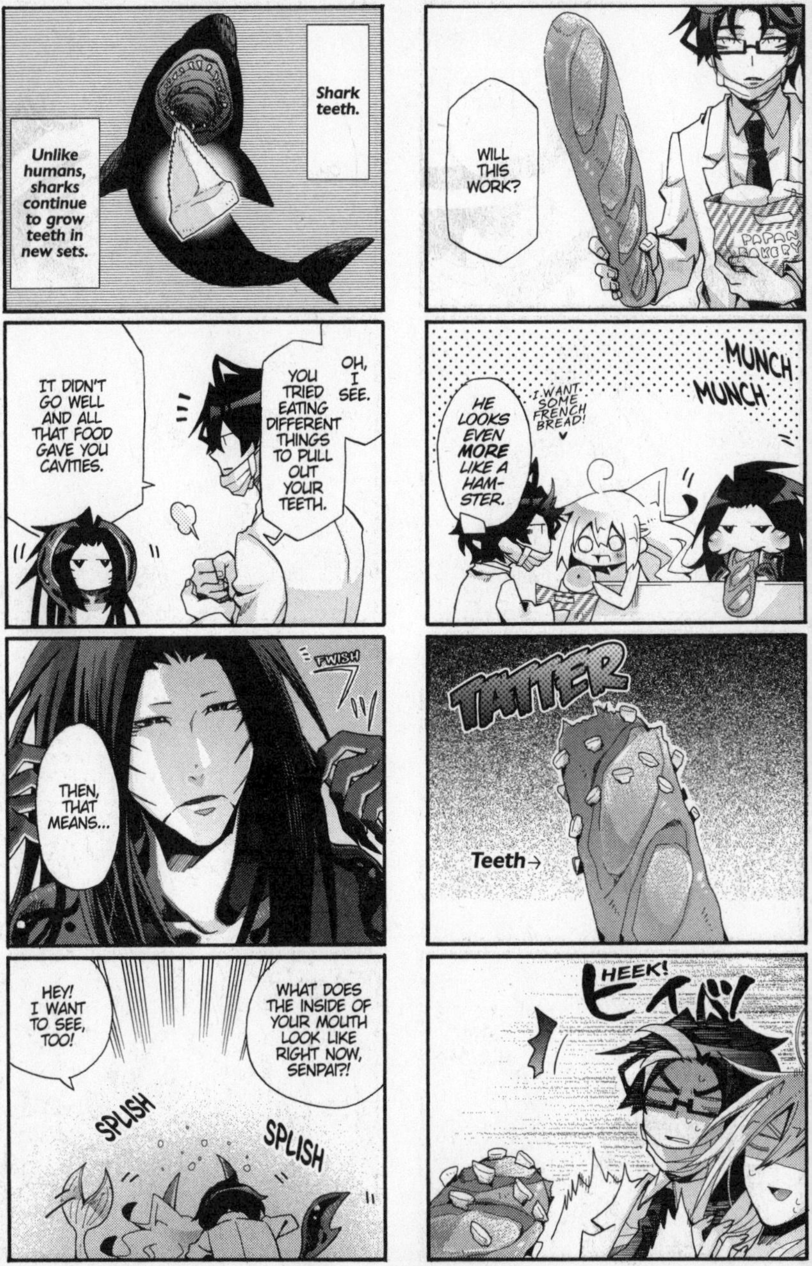
WILL THIS WORK?
PAPAN BAKERY
Shark teeth.
Unlike humans, sharks continue to grow teeth in new sets.
MUNCH MUNCH
I WANT SOME FRENCH BREAD!
HE LOOKS EVEN MORE LIKE A HAM-STER.
OH, I SEE.
YOU TRIED EATING DIFFERENT THINGS TO PULL OUT YOUR TEETH.
IT DIDN'T GO WELL AND ALL THAT FOOD GAVE YOU CAVITIES.
TATTER
Teeth→
FWISH
THEN, THAT MEANS...
HEEK!
WHAT DOES THE INSIDE OF YOUR MOUTH LOOK LIKE RIGHT NOW, SENPAI?!
HEY! I WANT TO SEE, TOO!
SPLISH
SPLISH

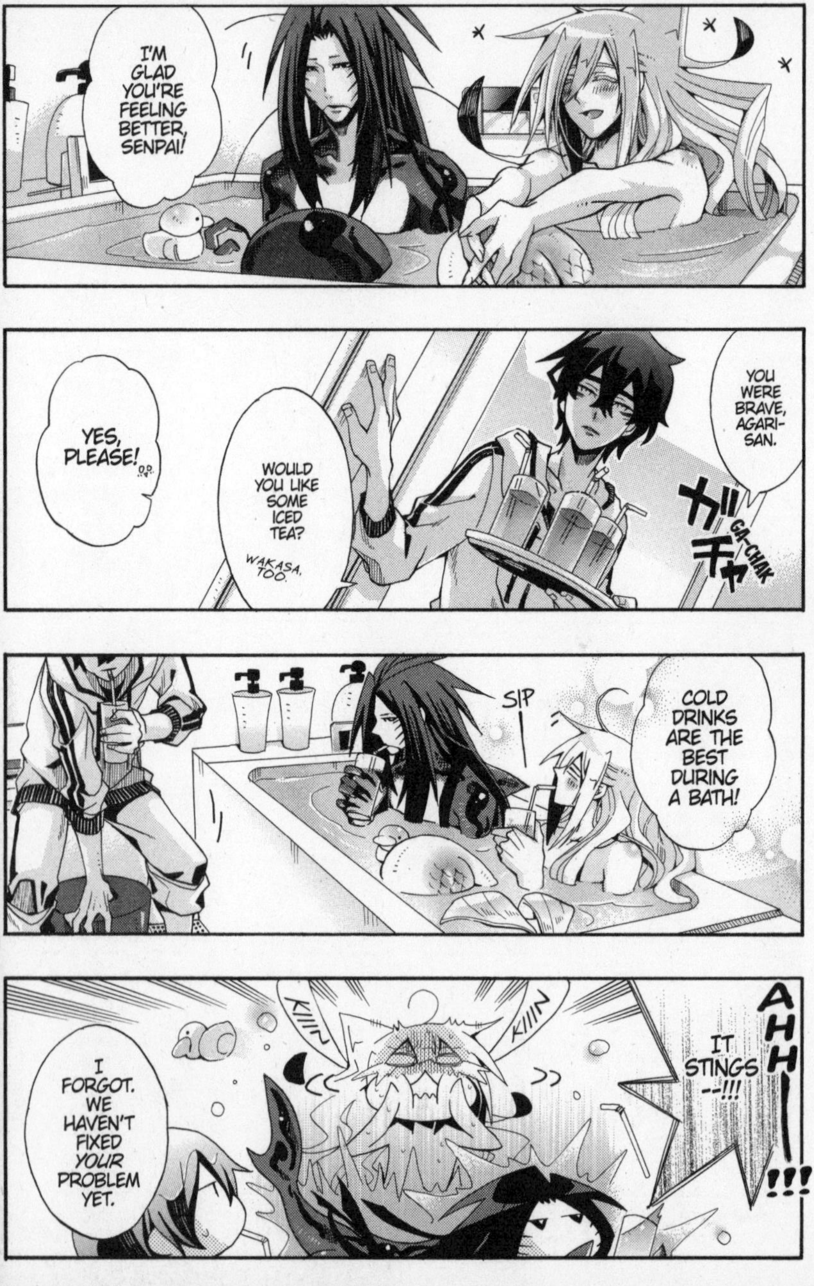
I'M GLAD YOU'RE FEELING BETTER, SENPAI!
YOU WERE BRAVE, AGARI-SAN.
GA-CHAK
WOULD YOU LIKE SOME ICED TEA?
WAKASA, TOO.
YES, PLEASE!
COLD DRINKS ARE THE BEST DURING A BATH!
SIP
AHH!!!
IT STINGS--!!!
KIIIN
KIIIN
I FORGOT. WE HAVEN'T FIXED YOUR PROBLEM YET.

Merman in My Tub

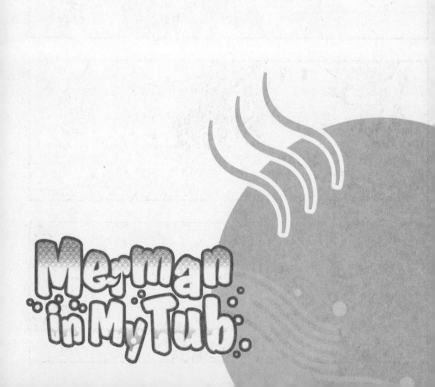

オレん家（ち）のフロ事情

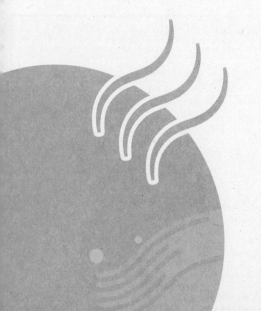

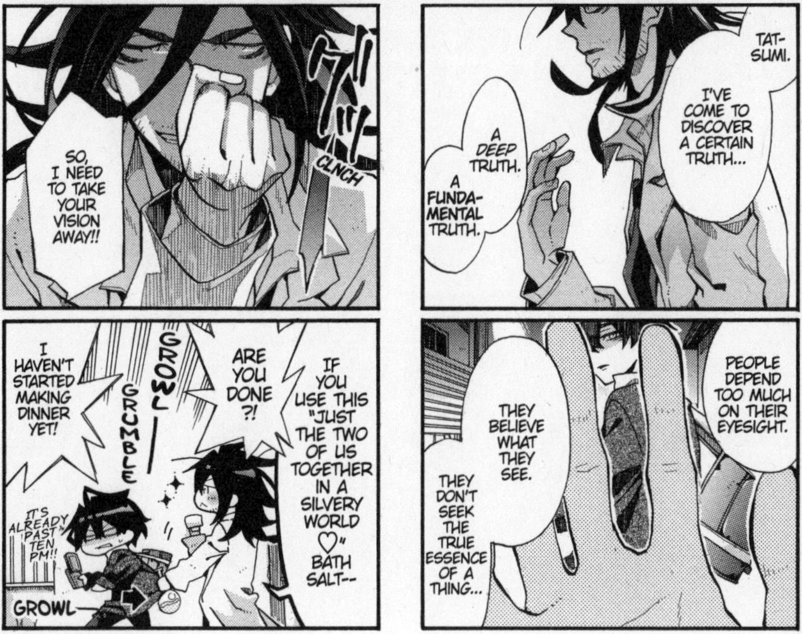
TAT-SUMI.
I'VE COME TO DISCOVER A CERTAIN TRUTH...
A DEEP TRUTH.
A FUNDA-MENTAL TRUTH.
CLNCH
SO, I NEED TO TAKE YOUR VISION AWAY!!
PEOPLE DEPEND TOO MUCH ON THEIR EYESIGHT.
THEY BELIEVE WHAT THEY SEE.
THEY DON'T SEEK THE TRUE ESSENCE OF A THING...
IF YOU USE THIS "JUST THE TWO OF US TOGETHER IN A SILVERY WORLD ♡" BATH SALT--
ARE YOU DONE ?!
GROWL
GRUMBLE
I HAVEN'T STARTED MAKING DINNER YET!
IT'S ALREADY PAST TEN PM!!
GROWL

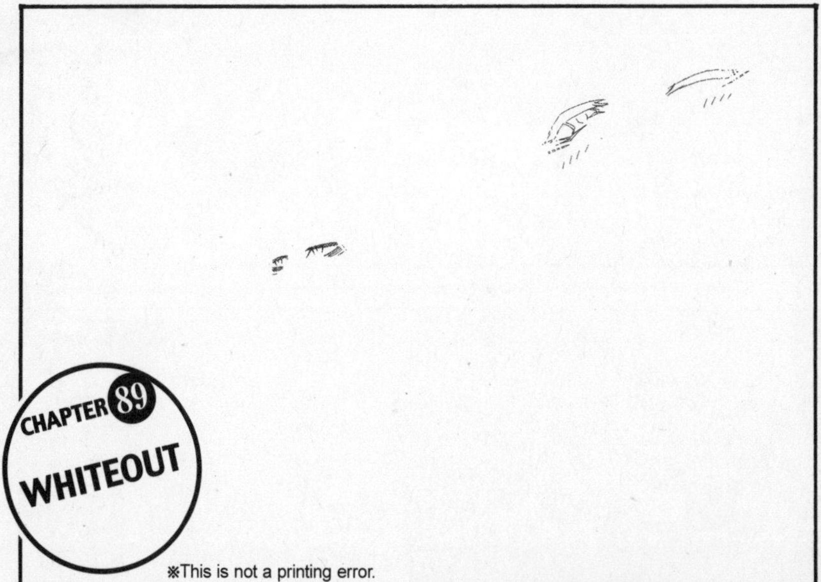
CHAPTER 89
WHITEOUT
※This is not a printing error.

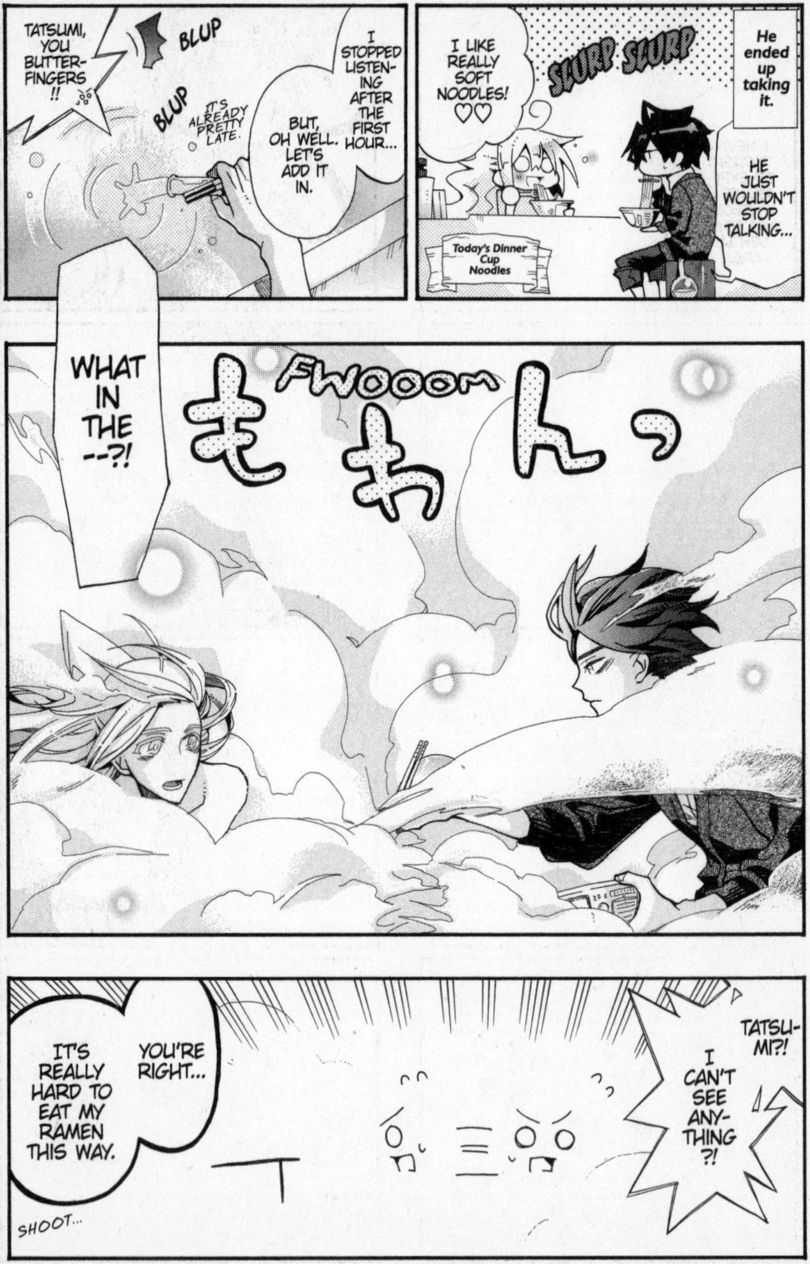
He ended up taking it.
HE JUST WOULDN'T STOP TALKING...
SLURP SLURP
I LIKE REALLY SOFT NOODLES! ♡♡
Today's Dinner Cup Noodles
I STOPPED LISTEN-ING AFTER THE FIRST HOUR...
BUT, OH WELL. LET'S ADD IT IN.
IT'S ALREADY PRETTY LATE.
BLUP
BLUP
TATSUMI, YOU BUTTER-FINGERS!!
WHAT IN THE--?!
もわんっ
FWOOOM
TATSU-MI?!
I CAN'T SEE ANY-THING?!
YOU'RE RIGHT...
IT'S REALLY HARD TO EAT MY RAMEN THIS WAY.
SHOOT...

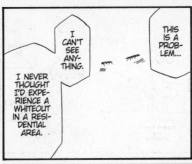

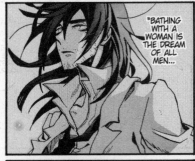

"BATHING WITH A WOMAN IS THE DREAM OF ALL MEN...
THIS IS A PROBLEM...
I CAN'T SEE ANYTHING.
I NEVER THOUGHT I'D EXPERIENCE A WHITEOUT IN A RESIDENTIAL AREA.
"BUT WOMEN GET TOO EMBARRASSED TO JOIN YOU.
"IT'S DIFFERENT IF YOU CAN'T SEE ONE ANOTHER, THOUGH.
Definition of "white-out":
When visibility is obscured by snow or clouds, making it impossible for one to find their bearings, or discern the surrounding area's elevation or terrain.
......
"IF THE BODY CAN'T BE SEEN, PEOPLE WILL BARE THEIR HEARTS!!
LIKE, "AHHN! I LOVE YOU, HISATORA-SAN"!
WE'LL HAVE TO MOVE AROUND CAREFULLY...
THAT WAS DELICIOUS!
WHAT SHOULD I DO ABOUT THE RAMEN BOX?
OH, I'LL TAKE THAT--
A BATH SALT THAT MAKES AN OPAQUE WHITE FOG...?
SMOKE
LOOK! LOOK!
SMOKE
EVEN IF I CAN'T SEE, I CAN STILL EAT MY RAMEN!
SLURP
SLURP
SPLASH
OW, HOT!!!

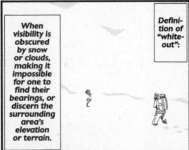

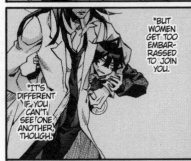

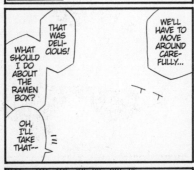

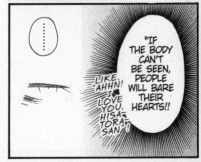

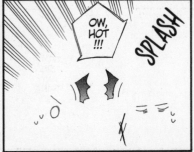

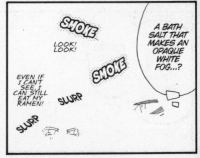

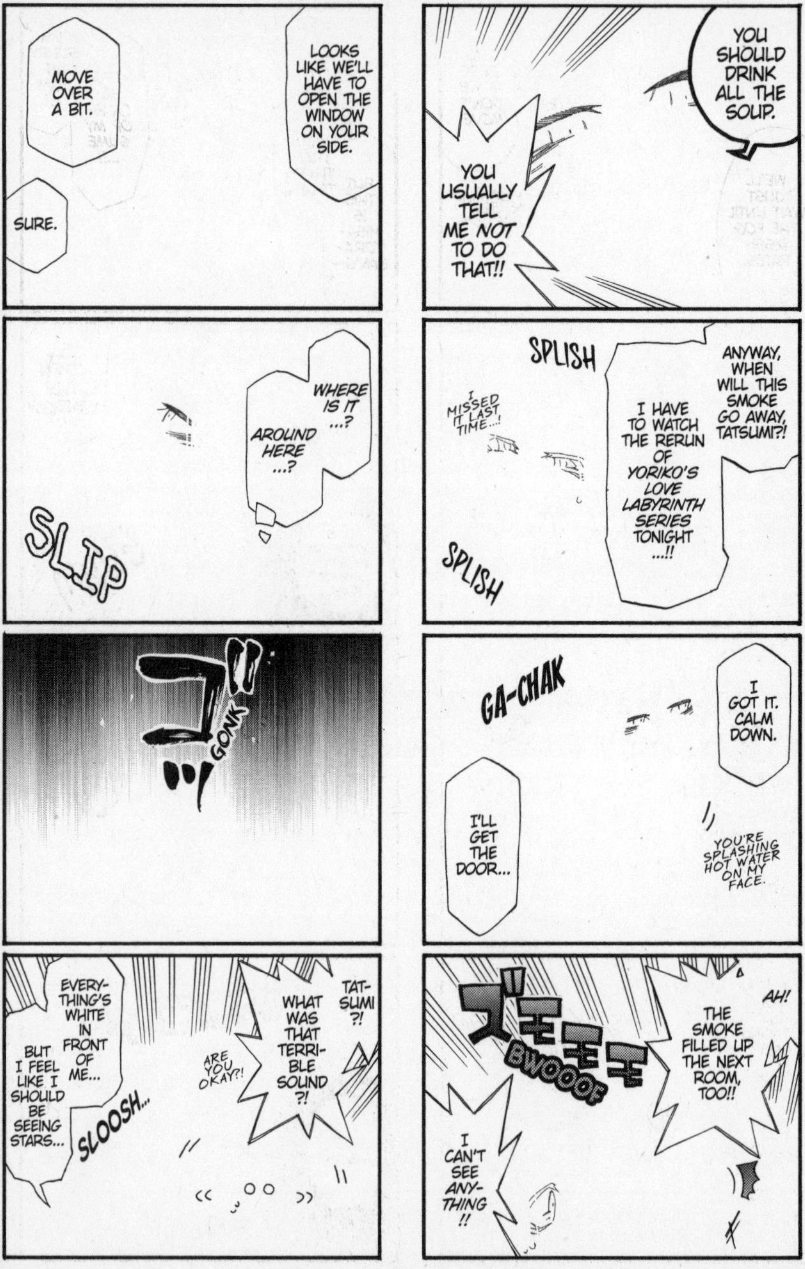
YOU SHOULD DRINK ALL THE SOUP.
YOU USUALLY TELL ME NOT TO DO THAT!!
LOOKS LIKE WE'LL HAVE TO OPEN THE WINDOW ON YOUR SIDE.
MOVE OVER A BIT.
SURE.
ANYWAY, WHEN WILL THIS SMOKE GO AWAY, TATSUMI?!
I HAVE TO WATCH THE RERUN OF YORIKO'S LOVE LABYRINTH SERIES TONIGHT ...!!
SPLISH
I MISSED IT LAST TIME...!
SPLISH
WHERE IS IT ...?
AROUND HERE ...?
SLIP
I GOT IT. CALM DOWN.
GA-CHAK
YOU'RE SPLASHING HOT WATER ON MY FACE.
I'LL GET THE DOOR...
ゴッ
GONK
AH!
THE SMOKE FILLED UP THE NEXT ROOM, TOO!!
ズモモモ
BWOOOF
I CAN'T SEE ANYTHING!!
TATSUMI?!
WHAT WAS THAT TERRIBLE SOUND?!
ARE YOU OKAY?!
EVERYTHING'S WHITE IN FRONT OF ME...
BUT I FEEL LIKE I SHOULD BE SEEING STARS...
SLOOSH...

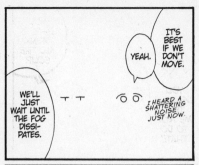

I'M SORRY, TAT-SUMI...!
IT'S BE-CAUSE OF MY SLIME...!!
WELL YEAH, THAT'S TRUE...
BUT THIS IS HISA-TORA-SAN'S--
I'LL OPEN THE WINDOW!!
WAIT A SECOND!!
I'VE GOT A BAD FEELING ABOUT THIS...
GUWA
SQUISH
HUH?!
I STEPPED ON SOME-THING.
SWAY
FLOP
KIISH!
SO HEAVY!
IT'S BEST IF WE DON'T MOVE.
YEAH.
I HEARD A SHATTERING NOISE JUST NOW.
WE'LL JUST WAIT UNTIL THE FOG DISSI-PATES.
TA... TAT-SUMI.
WHAT?
IS YOUR BOO-BOO OKAY, NOW?
PAT
PAT
I HIT MY HEAD.
THAT'S MY BUTT.
WHY IS YOUR BUTT FACING ME?!
ARE YOU MOONING ME?!

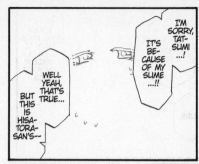

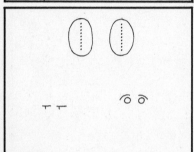

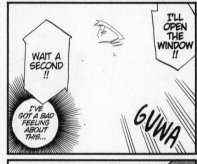

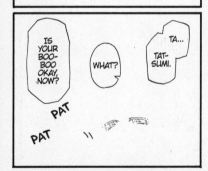

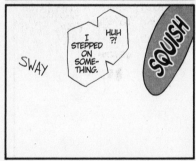

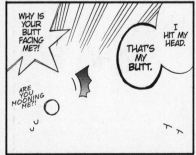

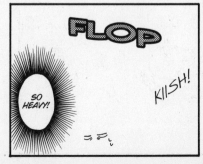

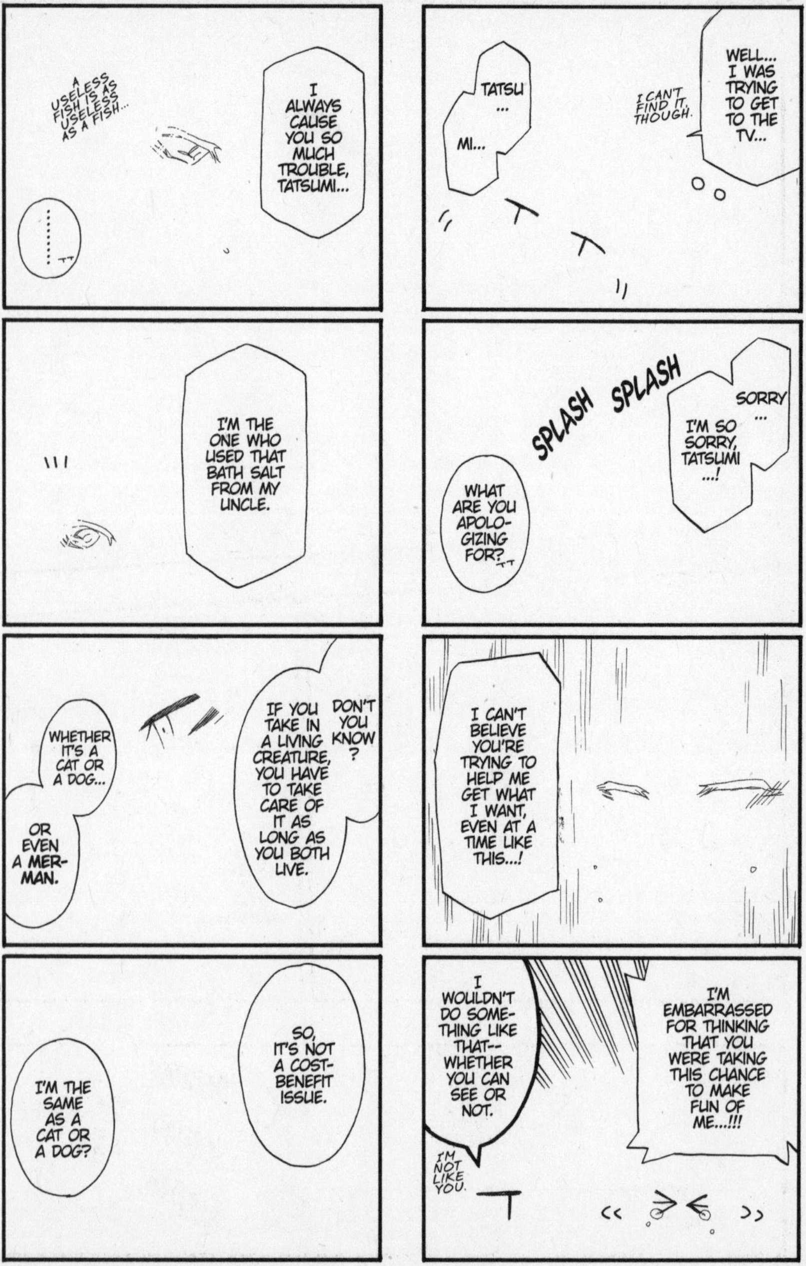

WELL... I WAS TRYING TO GET TO THE TV...
I CAN'T FIND IT, THOUGH.
TATSU... MI...
I ALWAYS CAUSE YOU SO MUCH TROUBLE, TATSUMI...
A USELESS FISH IS AS USELESS AS A FISH...
......
SORRY... I'M SO SORRY, TATSUMI...!
SPLASH SPLASH
WHAT ARE YOU APOLOGIZING FOR?
I'M THE ONE WHO USED THAT BATH SALT FROM MY UNCLE.
I CAN'T BELIEVE YOU'RE TRYING TO HELP ME GET WHAT I WANT, EVEN AT A TIME LIKE THIS...!
DON'T YOU KNOW?
IF YOU TAKE IN A LIVING CREATURE, YOU HAVE TO TAKE CARE OF IT AS LONG AS YOU BOTH LIVE.
WHETHER IT'S A CAT OR A DOG...
OR EVEN A MERMAN.
I'M EMBARRASSED FOR THINKING THAT YOU WERE TAKING THIS CHANCE TO MAKE FUN OF ME...!!!
I WOULDN'T DO SOMETHING LIKE THAT-- WHETHER YOU CAN SEE OR NOT.
I'M NOT LIKE YOU.
SO, IT'S NOT A COST-BENEFIT ISSUE.
I'M THE SAME AS A CAT OR A DOG?

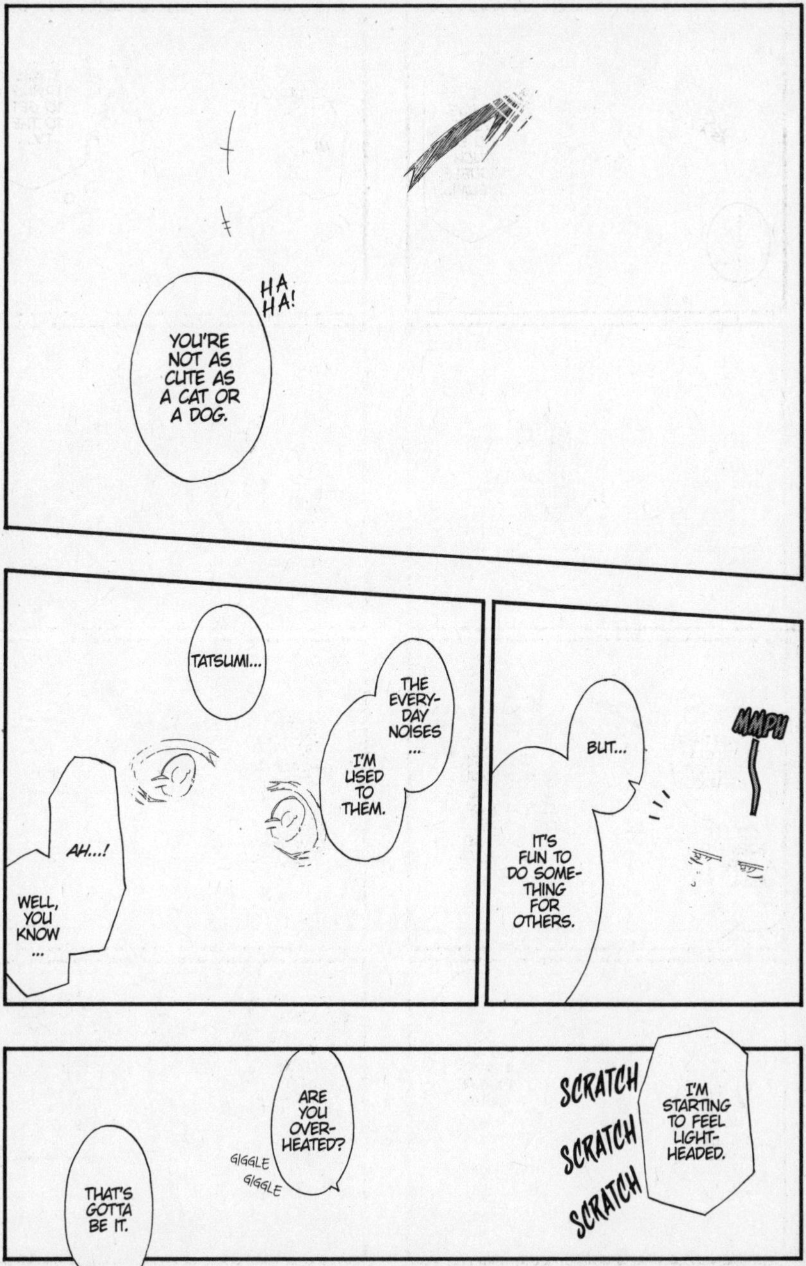
HA HA!
YOU'RE NOT AS CUTE AS A CAT OR A DOG.
MMPH
BUT...
IT'S FUN TO DO SOME-THING FOR OTHERS.
TATSUMI...
THE EVERY-DAY NOISES ...
I'M USED TO THEM.
AH...!
WELL, YOU KNOW ...
SCRATCH SCRATCH SCRATCH
I'M STARTING TO FEEL LIGHT-HEADED.
ARE YOU OVER-HEATED?
GIGGLE GIGGLE
THAT'S GOTTA BE IT.

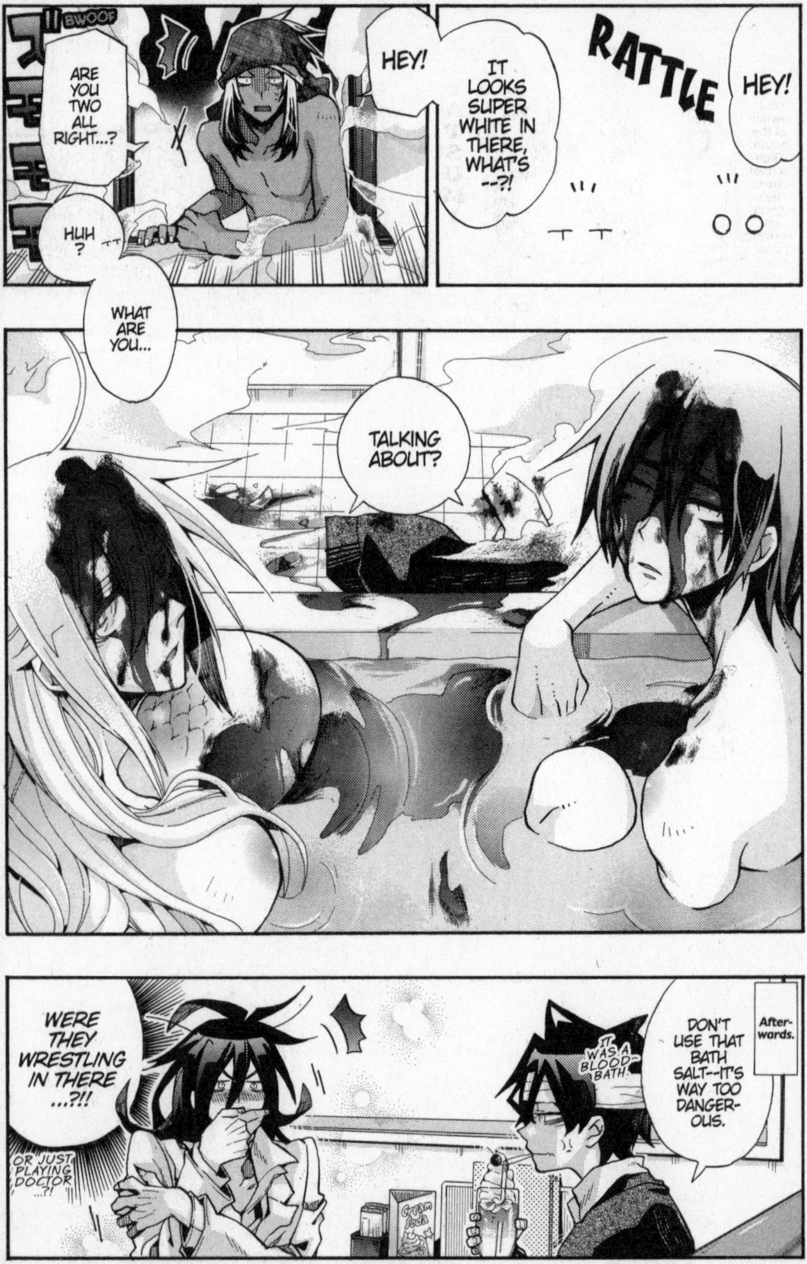
RATTLE
HEY!
HEY!
IT LOOKS SUPER WHITE IN THERE, WHAT'S --?!
BWOOF
ARE YOU TWO ALL RIGHT...?
HUH?
WHAT ARE YOU...
TALKING ABOUT?
After-wards.
DON'T USE THAT BATH SALT--IT'S WAY TOO DANGER-OUS.
IT WAS A BLOOD-BATH.
WERE THEY WRESTLING IN THERE ...?!!
OR JUST PLAYING DOCTOR ...?!
Cream Soda

Merman in My Tub

オレん家のフロ事情

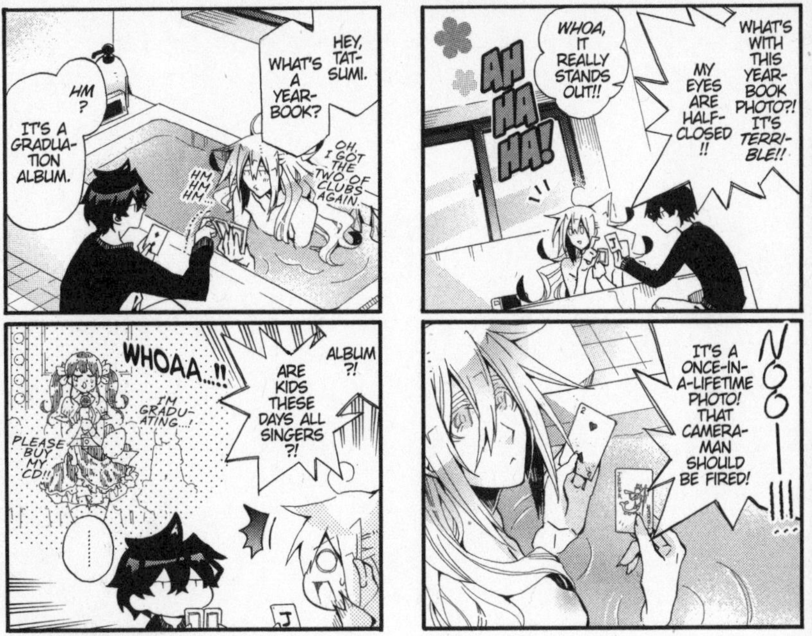
WHAT'S WITH THIS YEAR-BOOK PHOTO?! IT'S TERRI-BLE!!
MY EYES ARE HALF-CLOSED!!
WHOA, IT REALLY STANDS OUT!!
AH HA HA!
IT'S A ONCE-IN-A-LIFETIME PHOTO! THAT CAMERA-MAN SHOULD BE FIRED!
NOOO—!!!...
HEY, TATSUMI.
WHAT'S A YEAR-BOOK?
HM?
IT'S A GRADUA-TION ALBUM.
OH, I GOT THE TWO OF CLUBS AGAIN.
HM HM HM...
ALBUM?!
ARE KIDS THESE DAYS ALL SINGERS?!
WHOAA...!!
I'M GRADU-ATING...!
PLEASE BUY MY CD!!
......

CHAPTER 90 OUR SCHOOL ALBUM ☆

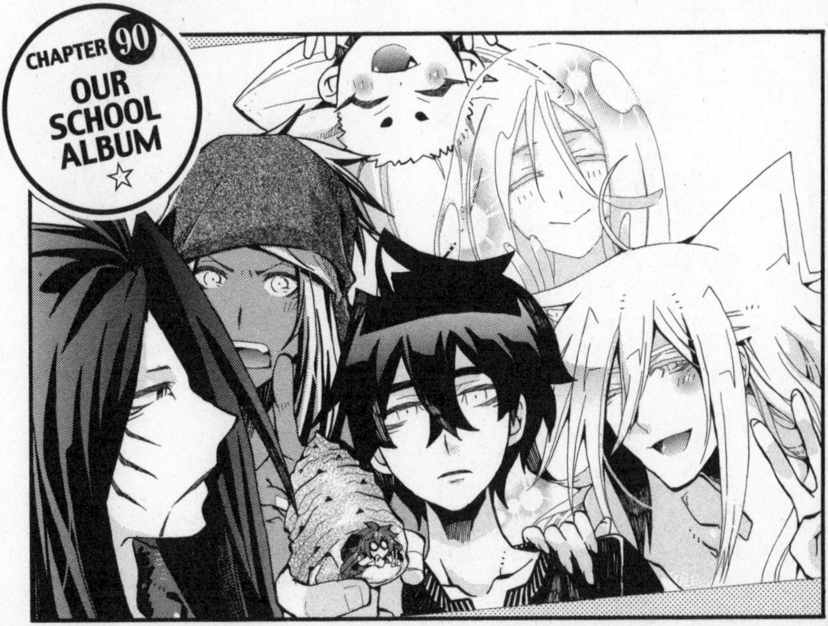

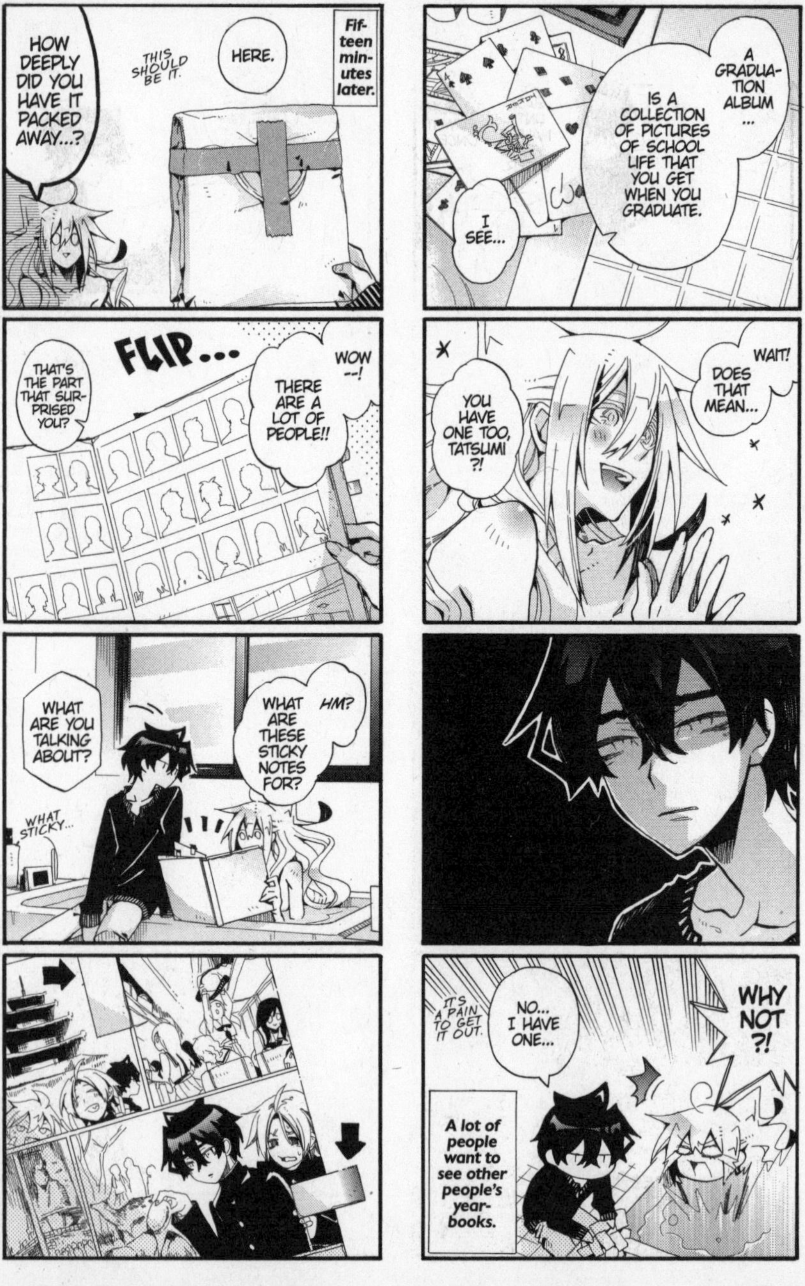
A GRADUATION ALBUM...
IS A COLLECTION OF PICTURES OF SCHOOL LIFE THAT YOU GET WHEN YOU GRADUATE.
I SEE...
Fifteen minutes later.
HERE.
THIS SHOULD BE IT.
HOW DEEPLY DID YOU HAVE IT PACKED AWAY...?
WAIT! DOES THAT MEAN...
YOU HAVE ONE TOO, TATSUMI?!
FLIP...
WOW--!
THERE ARE A LOT OF PEOPLE!!
THAT'S THE PART THAT SURPRISED YOU?
HM?
WHAT ARE THESE STICKY NOTES FOR?
WHAT ARE YOU TALKING ABOUT?
WHAT STICKY...
WHY NOT?!
NO... I HAVE ONE...
IT'S A PAIN TO GET IT OUT.
A lot of people want to see other people's yearbooks.

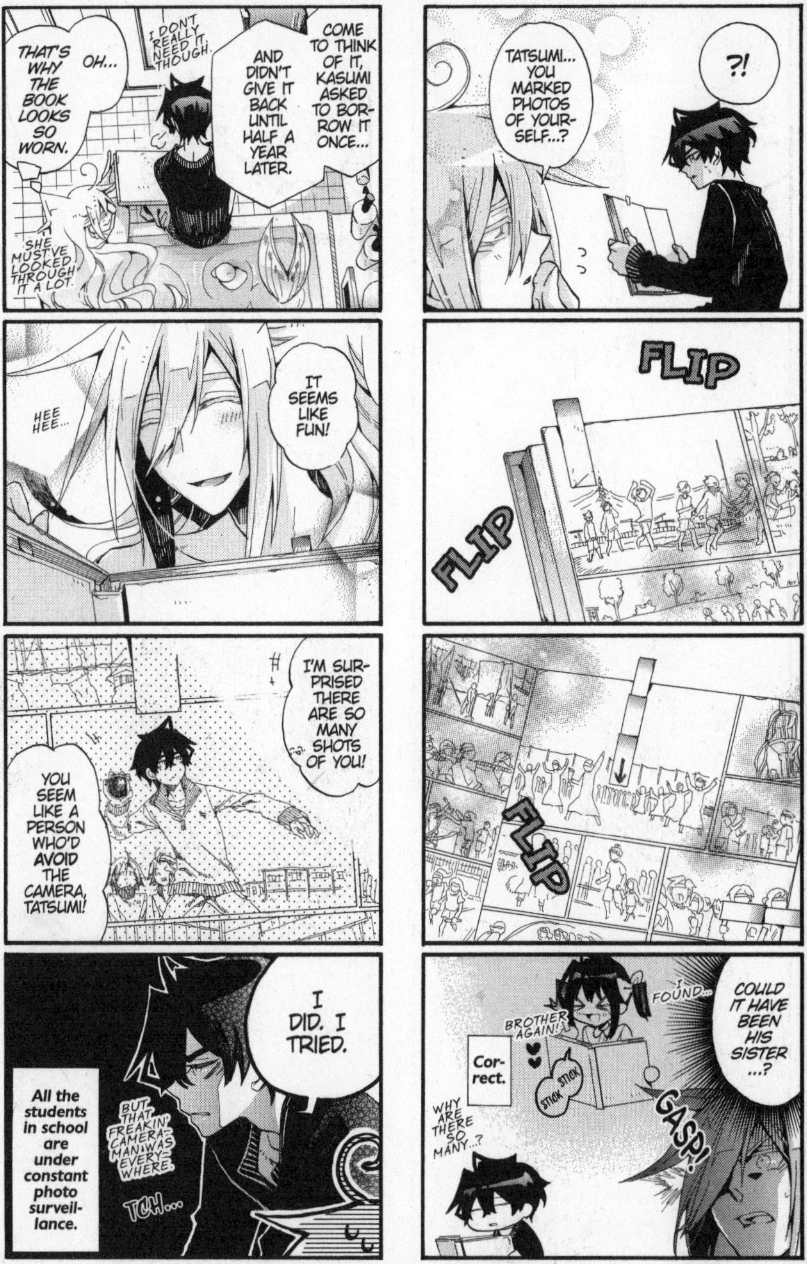
TATSUMI... YOU MARKED PHOTOS OF YOURSELF...?
?!
FLIP
FLIP
FLIP
COULD IT HAVE BEEN HIS SISTER...?
GASP!
I FOUND... BROTHER AGAIN!
STICK STICK
Correct.
WHY ARE THERE SO MANY...?
COME TO THINK OF IT, KASUMI ASKED TO BORROW IT ONCE...
AND DIDN'T GIVE IT BACK UNTIL HALF A YEAR LATER.
I DON'T REALLY NEED IT THOUGH.
OH...
THAT'S WHY THE BOOK LOOKS SO WORN.
SHE MUST'VE LOOKED THROUGH IT A LOT.
IT SEEMS LIKE FUN!
HEE HEE...
I'M SURPRISED THERE ARE SO MANY SHOTS OF YOU!
YOU SEEM LIKE A PERSON WHO'D AVOID THE CAMERA, TATSUMI!
I DID. I TRIED.
BUT THAT FREAKIN' CAMERAMAN WAS EVERYWHERE.
TCH...
All the students in school are under constant photo surveillance.

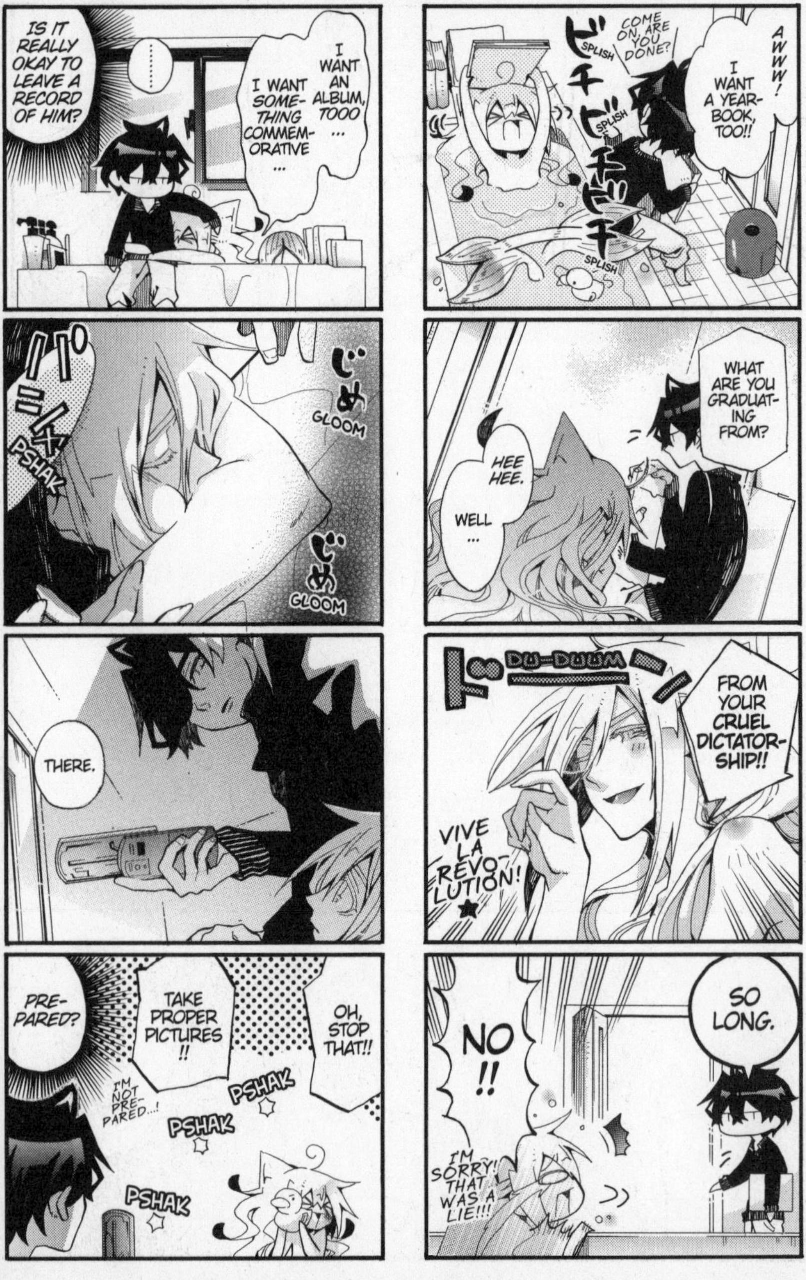
AWWW!
I WANT A YEAR-BOOK, TOO!!
COME ON, ARE YOU DONE?
SPLISH
SPLISH
SPLISH
I WANT AN ALBUM, TOOO ...
I WANT SOME-THING COMMEM-ORATIVE ...
......
IS IT REALLY OKAY TO LEAVE A RECORD OF HIM?
WHAT ARE YOU GRADUAT-ING FROM?
HEE HEE.
WELL ...
GLOOM
PSHAK
GLOOM
FROM YOUR CRUEL DICTATOR-SHIP!!
DU-DUUM
VIVE LA REVO-LUTION! ★
THERE.
SO LONG.
NO !!
I'M SORRY! THAT WAS A LIE!!!
OH, STOP THAT!!
TAKE PROPER PICTURES !!
PRE-PARED?
PSHAK
I'M NOT PRE-PARED...!
PSHAK
PSHAK

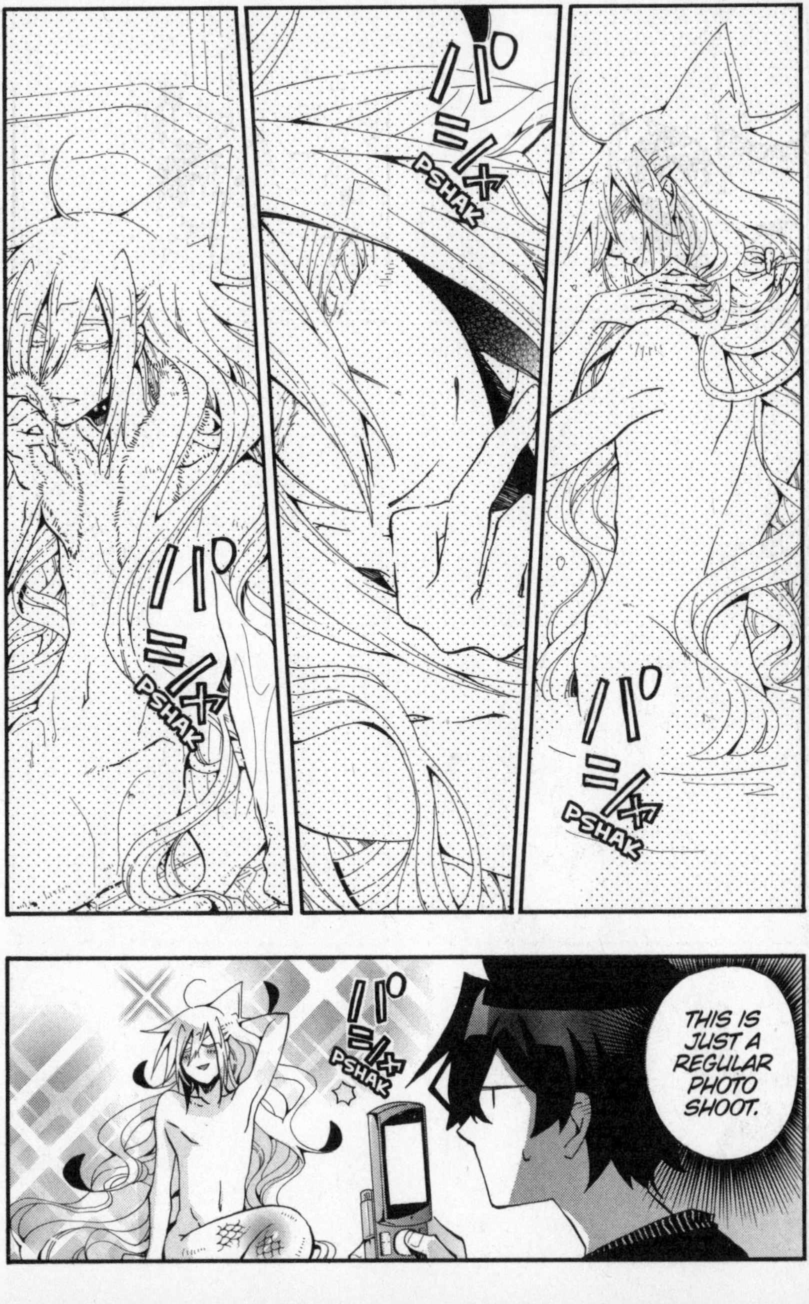
PSHAK
PSHAK
PSHAK
THIS IS JUST A REGULAR PHOTO SHOOT.
PSHAK

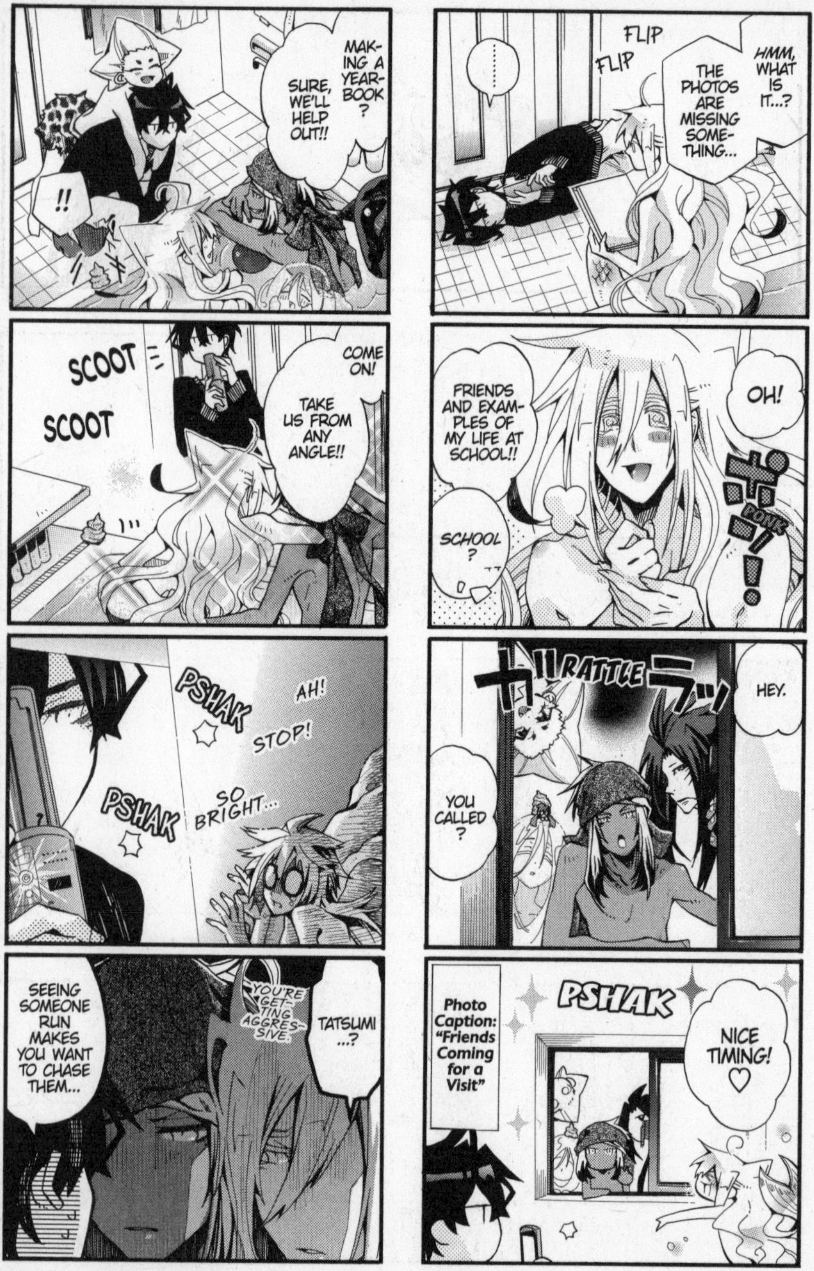
HMM, WHAT IS IT...?
THE PHOTOS ARE MISSING SOMETHING...
FLIP
FLIP
......
OH!
PONK
FRIENDS AND EXAMPLES OF MY LIFE AT SCHOOL!!
SCHOOL?
HEY.
RATTLE
YOU CALLED?
NICE TIMING! ♡
PSHAK
Photo Caption: "Friends Coming for a Visit"
MAKING A YEARBOOK?
SURE, WE'LL HELP OUT!!
!!
COME ON! TAKE US FROM ANY ANGLE!!
SCOOT
SCOOT
AH! STOP!
PSHAK
SO BRIGHT...
PSHAK
TATSUMI...?
YOU'RE GETTING AGGRESSIVE.
SEEING SOMEONE RUN MAKES YOU WANT TO CHASE THEM...

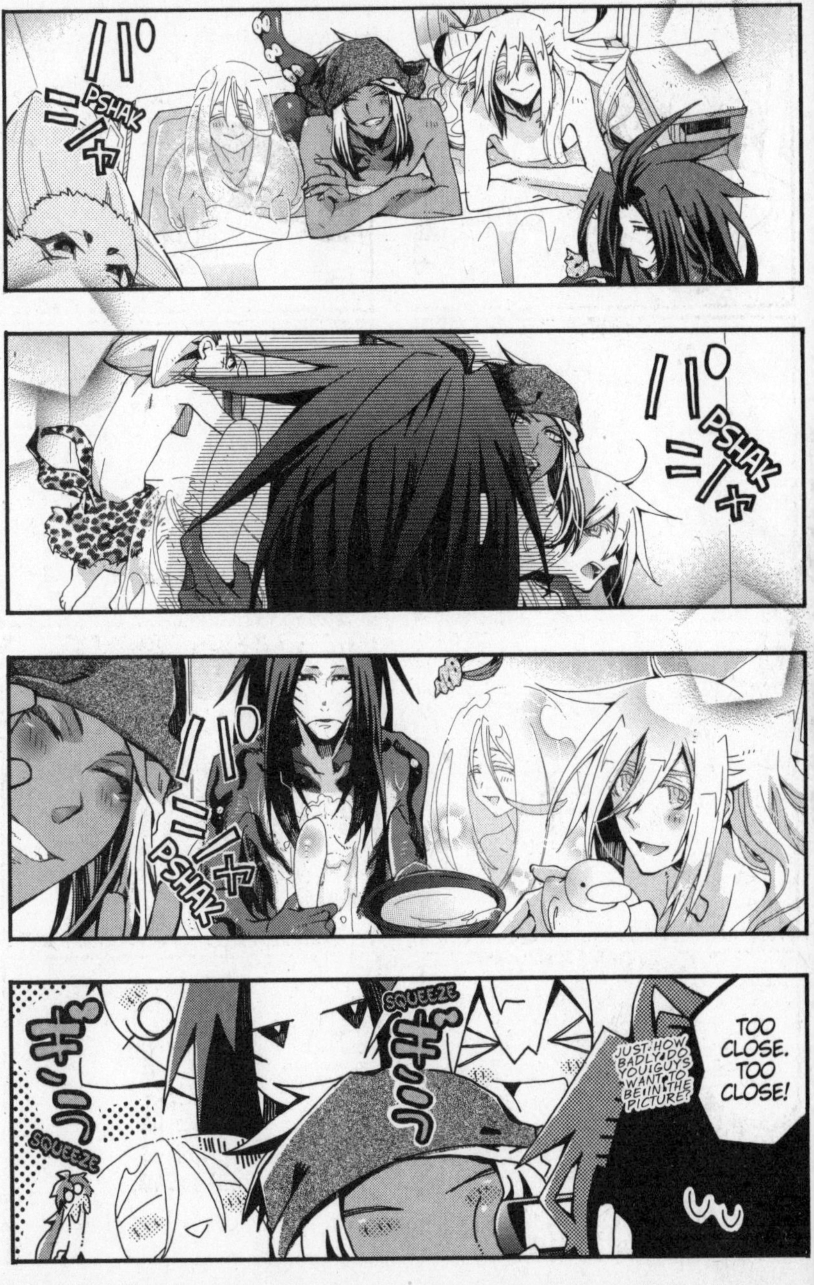
PSHAK
PSHAK
PSHAK
TOO CLOSE. TOO CLOSE!
JUST HOW BADLY DO YOU GUYS WANT TO BE IN THE PICTURE?
SQUEEZE
SQUEEZE

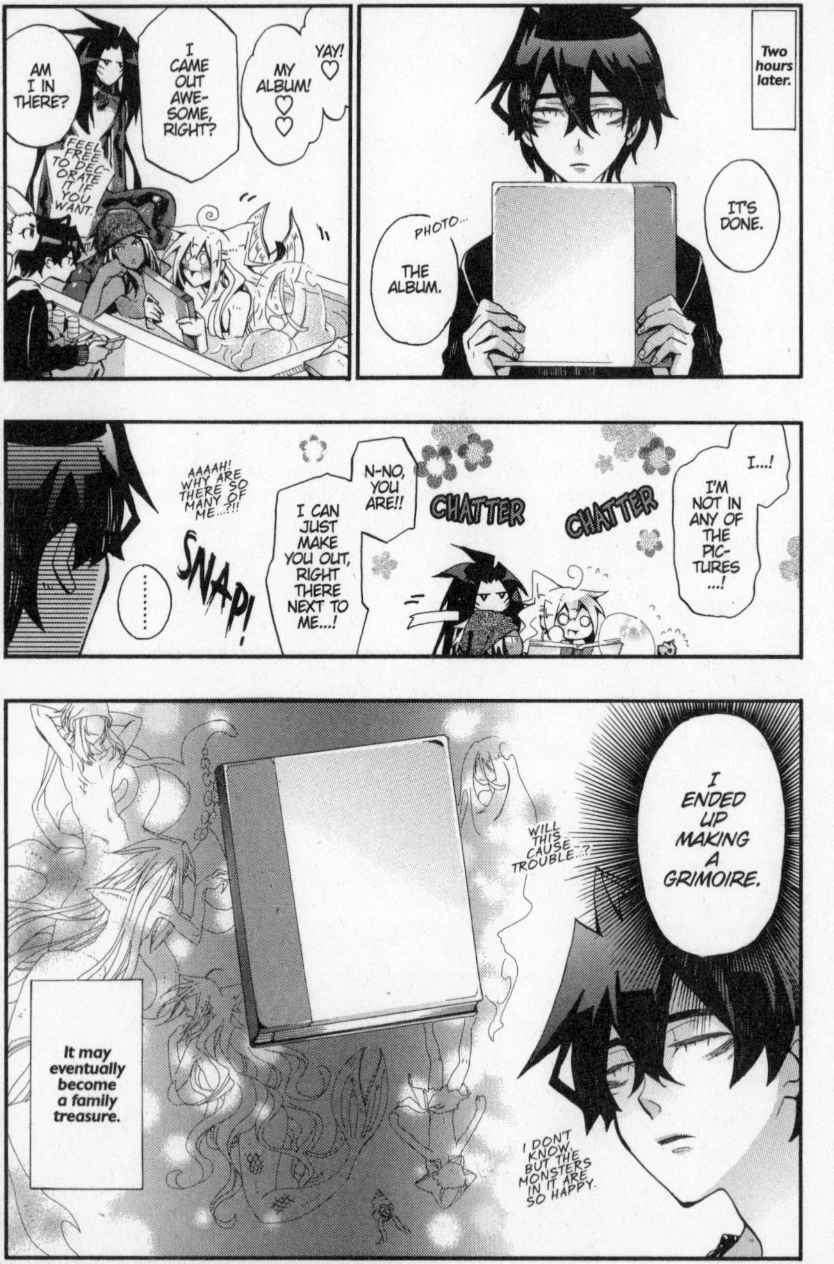
Two hours later.
IT'S DONE.
PHOTO... THE ALBUM.
YAY! ♡
MY ALBUM! ♡ ♡
I CAME OUT AWE-SOME, RIGHT?
AM I IN THERE?
FEEL FREE TO DEC-ORATE IT IF YOU WANT.
I...!
I'M NOT IN ANY OF THE PIC-TURES...!
CHATTER
CHATTER
N-NO, YOU ARE!!
I CAN JUST MAKE YOU OUT, RIGHT THERE NEXT TO ME...!
AAAAH! WHY ARE THERE SO MANY OF ME...?!!
SNAP!
......
I ENDED UP MAKING A GRIMOIRE.
WILL THIS CAUSE TROUBLE...?
I DON'T KNOW, BUT THE MONSTERS IN IT ARE SO HAPPY.
It may eventually become a family treasure.

Merman in My Tub

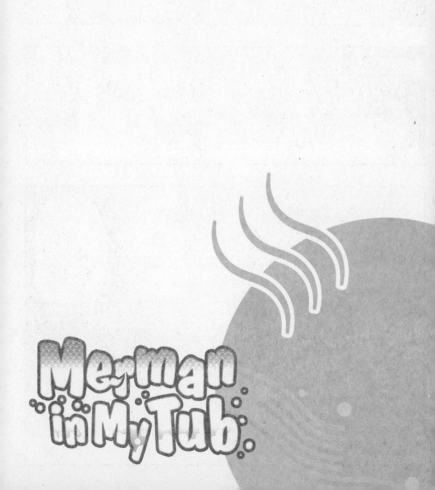

オレん家のフロ事情

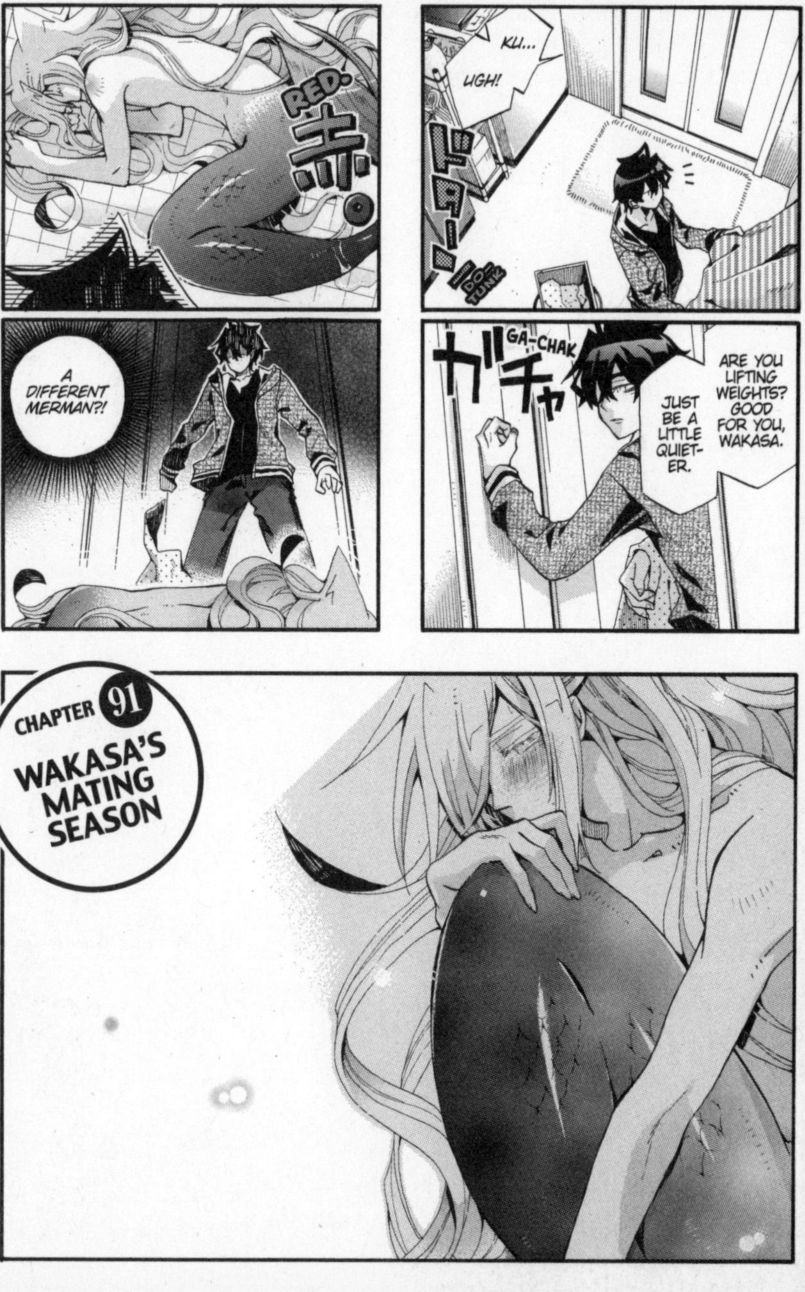
KU...
UGH!
ドターン
DO-TUNK
RED.
赤
ガチャ
GA-CHAK
ARE YOU LIFTING WEIGHTS? GOOD FOR YOU, WAKASA.
JUST BE A LITTLE QUIET-ER.
A DIFFERENT MERMAN?!
CHAPTER 91
WAKASA'S MATING SEASON

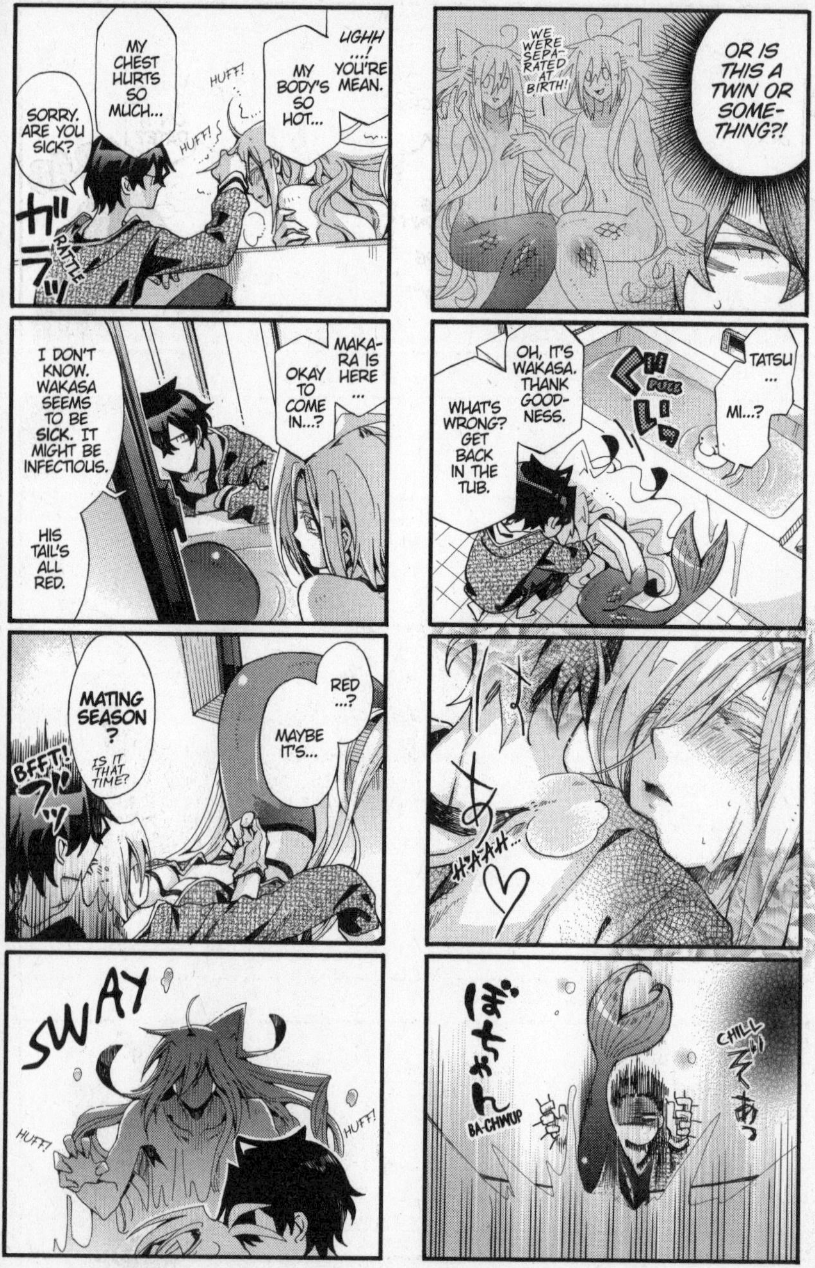
OR IS THIS A TWIN OR SOME-THING?!
WE WERE SEPA-RATED AT BIRTH!
UGHH ....! YOU'RE MEAN.
MY BODY'S SO HOT...
HUFF!
MY CHEST HURTS SO MUCH...
HUFF!
SORRY. ARE YOU SICK?
ガラッ
RATTLE
TATSU ... MI...?
ぐいっ
PULL
OH, IT'S WAKASA. THANK GOOD-NESS.
WHAT'S WRONG? GET BACK IN THE TUB.
MAKA-RA IS HERE ...
OKAY TO COME IN...?
I DON'T KNOW. WAKASA SEEMS TO BE SICK. IT MIGHT BE INFECTIOUS.
HIS TAIL'S ALL RED.
あ
HA-A-AH...
RED ...?
MAYBE IT'S...
MATING SEASON ?
IS IT THAT TIME?
BFFT!
ぼちゃん
BA-CHWUP
CHILL
ぞあっ
SWAY
HUFF!
HUFF!

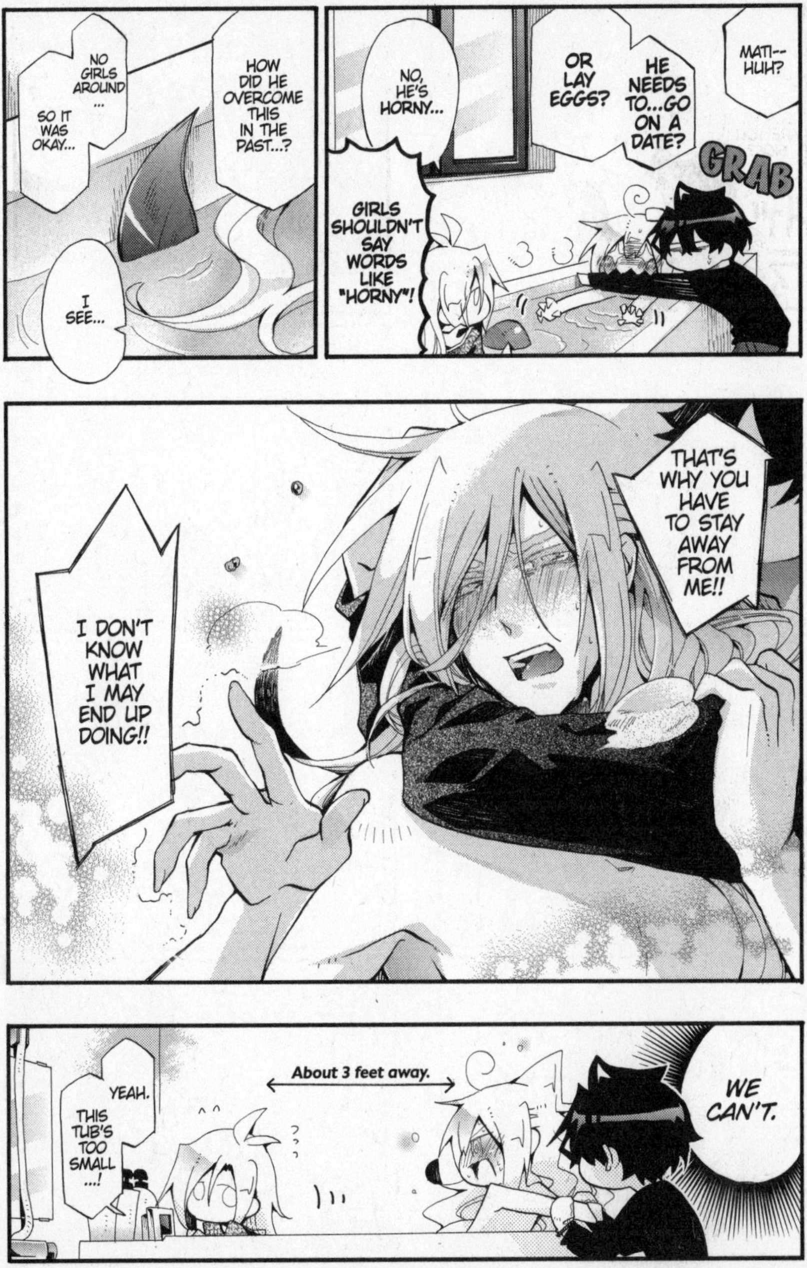
MATI-- HUH?
GRAB
HE NEEDS TO...GO ON A DATE?
OR LAY EGGS?
NO, HE'S HORNY...
GIRLS SHOULDN'T SAY WORDS LIKE "HORNY"!
HOW DID HE OVERCOME THIS IN THE PAST...?
NO GIRLS AROUND ...
SO IT WAS OKAY...
I SEE...
THAT'S WHY YOU HAVE TO STAY AWAY FROM ME!!
I DON'T KNOW WHAT I MAY END UP DOING!!
WE CAN'T.
About 3 feet away.
YEAH.
THIS TUB'S TOO SMALL ...!

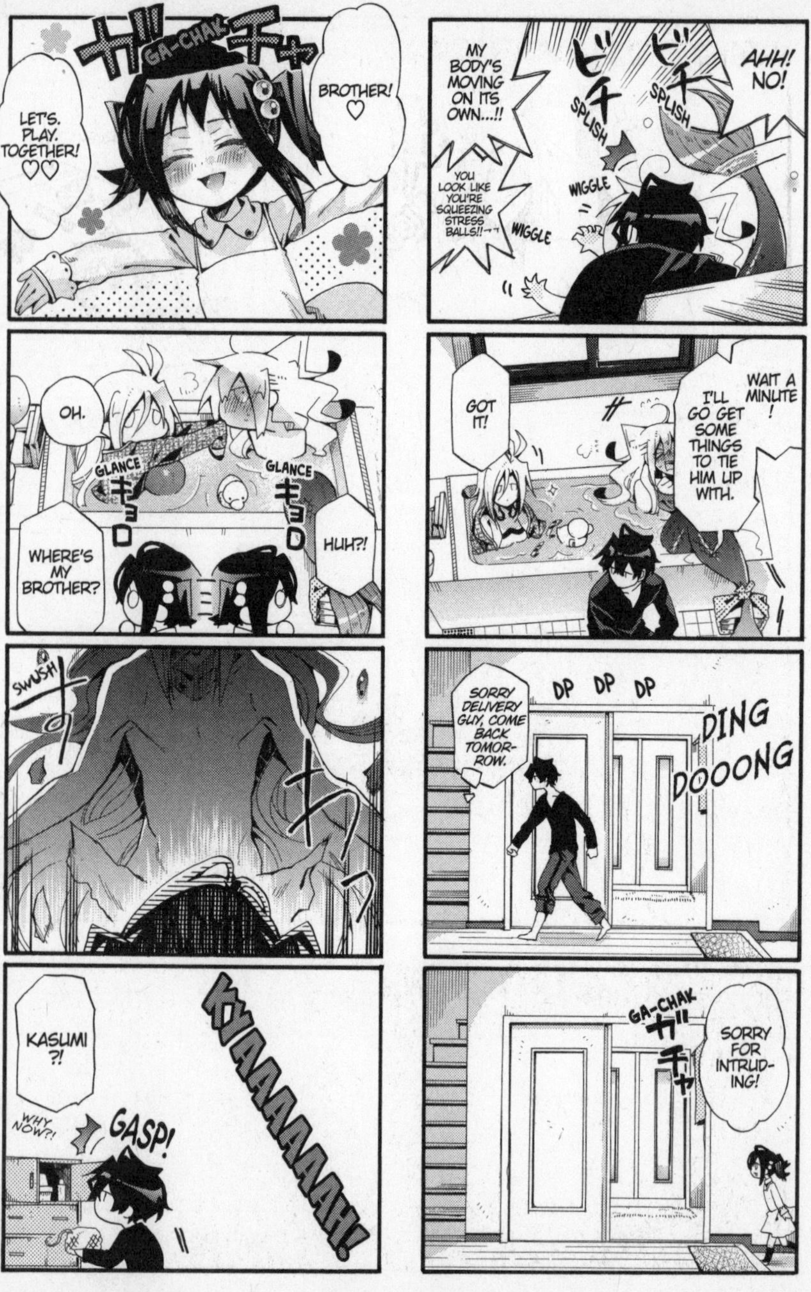
AHH! NO!
ビチ SPLISH
ビチ SPLISH
MY BODY'S MOVING ON ITS OWN...!!
WIGGLE
YOU LOOK LIKE YOU'RE SQUEEZING STRESS BALLS!!
WIGGLE
ガチャ GA-CHAK
BROTHER! ♡
LET'S. PLAY. TOGETHER! ♡♡
WAIT A MINUTE!
I'LL GO GET SOME THINGS TO TIE HIM UP WITH.
GOT IT!
GLANCE キョロ
OH.
GLANCE キョロ
HUH?!
WHERE'S MY BROTHER?
DP DP DP
DING DOOONG
SORRY DELIVERY GUY, COME BACK TOMORROW.
SWUSH
SORRY FOR INTRUDING!
GA-CHAK ガチャ
KYAAAAAAAH!
KASUMI?!
GASP!
WHY NOW?!

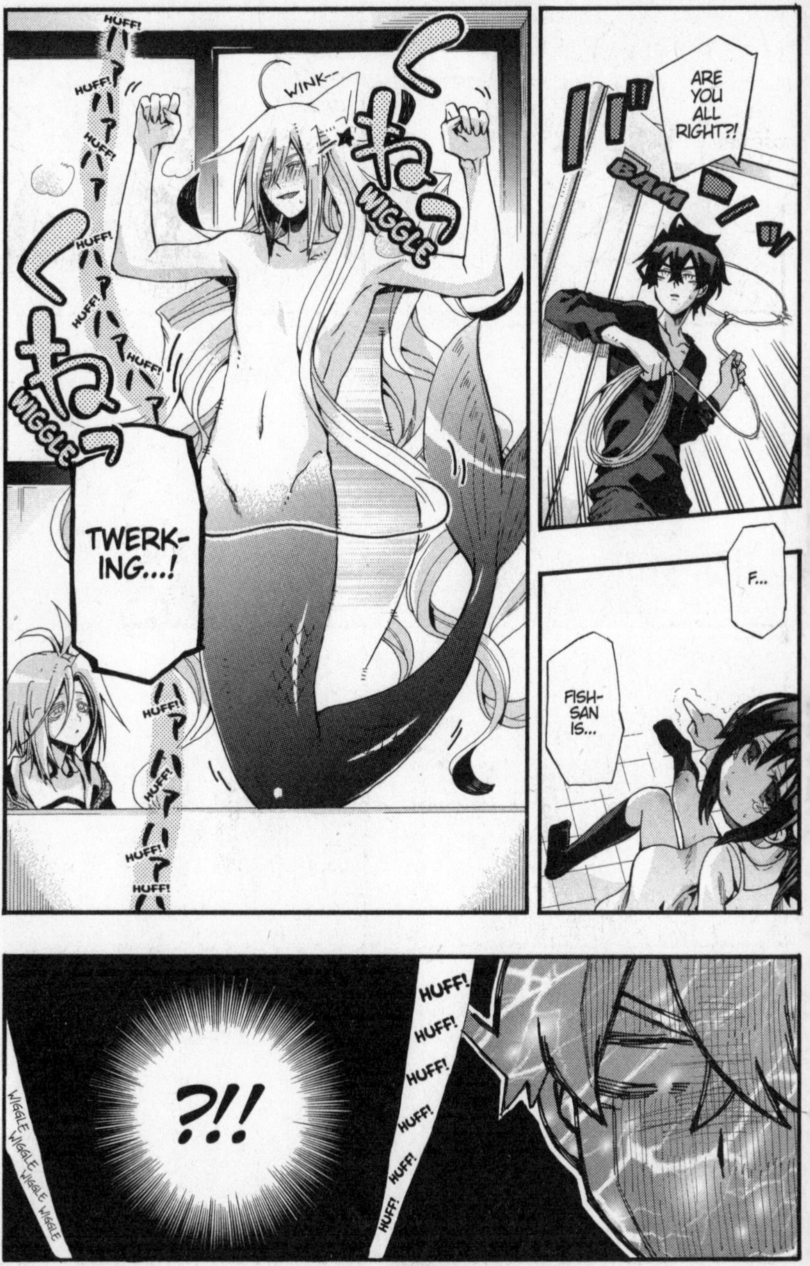

BAM
ARE YOU ALL RIGHT?!
F...
FISH-SAN IS...
WINK--
WIGGLE
WIGGLE
HUFF!
HUFF!
HUFF!
HUFF!
HUFF!
HUFF!
TWERKING...!
HUFF!
HUFF!
HUFF!
HUFF!
HUFF!
HUFF!
HUFF!
HUFF!
HUFF!
HUFF!
HUFF!
?!!
WIGGLE WIGGLE WIGGLE WIGGLE

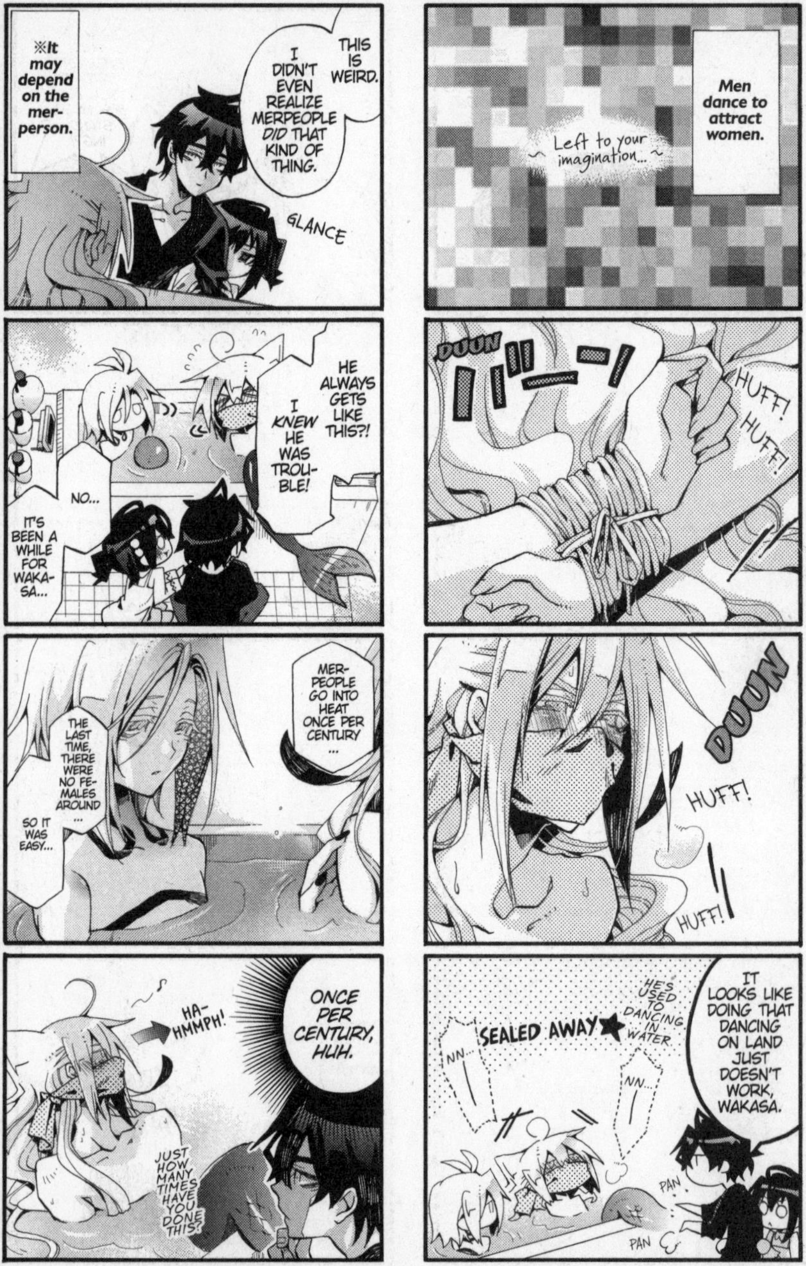
Men dance to attract women.
~ Left to your imagination... ~
DUUN
HUFF! HUFF!
DUUN
HUFF!
HUFF!
IT LOOKS LIKE DOING THAT DANCING ON LAND JUST DOESN'T WORK, WAKASA.
HE'S USED TO DANCING IN WATER.
SEALED AWAY★
NN...
NN...
PAN
PAN
THIS IS WEIRD.
I DIDN'T EVEN REALIZE MERPEOPLE *DID* THAT KIND OF THING.
※It may depend on the merperson.
GLANCE
HE ALWAYS GETS LIKE THIS?!
I *KNEW* HE WAS TROUBLE!
NO...
IT'S BEEN A WHILE FOR WAKASA...
MERPEOPLE GO INTO HEAT ONCE PER CENTURY...
THE LAST TIME, THERE WERE NO FEMALES AROUND...
SO IT WAS EASY...
ONCE PER CENTURY, HUH.
HA-HMMPH!
JUST HOW MANY TIMES HAVE YOU DONE THIS?

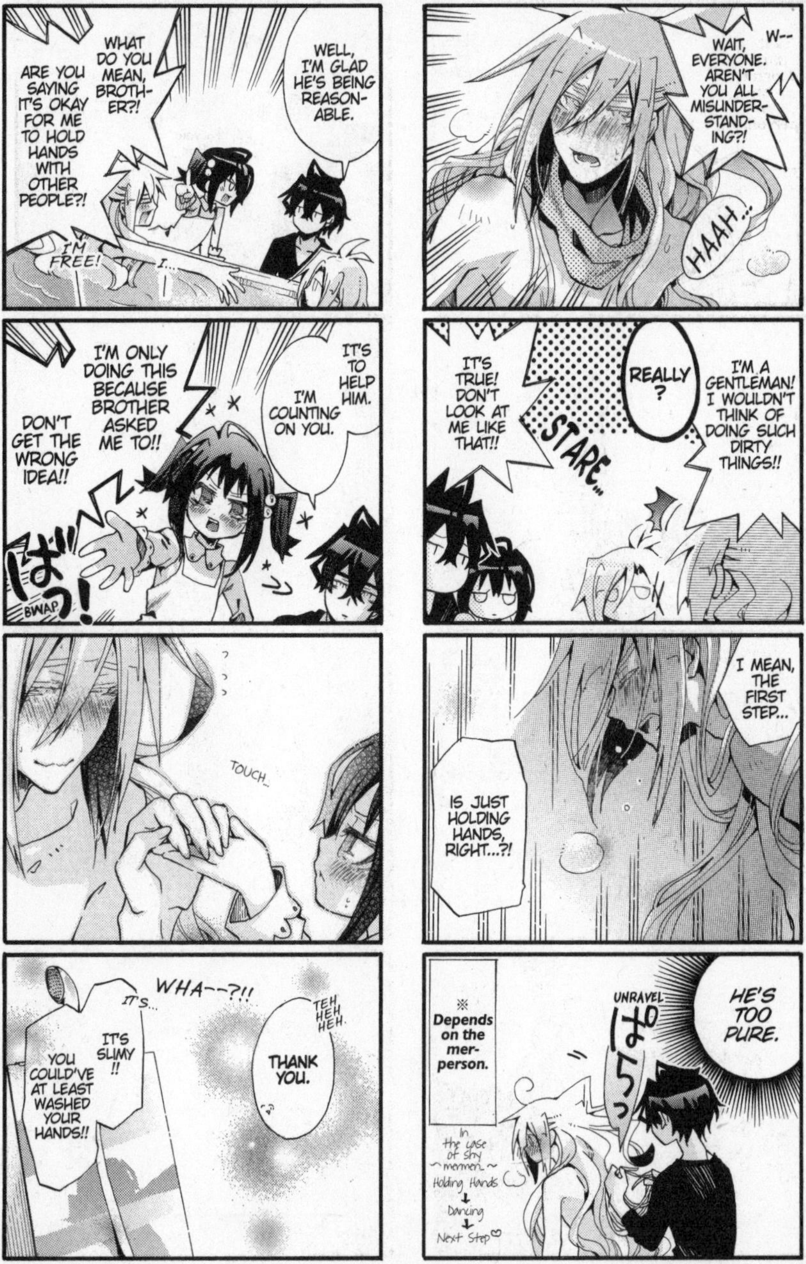
W--
WAIT, EVERYONE. AREN'T YOU ALL MISUNDER-STANDING?!
HAAH...
WELL, I'M GLAD HE'S BEING REASON-ABLE.
WHAT DO YOU MEAN, BROTH-ER?!
ARE YOU SAYING IT'S OKAY FOR ME TO HOLD HANDS WITH OTHER PEOPLE?!
I'M FREE!
I...
I'M A GENTLEMAN! I WOULDN'T THINK OF DOING SUCH DIRTY THINGS!!
REALLY?
STARE...
IT'S TRUE! DON'T LOOK AT ME LIKE THAT!!
IT'S TO HELP HIM.
I'M COUNTING ON YOU.
I'M ONLY DOING THIS BECAUSE BROTHER ASKED ME TO!!
DON'T GET THE WRONG IDEA!!
ばっ!
BWAP
I MEAN, THE FIRST STEP...
IS JUST HOLDING HANDS, RIGHT...?!
TOUCH...
HE'S TOO PURE.
UNRAVEL
ぱらっ
※ Depends on the mer-person.
In the case of shy mermen ~ Holding Hands → Dancing → Next Step♡
TEH HEH HEH.
THANK YOU.
WHA--?!!
IT'S...
IT'S SLIMY!!
YOU COULD'VE AT LEAST WASHED YOUR HANDS!!

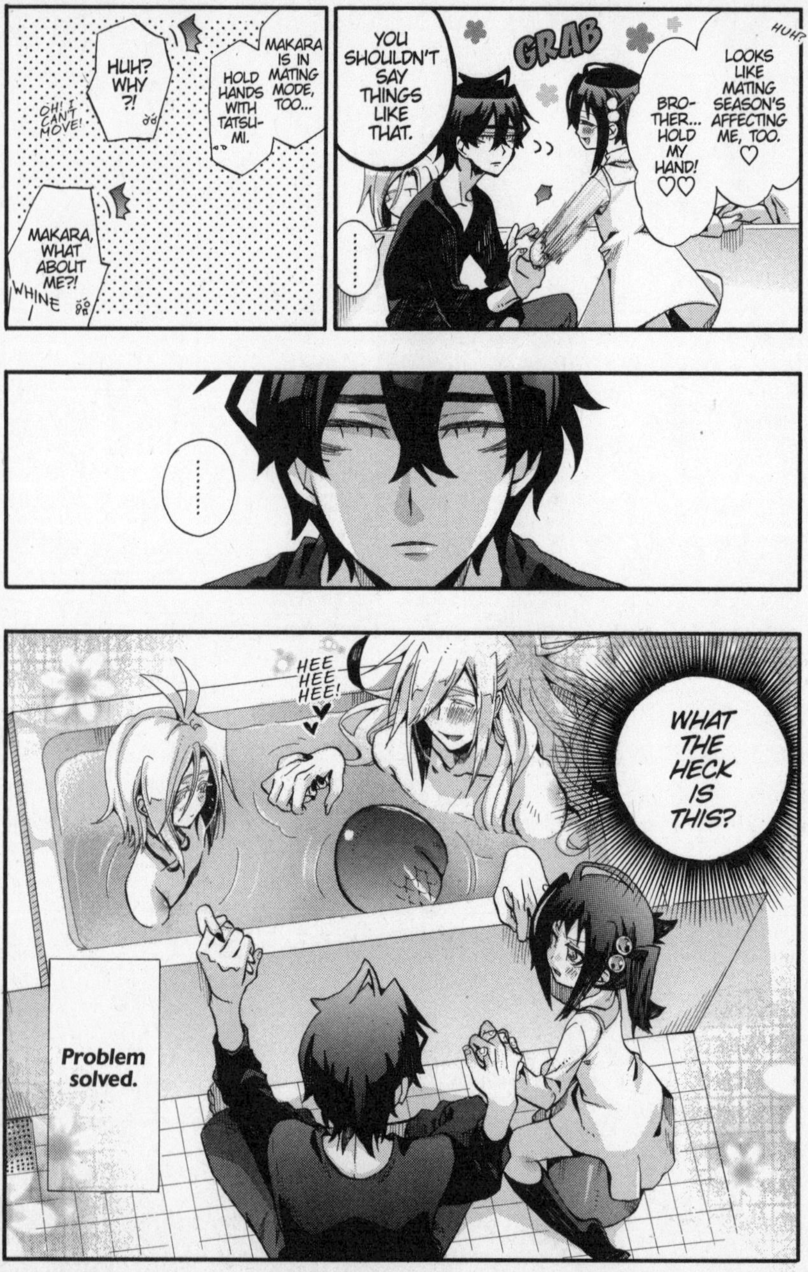
HUH?
LOOKS LIKE MATING SEASON'S AFFECTING ME, TOO. ♡
BRO-THER... HOLD MY HAND! ♡♡
GRAB
YOU SHOULDN'T SAY THINGS LIKE THAT.
......
MAKARA IS IN MATING MODE, TOO...
HOLD HANDS WITH TATSU-MI.
HUH? WHY?!
OH! I CAN'T MOVE!
MAKARA, WHAT ABOUT ME?!
WHINE
......
WHAT THE HECK IS THIS?
HEE HEE HEE! ♥
Problem solved.

Merman in My Tub

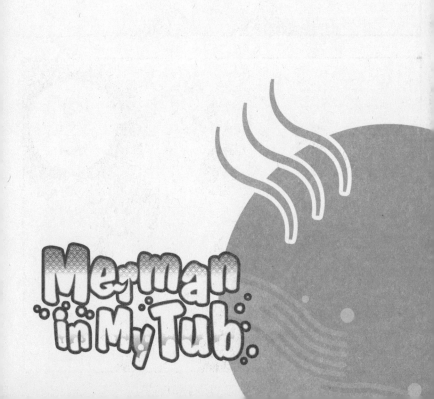

オレん家のフロ事情

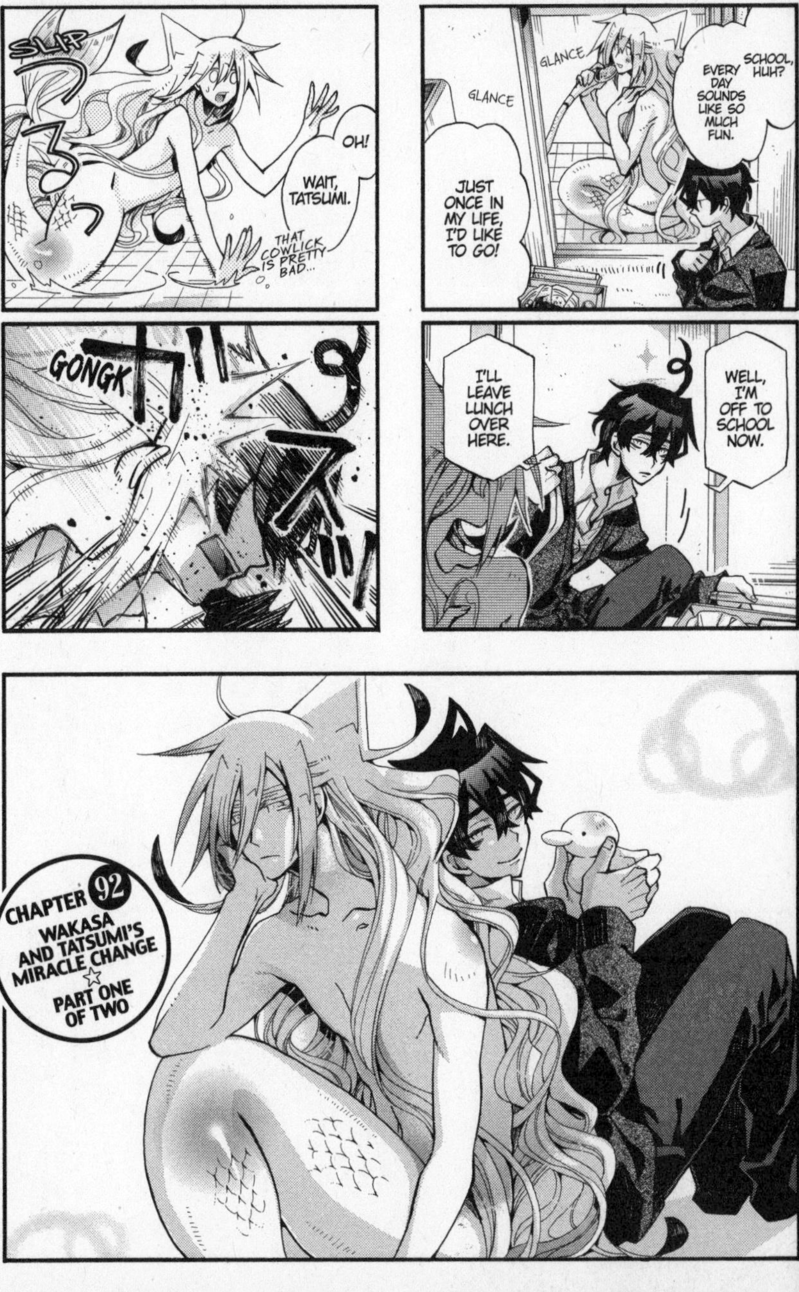
GLANCE
GLANCE
SCHOOL, HUH? EVERY DAY SOUNDS LIKE SO MUCH FUN.
JUST ONCE IN MY LIFE, I'D LIKE TO GO!
SLIP
OH!
WAIT, TATSUMI.
THAT COWLICK IS PRETTY BAD...
WELL, I'M OFF TO SCHOOL NOW.
I'LL LEAVE LUNCH OVER HERE.
GONGK
CHAPTER 92
WAKASA AND TATSUMI'S MIRACLE CHANGE ☆ PART ONE OF TWO

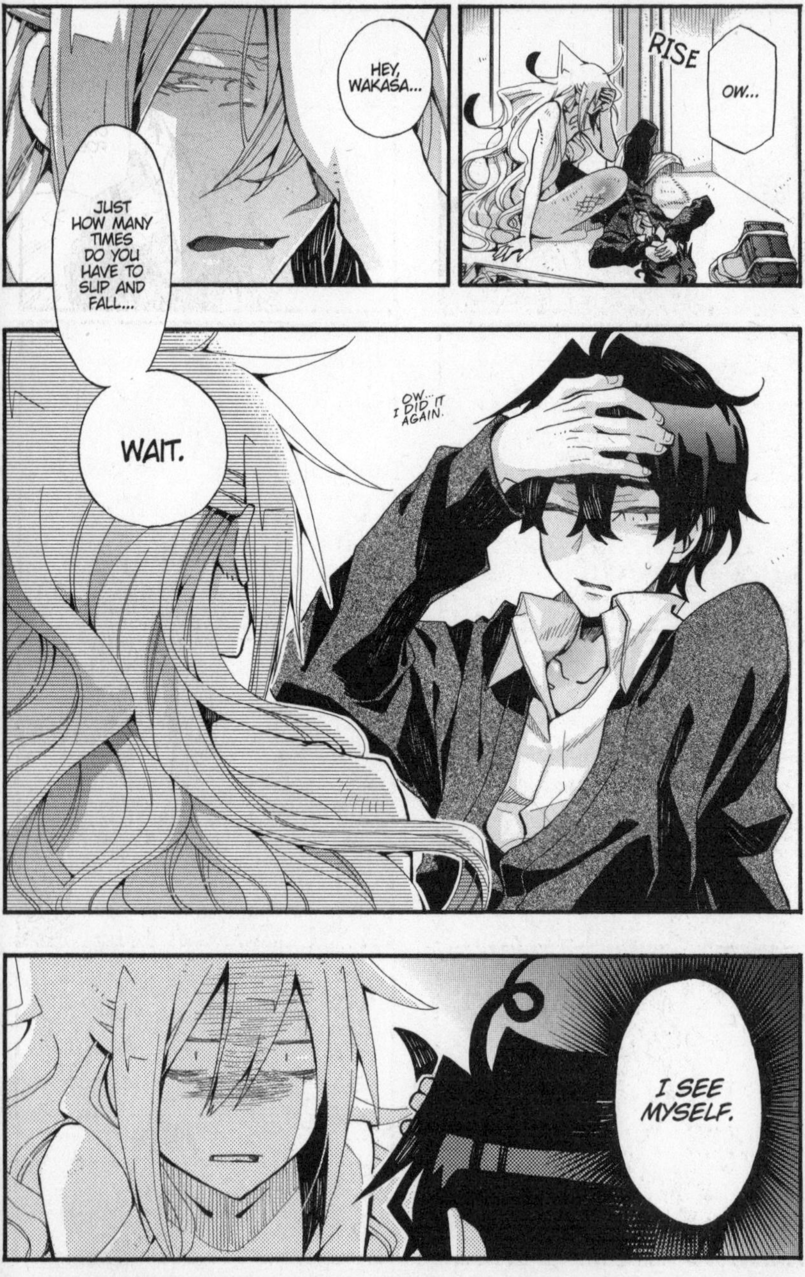
RISE
OW...
HEY, WAKASA...
JUST HOW MANY TIMES DO YOU HAVE TO SLIP AND FALL...
OW... I DID IT AGAIN.
WAIT.
I SEE MYSELF.

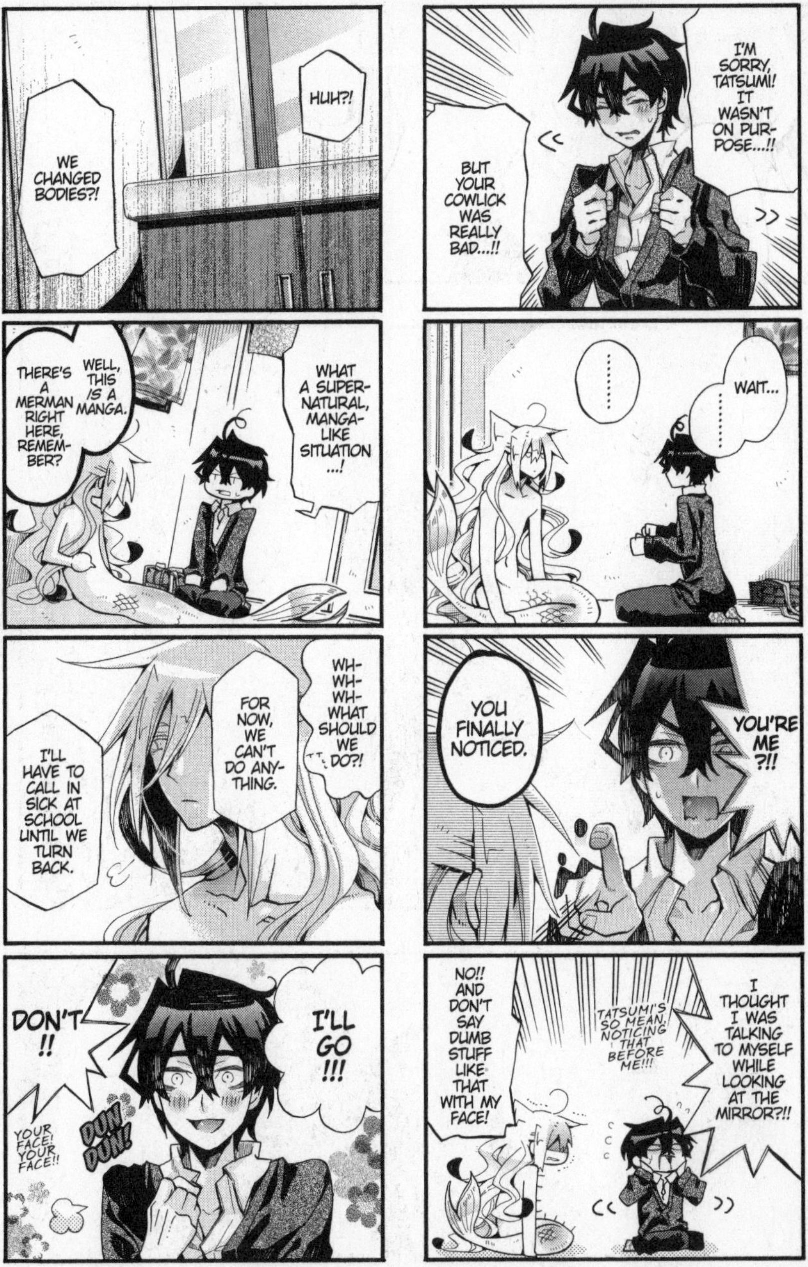
I'M SORRY, TATSUMI! IT WASN'T ON PURPOSE...!!
BUT YOUR COWLICK WAS REALLY BAD...!!
HUH?!
WE CHANGED BODIES?!
WAIT...
......
WHAT A SUPERNATURAL, MANGA-LIKE SITUATION...!
WELL, THIS IS A MANGA.
THERE'S A MERMAN RIGHT HERE, REMEMBER?
YOU'RE ME?!!
YOU FINALLY NOTICED.
WH-WH-WH-WHAT SHOULD WE DO?!
FOR NOW, WE CAN'T DO ANYTHING.
I'LL HAVE TO CALL IN SICK AT SCHOOL UNTIL WE TURN BACK.
I THOUGHT I WAS TALKING TO MYSELF WHILE LOOKING AT THE MIRROR?!!
TATSUMI'S SO MEAN, NOTICING THAT BEFORE ME!!!
NO!! AND DON'T SAY DUMB STUFF LIKE THAT WITH MY FACE!
I'LL GO!!!
DON'T!!
DUN DUN!
YOUR FACE! YOUR FACE!!

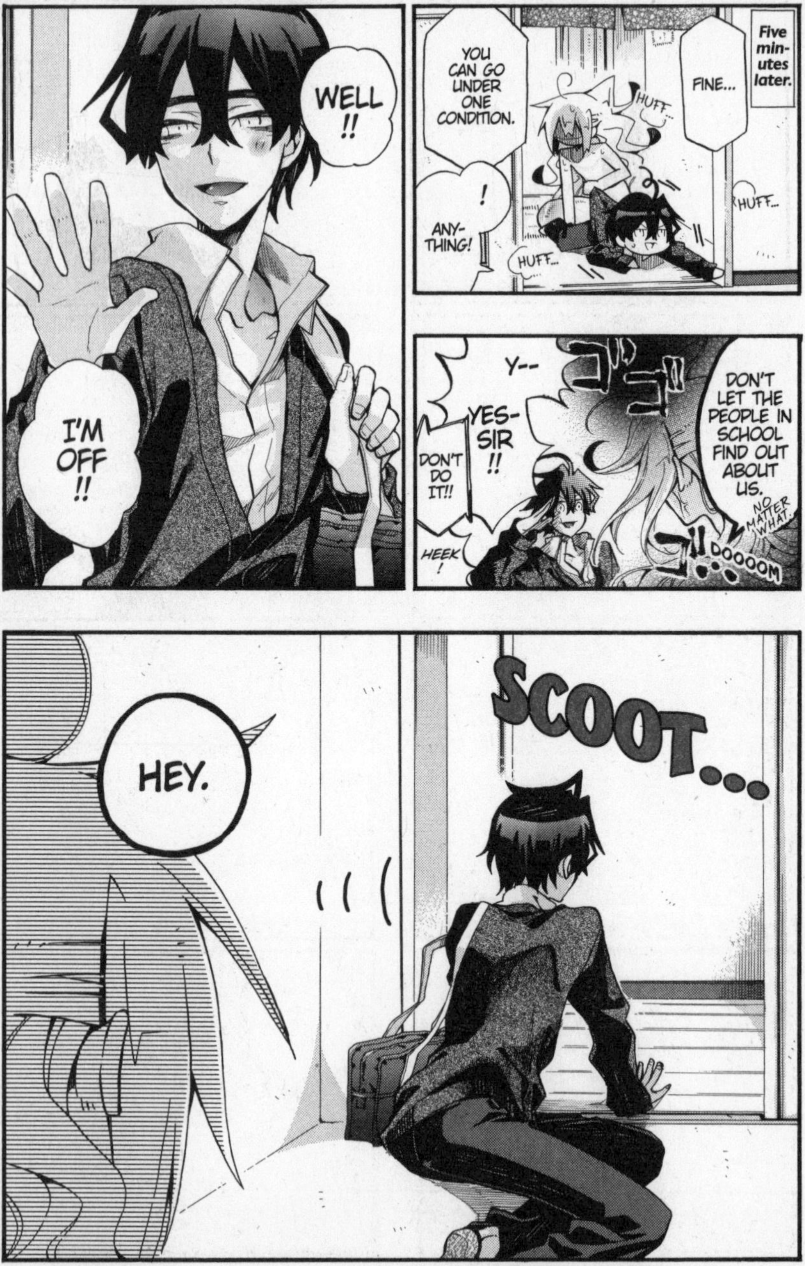
Five minutes later.
FINE...
HUFF...
HUFF...
YOU CAN GO UNDER ONE CONDITION.
HUFF...
! ANYTHING!
DON'T LET THE PEOPLE IN SCHOOL FIND OUT ABOUT US.
NO MATTER WHAT.
DOOOOM
Y--
YES-SIR!!
DON'T DO IT!!
HEEK!
WELL!!
I'M OFF!!
SCOOT...
HEY.

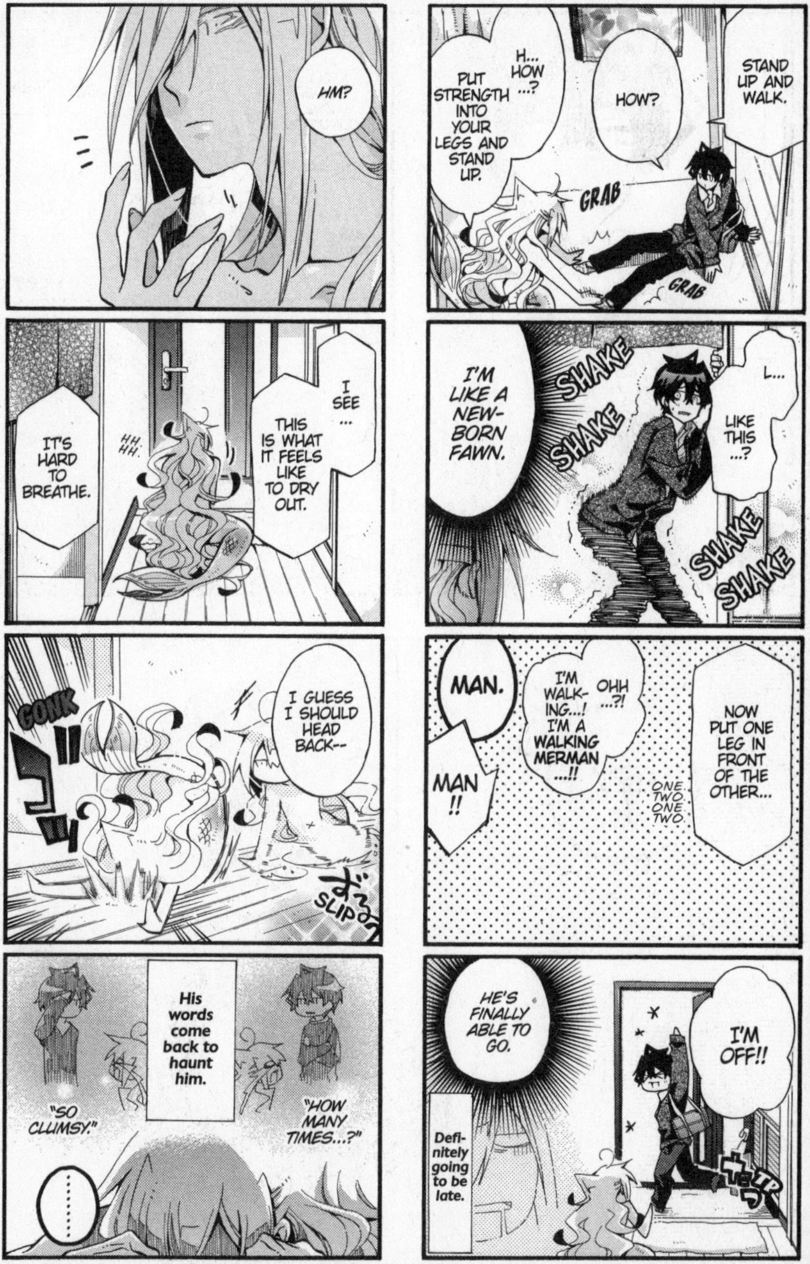
STAND UP AND WALK.
HOW?
H... HOW ...?
PUT STRENGTH INTO YOUR LEGS AND STAND UP.
GRAB
GRAB
L... LIKE THIS ...?
SHAKE
SHAKE
SHAKE
SHAKE
I'M LIKE A NEW-BORN FAWN.
NOW PUT ONE LEG IN FRONT OF THE OTHER...
ONE TWO ONE TWO
OHH ...?!
I'M WALKING...! I'M A WALKING MERMAN ...!!
MAN.
MAN !!
I'M OFF!!
TRP
HE'S FINALLY ABLE TO GO.
Definitely going to be late.
HM?
I SEE ...
THIS IS WHAT IT FEELS LIKE TO DRY OUT.
HH HH
IT'S HARD TO BREATHE.
I GUESS I SHOULD HEAD BACK--
CONK
SLIP
His words come back to haunt him.
"HOW MANY TIMES...?"
"SO CLUMSY."
......

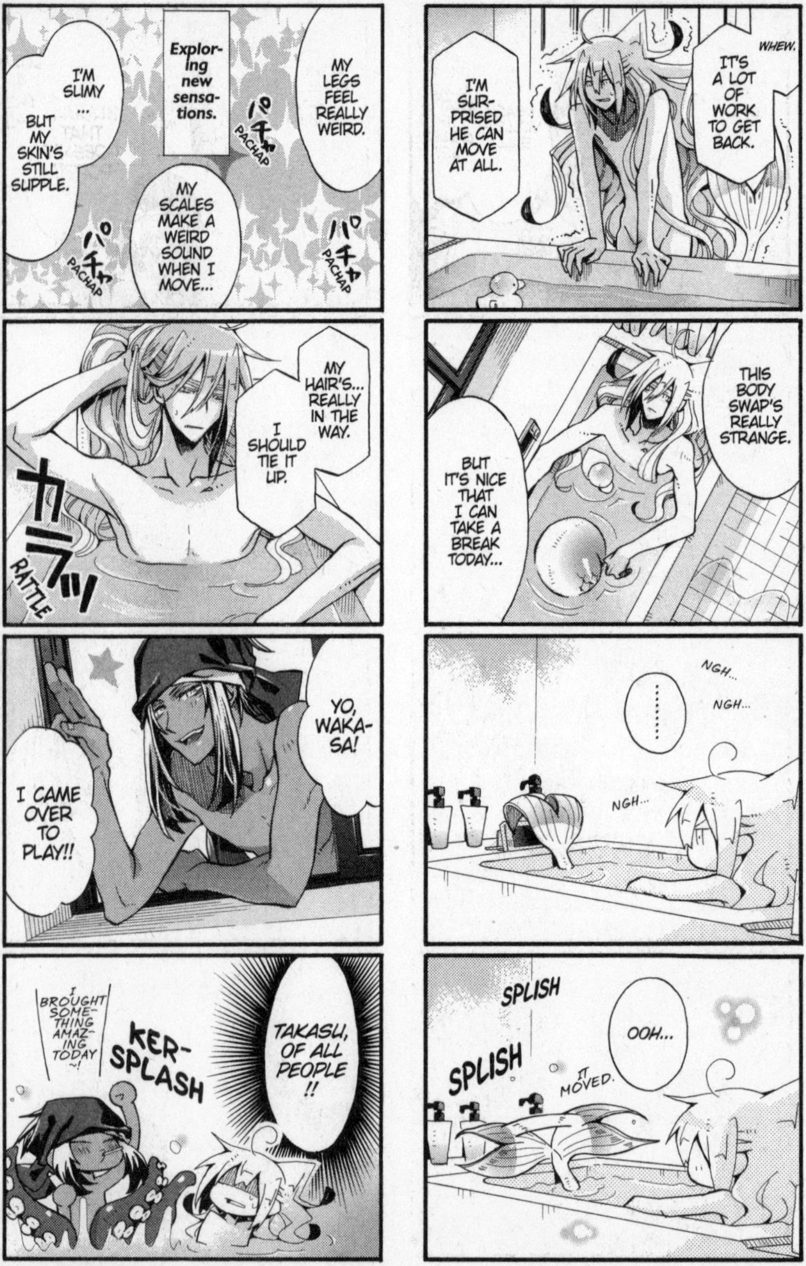
WHEW.
IT'S A LOT OF WORK TO GET BACK.
I'M SURPRISED HE CAN MOVE AT ALL.
MY LEGS FEEL REALLY WEIRD.
パチャ PACHAP
Exploring new sensations.
MY SCALES MAKE A WEIRD SOUND WHEN I MOVE...
パチャ PACHAP
I'M SLIMY... BUT MY SKIN'S STILL SUPPLE.
パチャ PACHAP
THIS BODY SWAP'S REALLY STRANGE.
BUT IT'S NICE THAT I CAN TAKE A BREAK TODAY...
MY HAIR'S... REALLY IN THE WAY.
I SHOULD TIE IT UP.
カラッ RATTLE
NGH...
NGH...
......
NGH...
YO, WAKASA!
I CAME OVER TO PLAY!!
SPLISH
OOH...
SPLISH
IT MOVED.
TAKASU, OF ALL PEOPLE!!
KER-SPLASH
I BROUGHT SOMETHING AMAZING TODAY~!

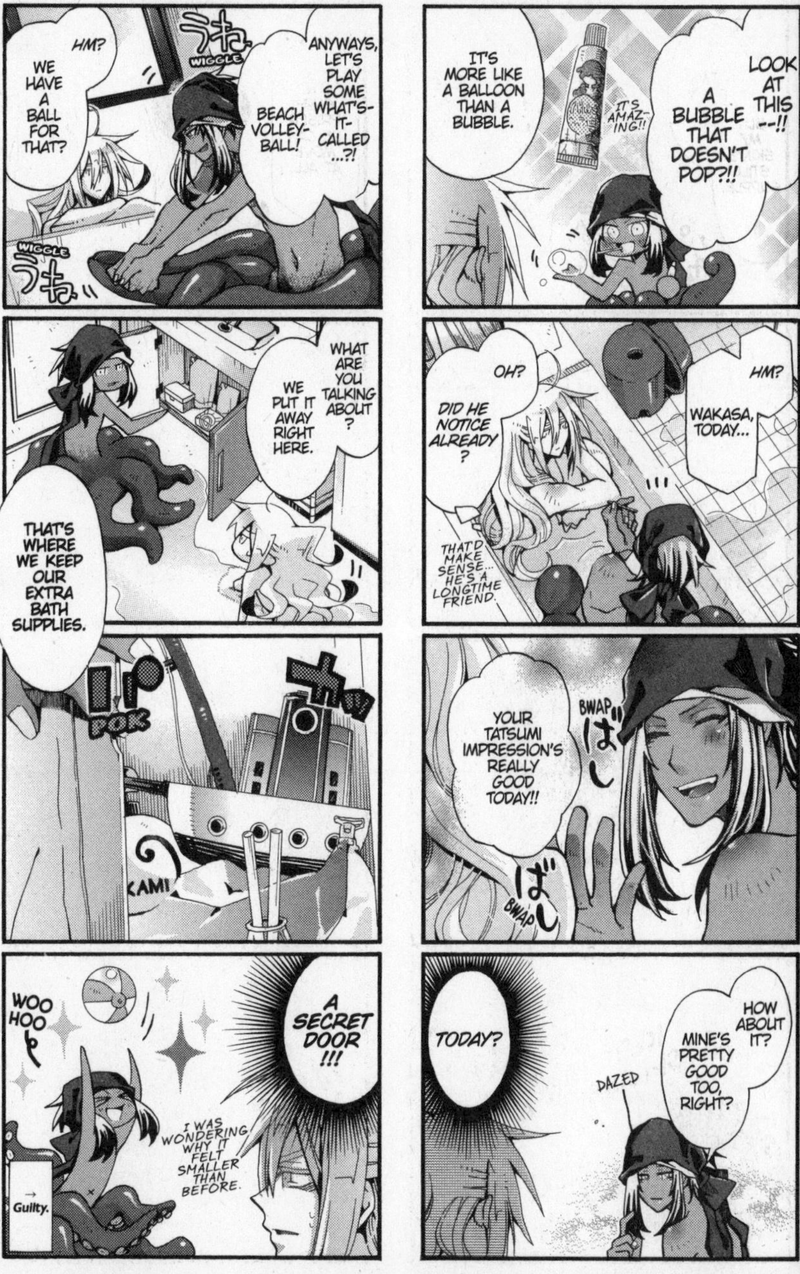
LOOK AT THIS--!!
A BUBBLE THAT DOESN'T POP?!!
IT'S AMAZING!!
IT'S MORE LIKE A BALLOON THAN A BUBBLE.
HM?
WAKASA, TODAY...
OH?
DID HE NOTICE ALREADY?
THAT'D MAKE SENSE... HE'S A LONGTIME FRIEND.
BWAP ぱし
YOUR TATSUMI IMPRESSION'S REALLY GOOD TODAY!!
ぱし BWAP
HOW ABOUT IT?
MINE'S PRETTY GOOD TOO, RIGHT?
DAZED
TODAY?
ANYWAYS, LET'S PLAY SOME WHAT'S-IT-CALLED...?!
BEACH VOLLEYBALL!
うね WIGGLE
HM?
WE HAVE A BALL FOR THAT?
WIGGLE うね
WHAT ARE YOU TALKING ABOUT?
WE PUT IT AWAY RIGHT HERE.
THAT'S WHERE WE KEEP OUR EXTRA BATH SUPPLIES.
カッ
POK
A SECRET DOOR!!!
WOO HOO
I WAS WONDERING WHY IT FELT SMALLER THAN BEFORE.
→ Guilty.

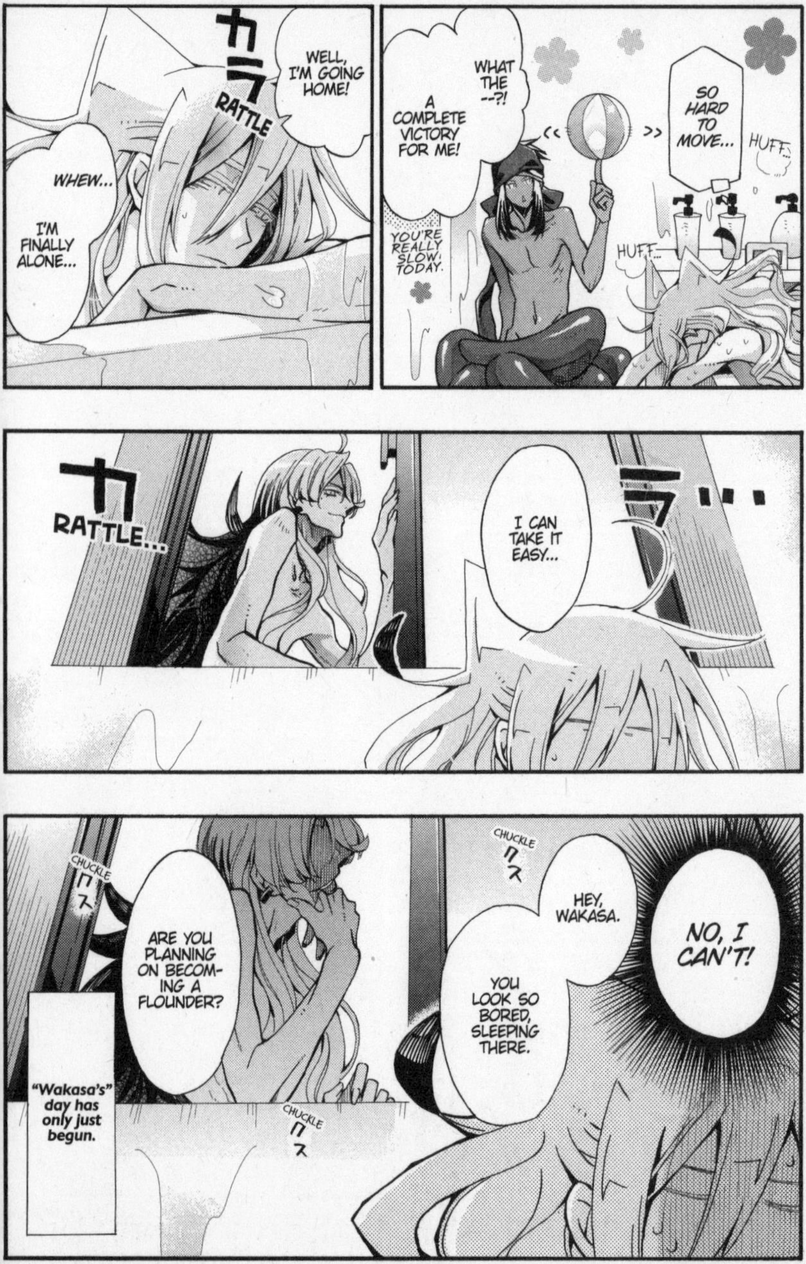
SO HARD TO MOVE...
HUFF...
HUFF...
WHAT THE --?!
A COMPLETE VICTORY FOR ME!
YOU'RE REALLY SLOW TODAY.
カラ
RATTLE
WELL, I'M GOING HOME!
WHEW...
I'M FINALLY ALONE...
ラ...
I CAN TAKE IT EASY...
カ
RATTLE...
NO, I CAN'T!
CHUCKLE
クス
HEY, WAKASA.
YOU LOOK SO BORED, SLEEPING THERE.
CHUCKLE
クス
ARE YOU PLANNING ON BECOMING A FLOUNDER?
CHUCKLE
クス
"Wakasa's" day has only just begun.

Merman in My Tub

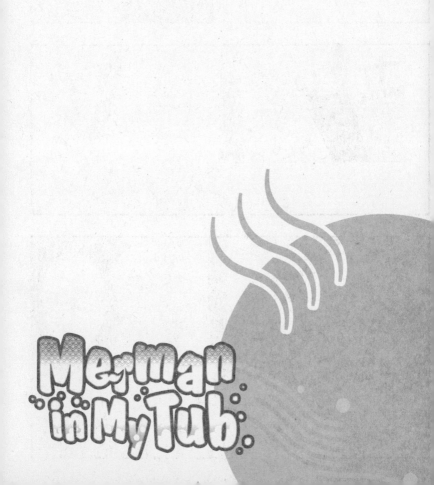

オレん家(ち)のフロ事情

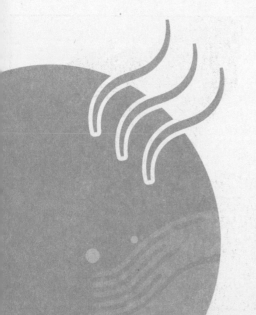

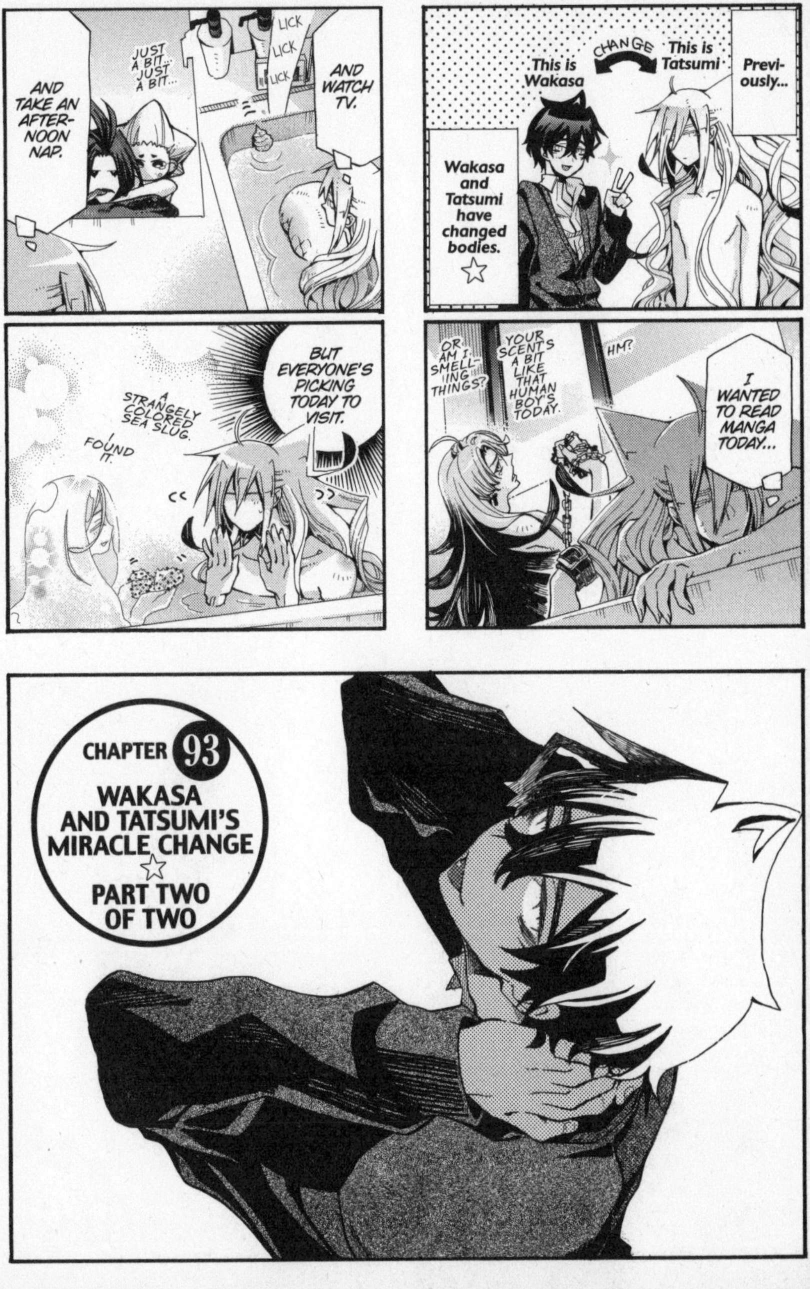
Previ-ously...
This is Tatsumi
CHANGE
This is Wakasa
Wakasa and Tatsumi have changed bodies. ☆
I WANTED TO READ MANGA TODAY...
HM?
YOUR SCENT'S A BIT LIKE THAT HUMAN BOY'S TODAY.
OR AM I SMELL-ING THINGS?
AND WATCH TV.
LICK
LICK
LICK
JUST A BIT... JUST A BIT...
AND TAKE AN AFTER-NOON NAP.
BUT EVERYONE'S PICKING TODAY TO VISIT.
A STRANGELY COLORED SEA SLUG.
I FOUND IT.
CHAPTER 93
WAKASA AND TATSUMI'S MIRACLE CHANGE
☆
PART TWO OF TWO

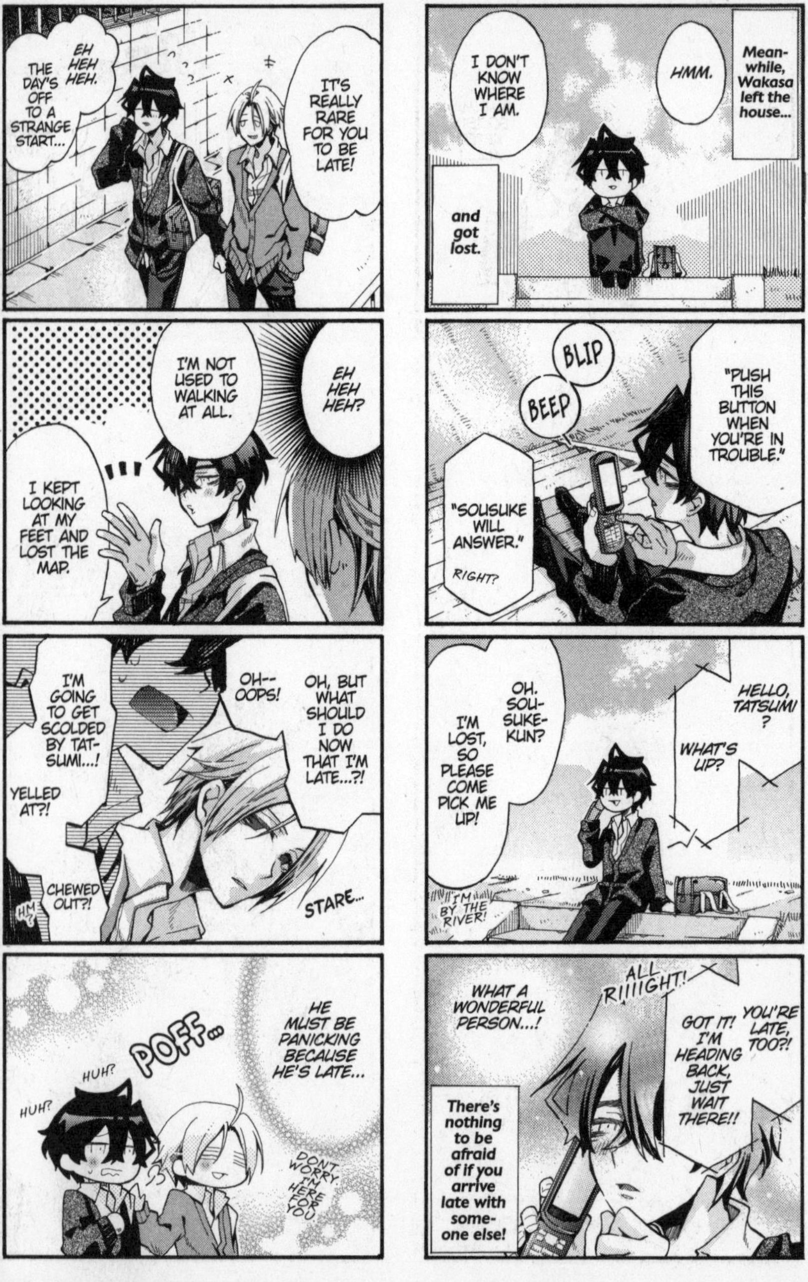
Meanwhile, Wakasa left the house...
HMM.
I DON'T KNOW WHERE I AM.
and got lost.
"PUSH THIS BUTTON WHEN YOU'RE IN TROUBLE."
BLIP
BEEP
"SOUSUKE WILL ANSWER."
RIGHT?
HELLO, TATSUMI?
WHAT'S UP?
OH. SOUSUKE-KUN?
I'M LOST, SO PLEASE COME PICK ME UP!
I'M BY THE RIVER!
ALL R!!!!GHT!
YOU'RE LATE, TOO?!
GOT IT! I'M HEADING BACK, JUST WAIT THERE!!
WHAT A WONDERFUL PERSON...!
There's nothing to be afraid of if you arrive late with someone else!
IT'S REALLY RARE FOR YOU TO BE LATE!
EH HEH HEH.
THE DAY'S OFF TO A STRANGE START...
EH HEH HEH?
I'M NOT USED TO WALKING AT ALL.
I KEPT LOOKING AT MY FEET AND LOST THE MAP.
OH, BUT WHAT SHOULD I DO NOW THAT I'M LATE...?!
OH-- OOPS!
I'M GOING TO GET SCOLDED BY TATSUMI...!
YELLED AT?!
CHEWED OUT?!
HM?
STARE...
HE MUST BE PANICKING BECAUSE HE'S LATE...
POFF...
HUH?
HUH?
DON'T WORRY. I'M HERE FOR YOU

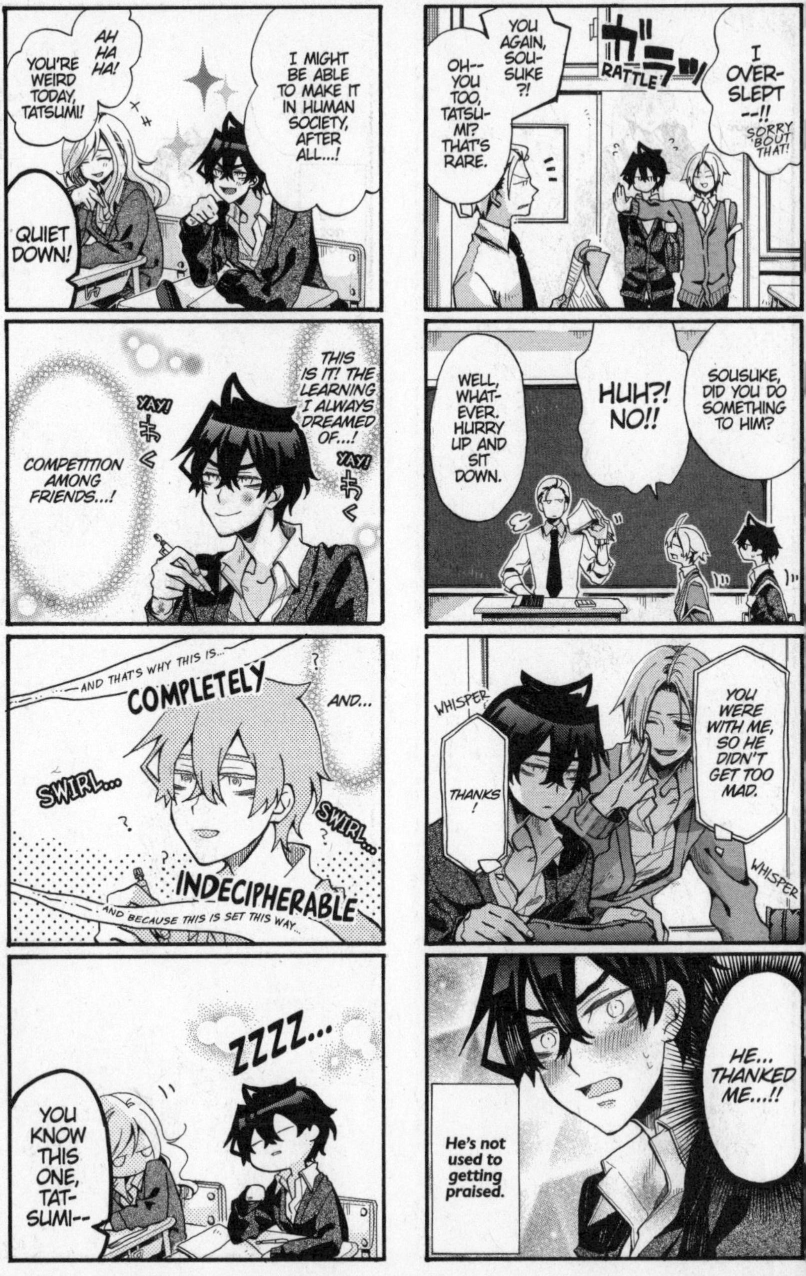
I OVER-SLEPT--!!
SORRY 'BOUT THAT!
RATTLE
YOU AGAIN, SOU-SUKE?!
OH-- YOU TOO, TATSU-MI? THAT'S RARE.
SOUSUKE, DID YOU DO SOMETHING TO HIM?
HUH?! NO!!
WELL, WHAT-EVER. HURRY UP AND SIT DOWN.
YOU WERE WITH ME, SO HE DIDN'T GET TOO MAD.
WHISPER
WHISPER
THANKS!
HE... THANKED ME...!!
He's not used to getting praised.
I MIGHT BE ABLE TO MAKE IT IN HUMAN SOCIETY, AFTER ALL...!
AH HA HA!
YOU'RE WEIRD TODAY, TATSUMI!
QUIET DOWN!
THIS IS IT! THE LEARNING I ALWAYS DREAMED OF...!
YAY!
YAY!
COMPETITION AMONG FRIENDS...!
AND THAT'S WHY THIS IS...
COMPLETELY
AND...
SWIRL...
SWIRL...
INDECIPHERABLE
AND BECAUSE THIS IS SET THIS WAY...
ZZZZ...
YOU KNOW THIS ONE, TAT-SUMI--

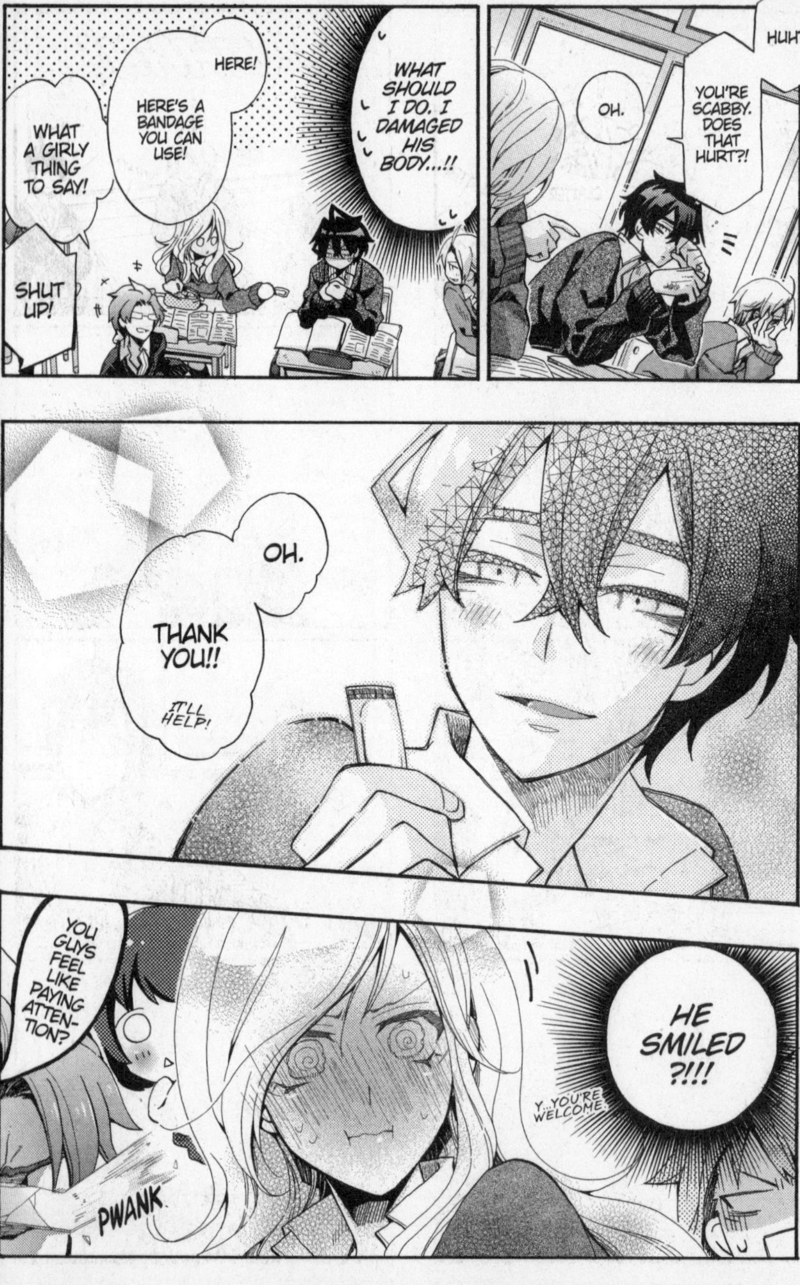
HUH?!
YOU'RE SCABBY. DOES THAT HURT?!
OH.
WHAT SHOULD I DO. I DAMAGED HIS BODY...!!
HERE!
HERE'S A BANDAGE YOU CAN USE!
WHAT A GIRLY THING TO SAY!
SHUT UP!
OH.
THANK YOU!!
IT'LL HELP!
HE SMILED?!!!
Y...YOU'RE WELCOME.
YOU GUYS FEEL LIKE PAYING ATTENTION?
PWANK

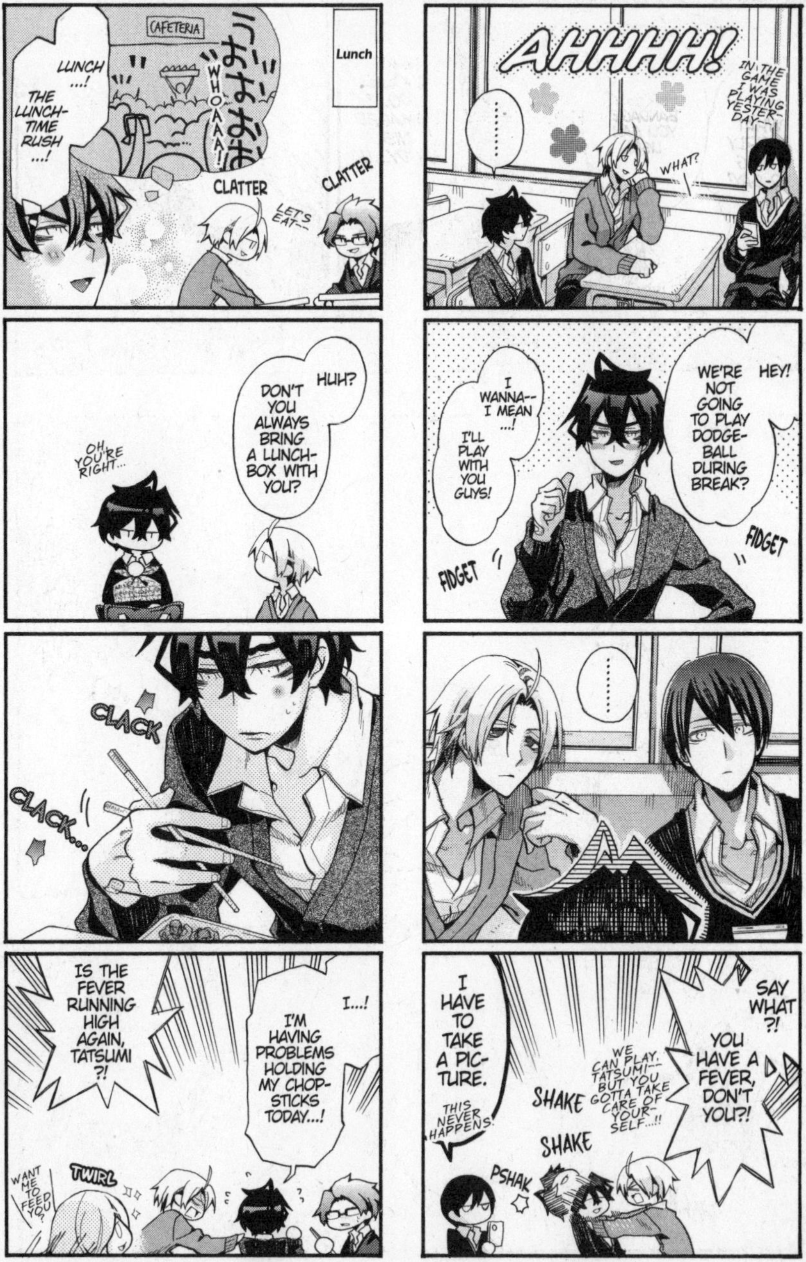
AHHHH!
IN THE GAME I WAS PLAYING YESTERDAY--
WHAT?
......
HEY! WE'RE NOT GOING TO PLAY DODGE-BALL DURING BREAK?
FIDGET
I WANNA-- I MEAN ...! I'LL PLAY WITH YOU GUYS!
FIDGET
......
SAY WHAT?! YOU HAVE A FEVER, DON'T YOU?!
WE CAN PLAY, TATSUMI-- BUT YOU GOTTA TAKE CARE OF YOUR-SELF...!!
SHAKE
SHAKE
I HAVE TO TAKE A PIC-TURE.
THIS NEVER HAPPENS!
PSHAK
Lunch
うおおお WHOAAA!
CAFETERIA
LUNCH ...! THE LUNCH-TIME RUSH ...!
CLATTER
CLATTER
LET'S EAT--
HUH? DON'T YOU ALWAYS BRING A LUNCH-BOX WITH YOU?
OH, YOU'RE RIGHT...
CLACK
CLACK...
I...! I'M HAVING PROBLEMS HOLDING MY CHOP-STICKS TODAY...!
IS THE FEVER RUNNING HIGH AGAIN, TATSUMI?!
TWIRL
WANT ME TO FEED YOU?

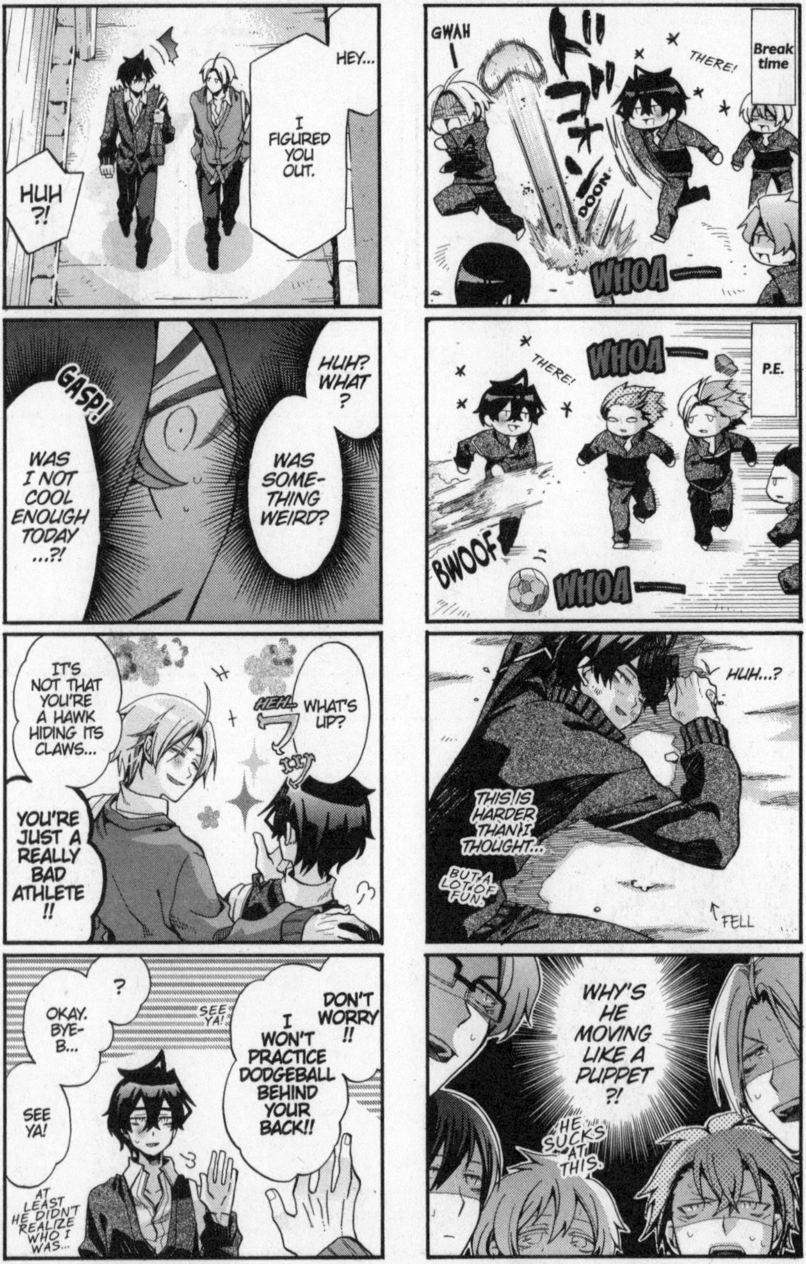
Break time
GWAH
THERE!
DOON
WHOA—
P.E.
WHOA—
THERE!
BWOOF
WHOA—
HUH...?
THIS IS HARDER THAN I THOUGHT...
BUT A LOT OF FUN.
FELL
WHY'S HE MOVING LIKE A PUPPET?!
HE SUCKS AT THIS.
HEY...
I FIGURED YOU OUT.
HUH?!
HUH? WHAT?
WAS SOMETHING WEIRD?
GASP!
WAS I NOT COOL ENOUGH TODAY...?!
WHAT'S UP?
HEH
IT'S NOT THAT YOU'RE A HAWK HIDING ITS CLAWS...
YOU'RE JUST A REALLY BAD ATHLETE!!
DON'T WORRY!!
I WON'T PRACTICE DODGEBALL BEHIND YOUR BACK!!
SEE YA!
?
OKAY. BYE-B...
SEE YA!
AT LEAST HE DIDN'T REALIZE WHO I WAS...

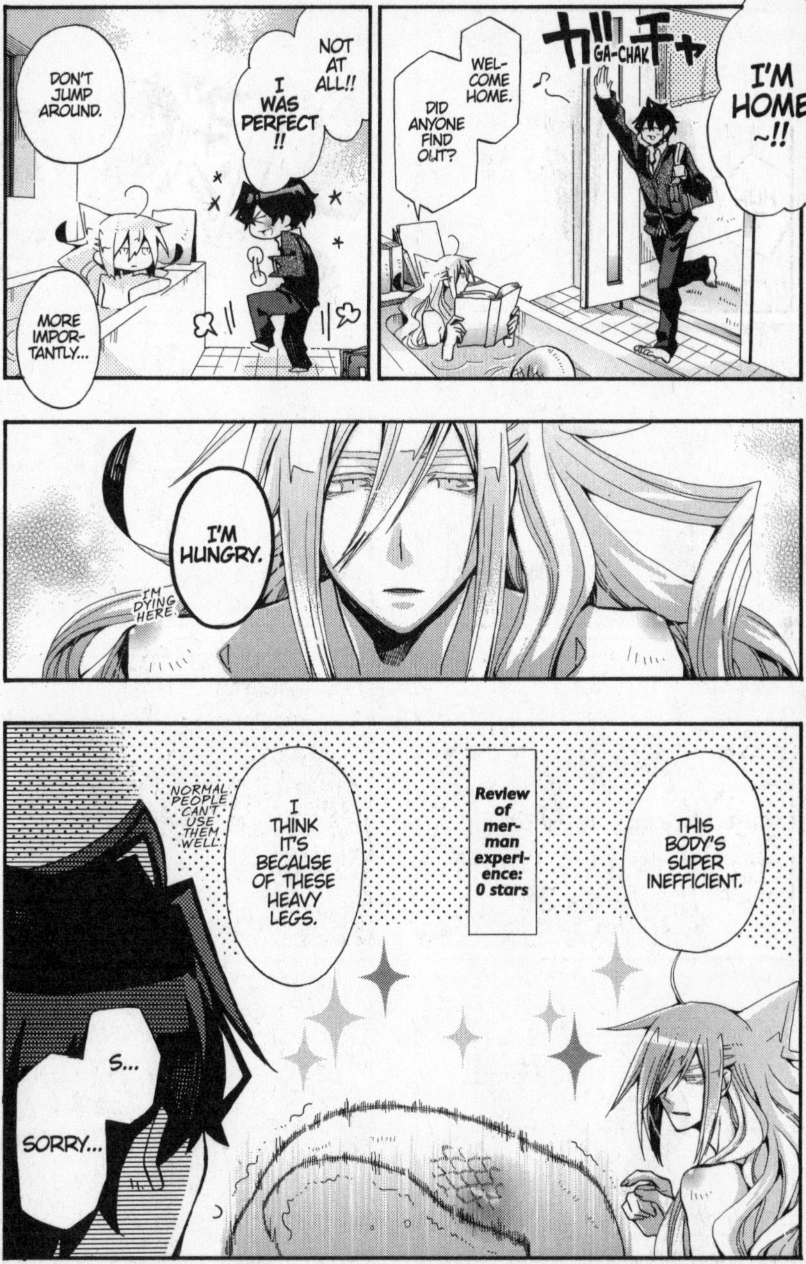
I'M HOME ~!!
ガチャ
GA-CHAK
WEL-COME HOME.
DID ANYONE FIND OUT?
NOT AT ALL!!
I WAS PERFECT !!
DON'T JUMP AROUND.
MORE IMPOR-TANTLY...
I'M HUNGRY.
I'M DYING HERE.
THIS BODY'S SUPER INEFFICIENT.
Review of mer-man experi-ence: 0 stars
I THINK IT'S BECAUSE OF THESE HEAVY LEGS.
NORMAL PEOPLE CAN'T USE THEM WELL.
S...
SORRY...

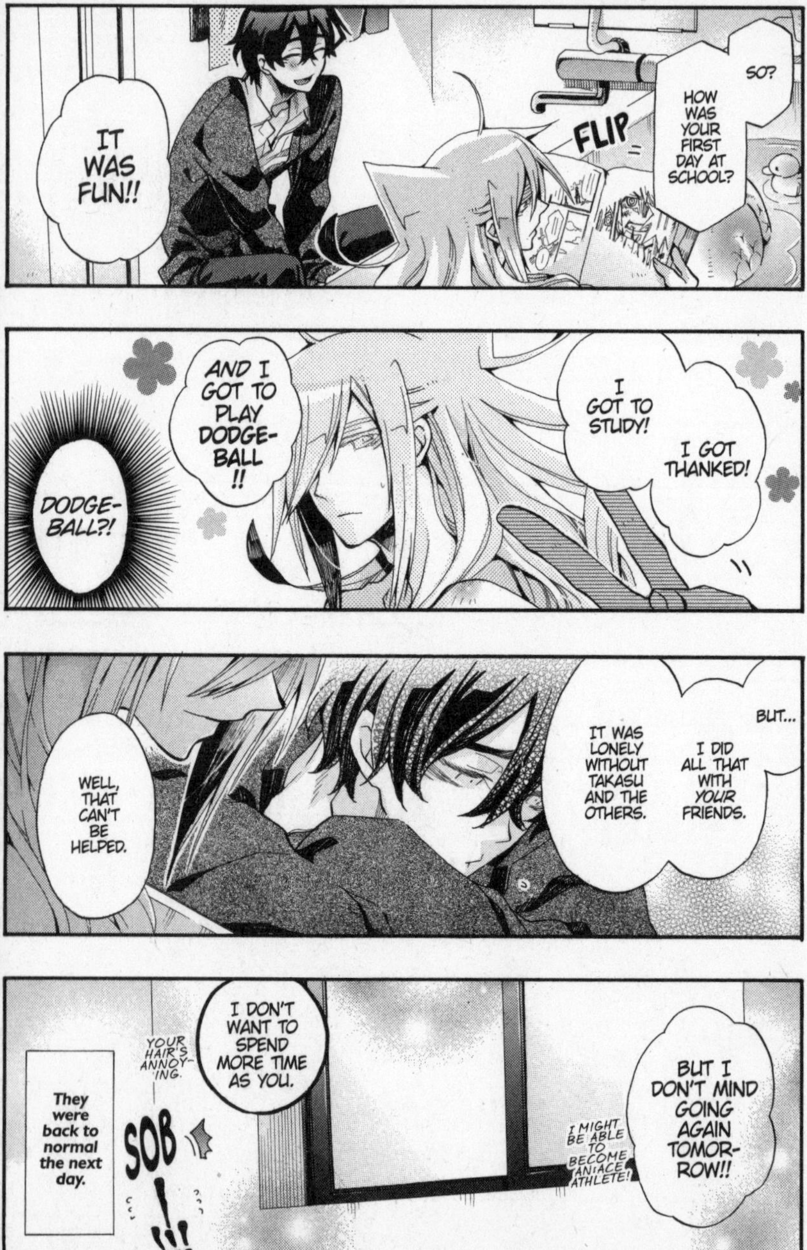
SO?
HOW WAS YOUR FIRST DAY AT SCHOOL?
FLIP
IT WAS FUN!!
I GOT TO STUDY!
I GOT THANKED!
AND I GOT TO PLAY DODGE-BALL!!
DODGE-BALL?!
BUT...
I DID ALL THAT WITH *YOUR* FRIENDS.
IT WAS LONELY WITHOUT TAKASU AND THE OTHERS.
WELL, THAT CAN'T BE HELPED.
BUT I DON'T MIND GOING AGAIN TOMOR-ROW!!
I MIGHT BE ABLE TO BECOME AN ACE ATHLETE!
I DON'T WANT TO SPEND MORE TIME AS YOU.
YOUR HAIR'S ANNOY-ING.
SOB
They were back to normal the next day.

Merman in My Tub

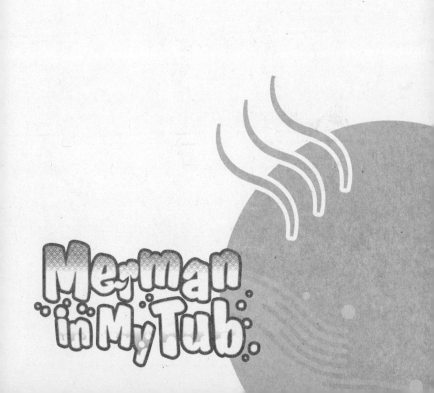

オレん家(ち)のフロ事情

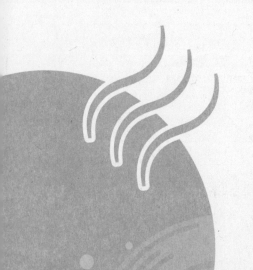

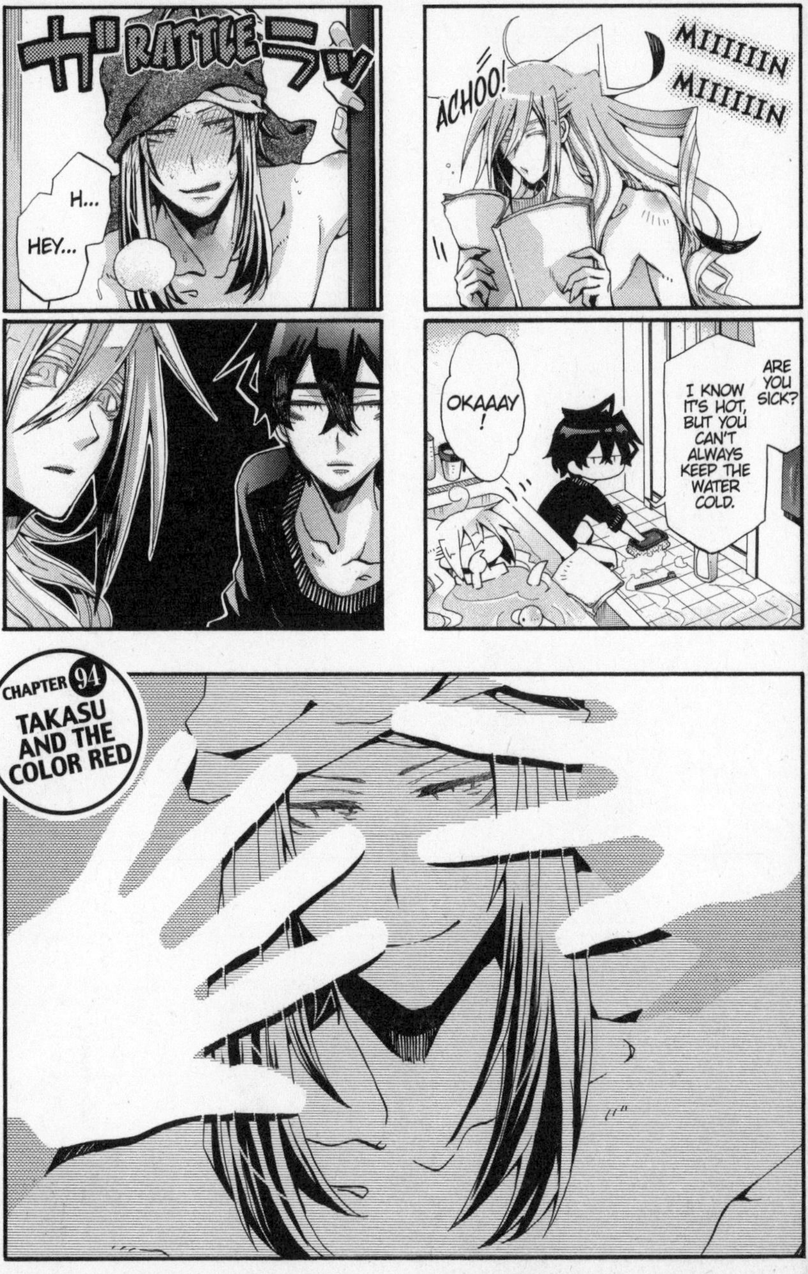
ACHOO!
MIIIIIN MIIIIIN
RATTLE
H... HEY...
ARE YOU SICK?
I KNOW IT'S HOT, BUT YOU CAN'T ALWAYS KEEP THE WATER COLD.
OKAAAY!
CHAPTER 94
TAKASU AND THE COLOR RED

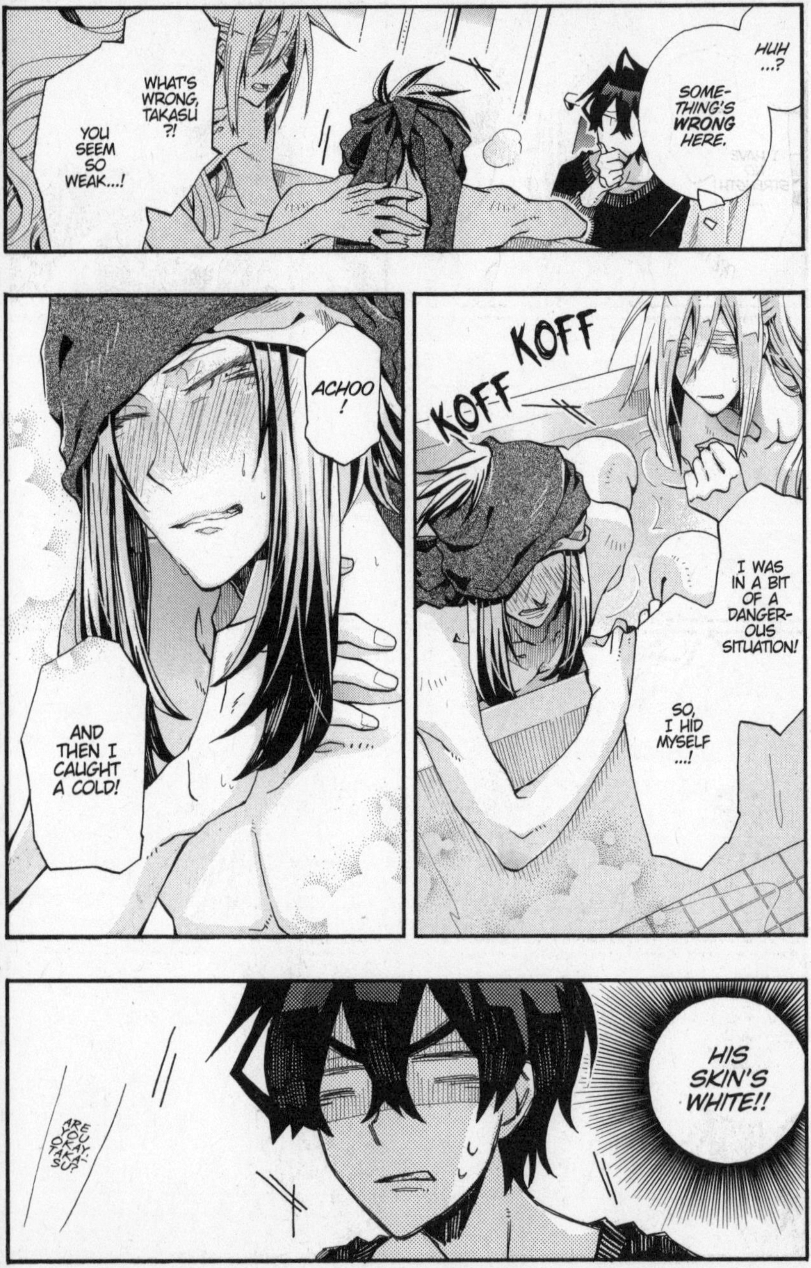
HUH ...?
SOMETHING'S WRONG HERE.
WHAT'S WRONG, TAKASU?!
YOU SEEM SO WEAK...!
KOFF KOFF
I WAS IN A BIT OF A DANGEROUS SITUATION!
SO, I HID MYSELF ...!
ACHOO!
AND THEN I CAUGHT A COLD!
HIS SKIN'S WHITE!!
ARE YOU OKAY, TAKASU?

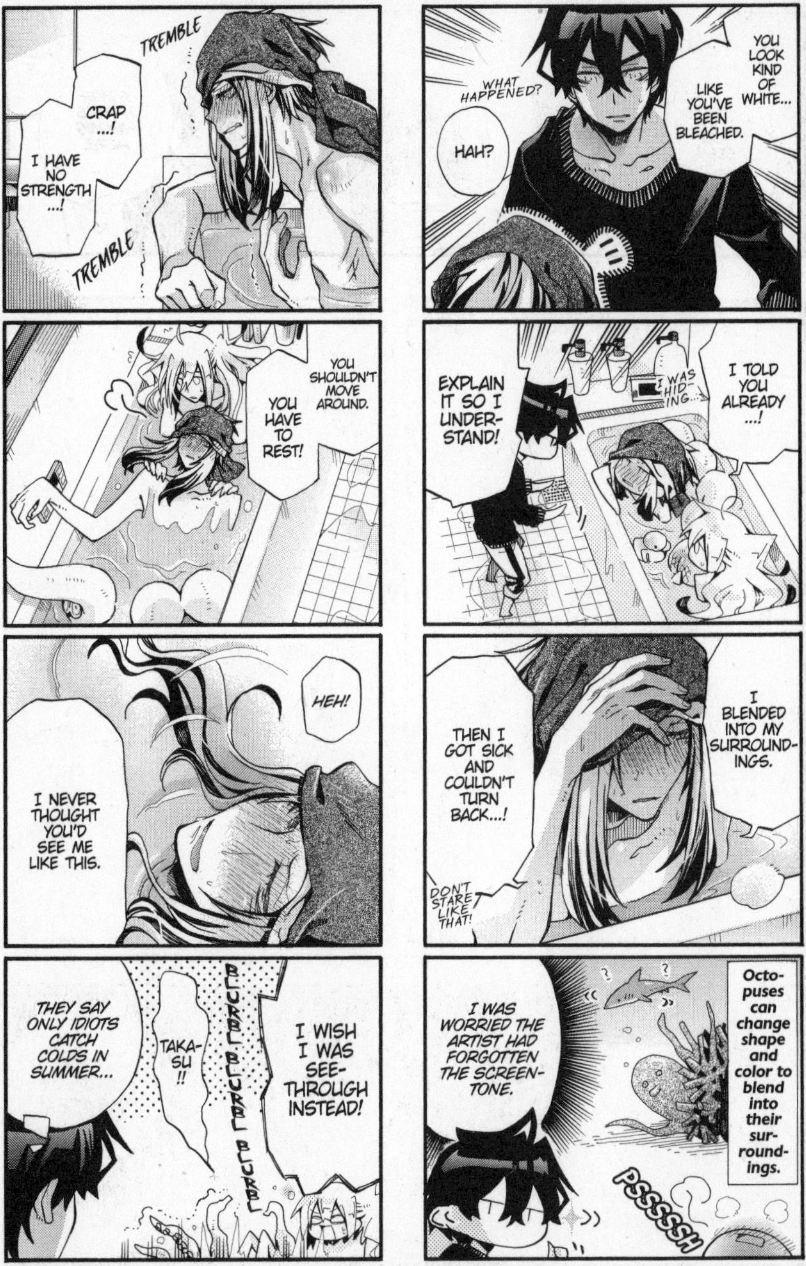
YOU LOOK KIND OF WHITE...
LIKE YOU'VE BEEN BLEACHED.
WHAT HAPPENED?
HAH?
TREMBLE
CRAP ...!
I HAVE NO STRENGTH ...!
TREMBLE
I TOLD YOU ALREADY ...!
I WAS HIDING...
EXPLAIN IT SO I UNDER-STAND!
YOU SHOULDN'T MOVE AROUND.
YOU HAVE TO REST!
I BLENDED INTO MY SURROUND-INGS.
THEN I GOT SICK AND COULDN'T TURN BACK...!
DON'T STARE LIKE THAT!
HEH!
I NEVER THOUGHT YOU'D SEE ME LIKE THIS.
Octo-puses can change shape and color to blend into their sur-round-ings.
I WAS WORRIED THE ARTIST HAD FORGOTTEN THE SCREEN-TONE.
PSSSSSH
I WISH I WAS SEE-THROUGH INSTEAD!
BLURBL BLURBL BLURBL
TAKA-SU !!
THEY SAY ONLY IDIOTS CATCH COLDS IN SUMMER...

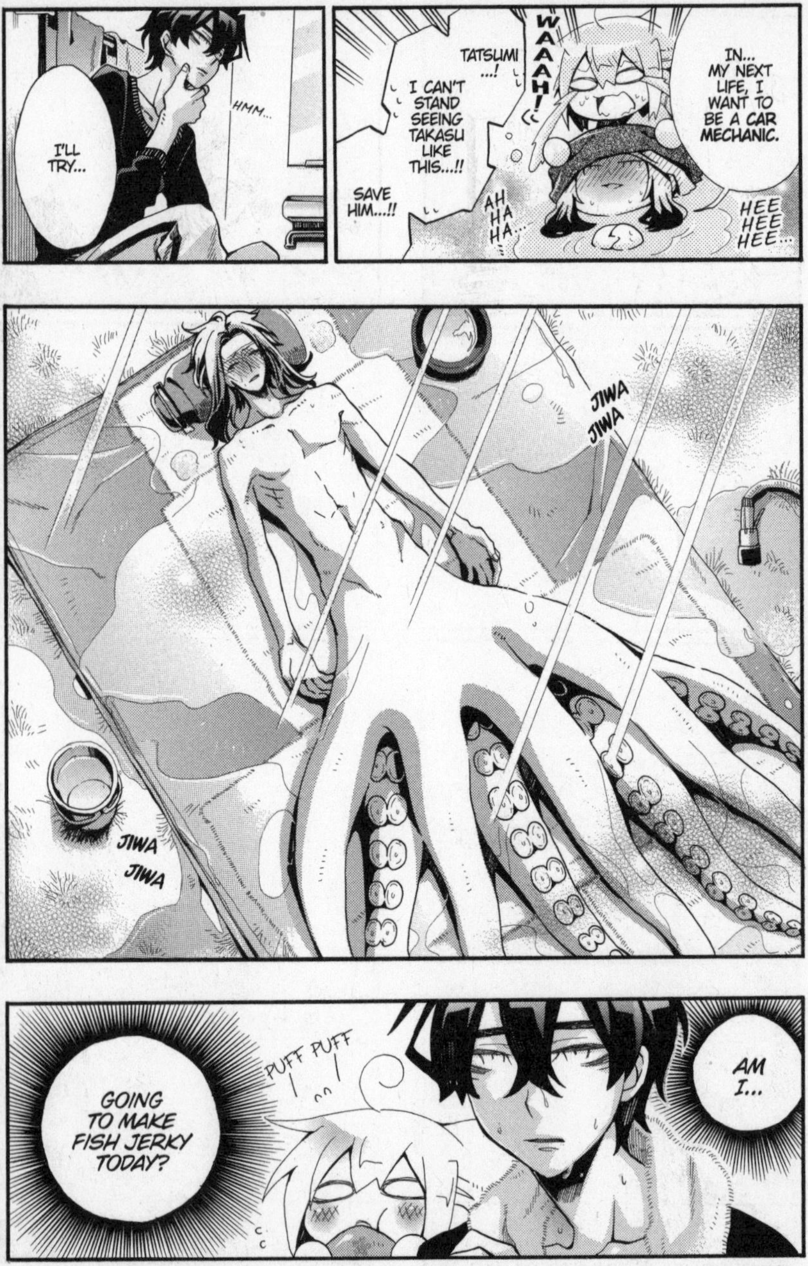
IN... MY NEXT LIFE, I WANT TO BE A CAR MECHANIC.
HEE HEE HEE...
WAAAAH!
TATSUMI ...!
I CAN'T STAND SEEING TAKASU LIKE THIS...!!
AH HA HA...
SAVE HIM...!!
HMM...
I'LL TRY...
JIWA JIWA
JIWA JIWA
AM I...
PUFF PUFF
GOING TO MAKE FISH JERKY TODAY?

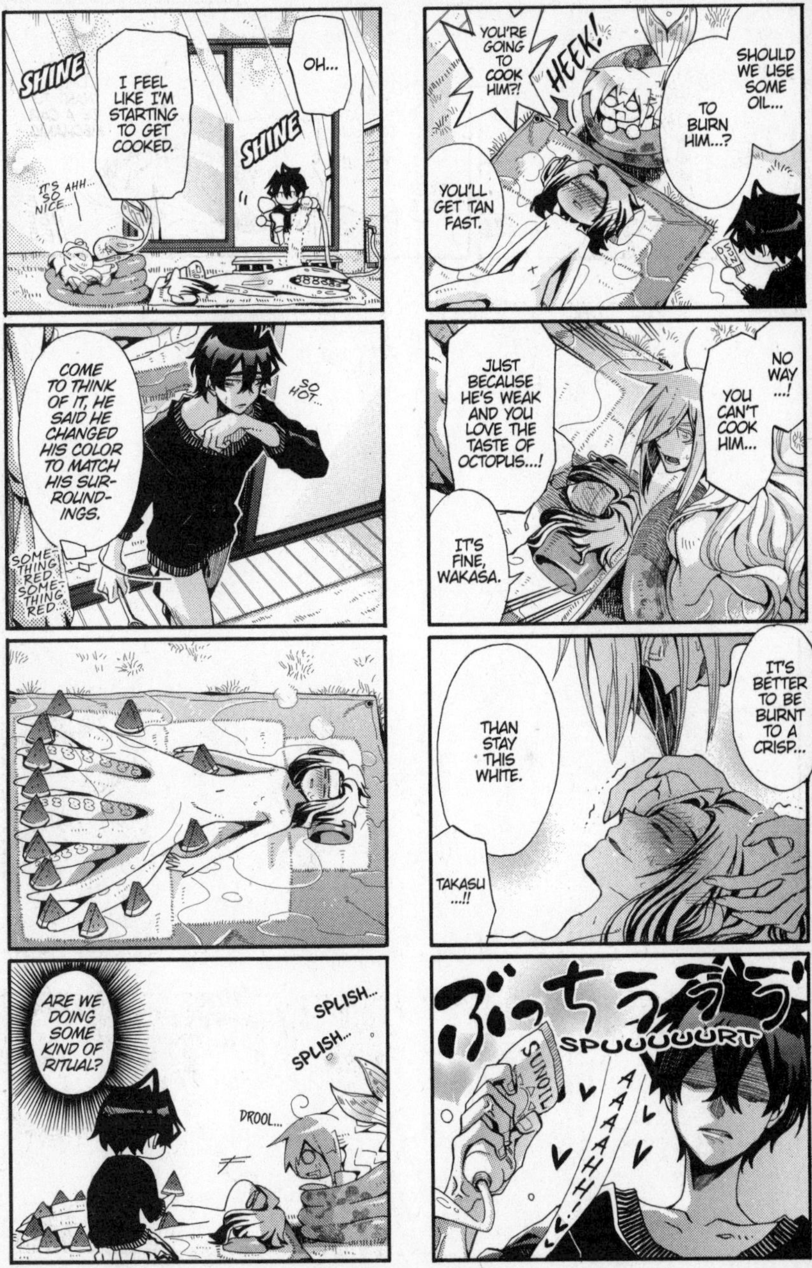
SHOULD WE USE SOME OIL...
TO BURN HIM...?
HEEK!
YOU'RE GOING TO COOK HIM?!
YOU'LL GET TAN FAST.
OH...
SHINE
I FEEL LIKE I'M STARTING TO GET COOKED.
SHINE
IT'S AHH... SO NICE...
NO WAY...!
YOU CAN'T COOK HIM...
JUST BECAUSE HE'S WEAK AND YOU LOVE THE TASTE OF OCTOPUS...!
IT'S FINE, WAKASA.
SO HOT...
COME TO THINK OF IT, HE SAID HE CHANGED HIS COLOR TO MATCH HIS SURROUNDINGS.
SOMETHING RED. SOMETHING RED...
IT'S BETTER TO BE BURNT TO A CRISP...
THAN STAY THIS WHITE.
TAKASU...!!
ぶっちううゔ
SPUUUUURT
SUNOIL
AAAAAHH...!
ARE WE DOING SOME KIND OF RITUAL?
SPLISH...
SPLISH...
DROOL...

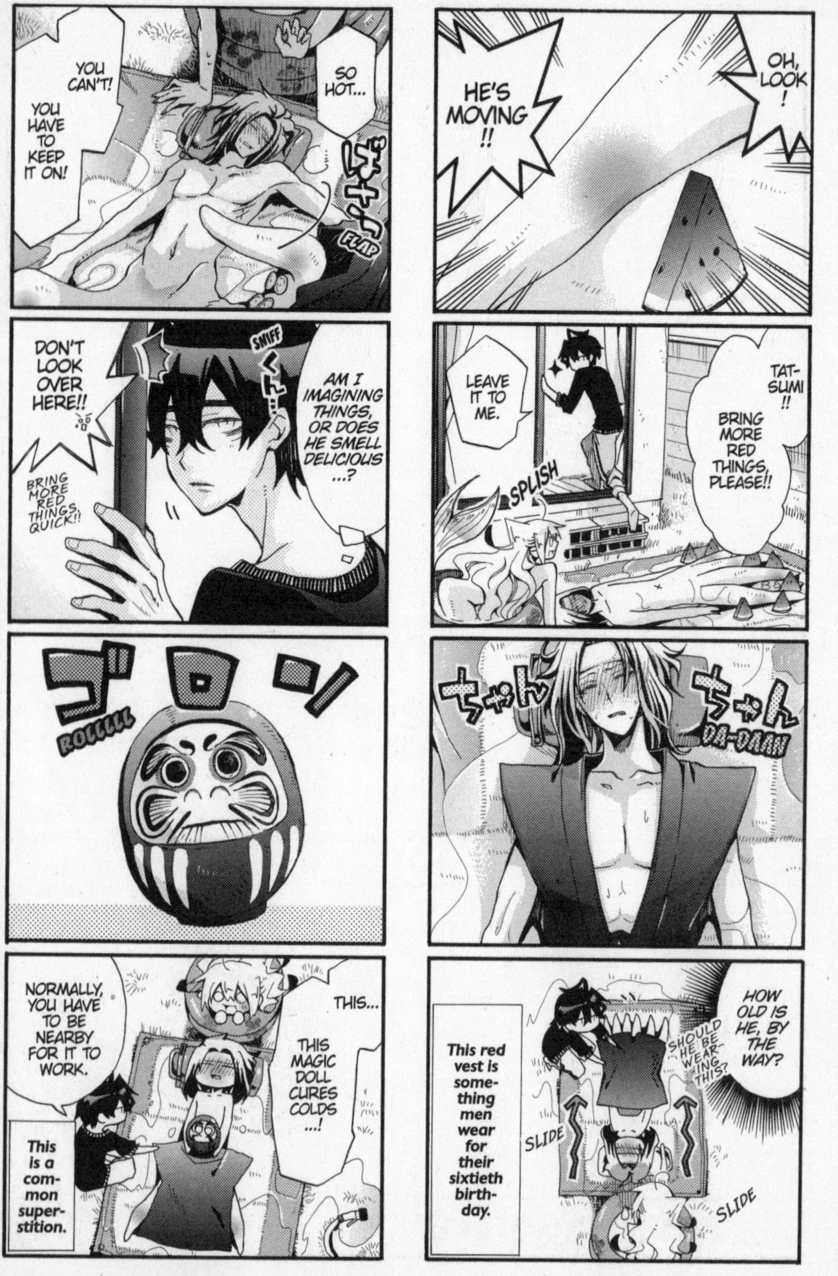
OH, LOOK!
HE'S MOVING!!
SO HOT...
YOU CAN'T!
YOU HAVE TO KEEP IT ON!
FLAP
TATSUMI!!
BRING MORE RED THINGS, PLEASE!!
LEAVE IT TO ME.
SPLISH
AM I IMAGINING THINGS, OR DOES HE SMELL DELICIOUS...?
SNIFF
くん
DON'T LOOK OVER HERE!!
BRING MORE RED THINGS, QUICK!!
ちゃん ちゃん
DA-DAAN
ゴロン
ROLLLLL
HOW OLD IS HE, BY THE WAY?
SHOULD HE BE WEARING THIS?
This red vest is something men wear for their sixtieth birthday.
SLIDE
SLIDE
THIS...
THIS MAGIC DOLL CURES COLDS...!
NORMALLY, YOU HAVE TO BE NEARBY FOR IT TO WORK.
This is a common superstition.

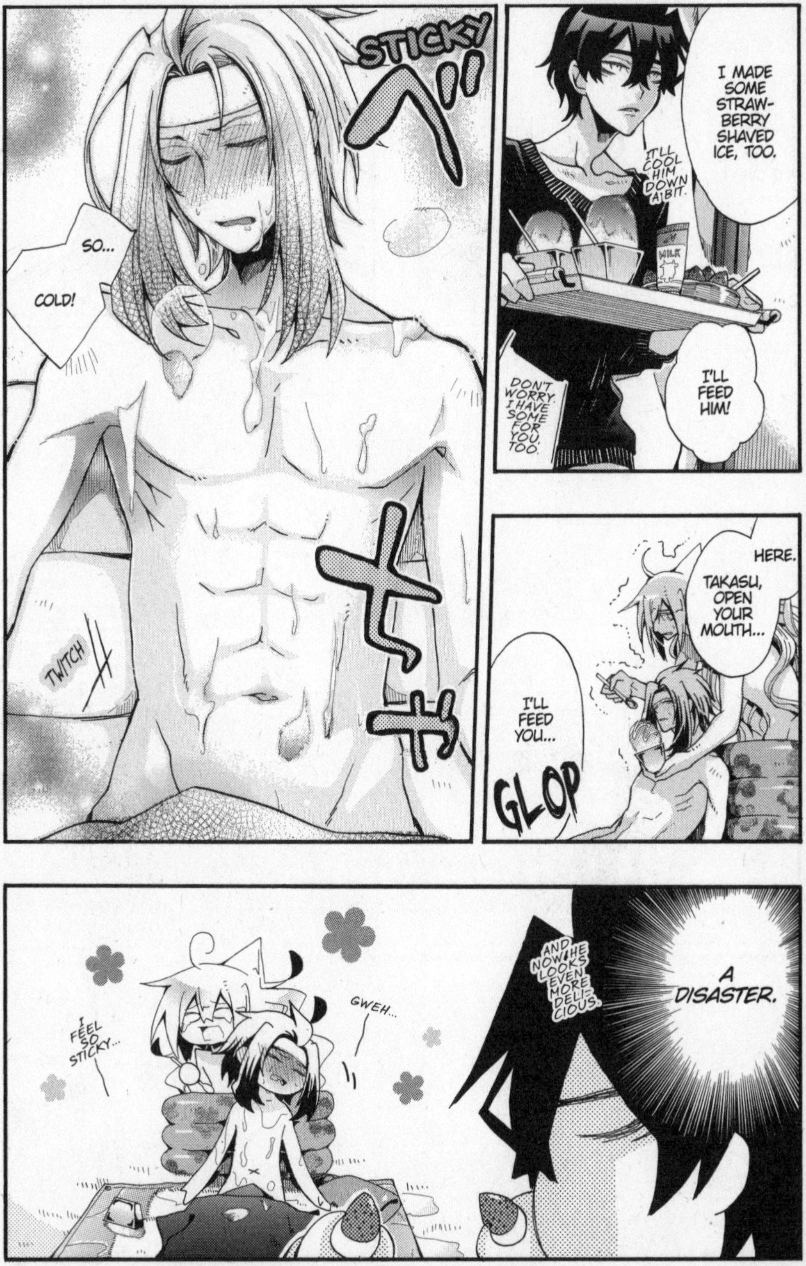
I MADE SOME STRAWBERRY SHAVED ICE, TOO.
IT'LL COOL HIM DOWN A BIT.
I'LL FEED HIM!
DON'T WORRY. I HAVE SOME FOR YOU, TOO.
HERE.
TAKASU, OPEN YOUR MOUTH...
I'LL FEED YOU...
GLOP
STICKY
SO...
COLD!
TWITCH
A DISASTER.
AND NOW HE LOOKS EVEN MORE DELICIOUS.
GWEH...
I FEEL SO STICKY...

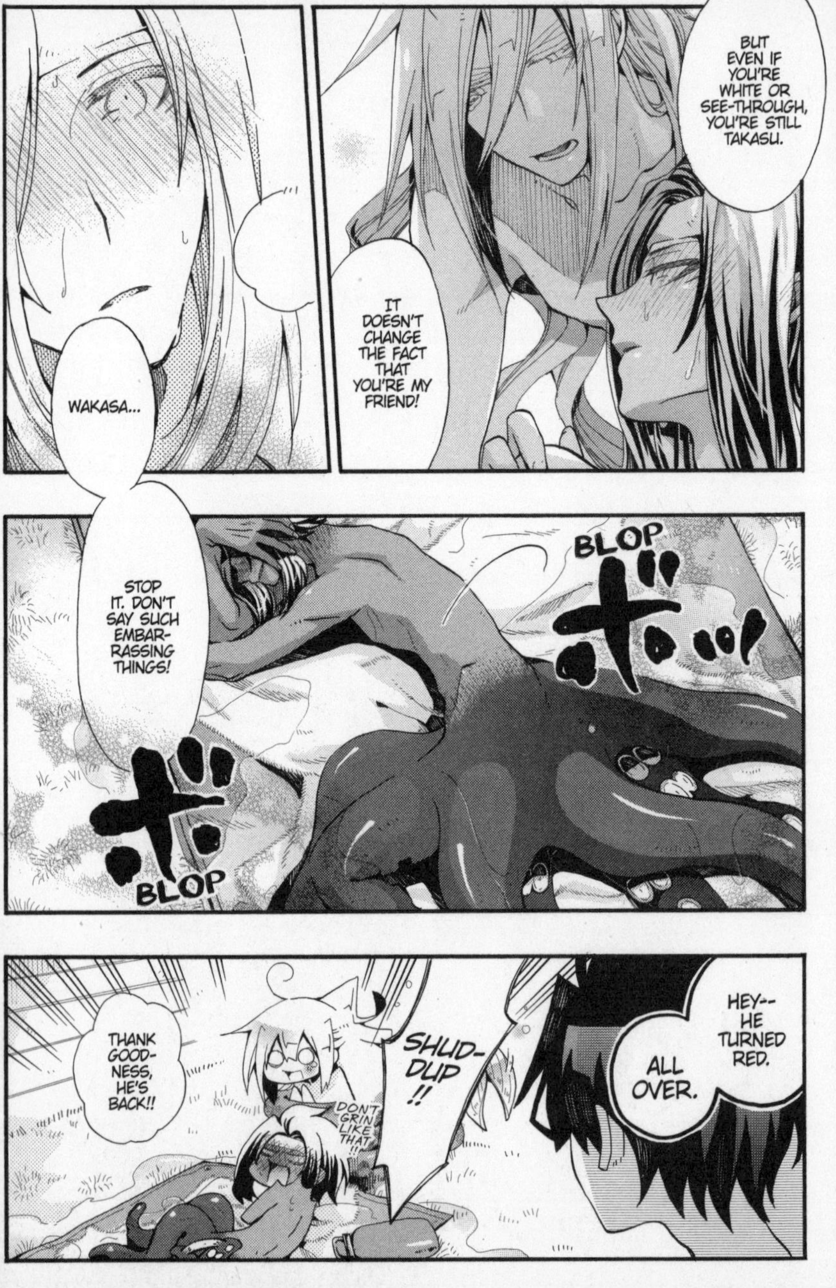
BUT EVEN IF YOU'RE WHITE OR SEE-THROUGH, YOU'RE STILL TAKASU.
IT DOESN'T CHANGE THE FACT THAT YOU'RE MY FRIEND!
WAKASA...
STOP IT. DON'T SAY SUCH EMBAR-RASSING THINGS!
BLOP
BLOP
HEY-- HE TURNED RED.
ALL OVER.
SHUD-DUP!!
DON'T GRIN LIKE THAT!!
THANK GOOD-NESS, HE'S BACK!!

Merman in My Tub

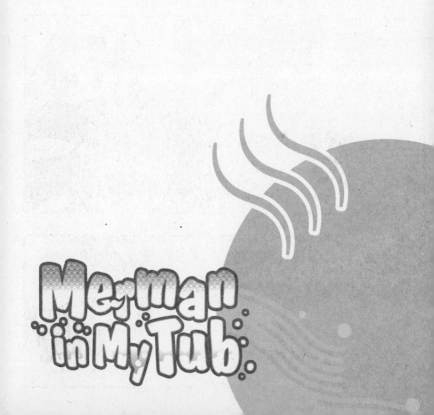

オレん家（ち）のフロ事情

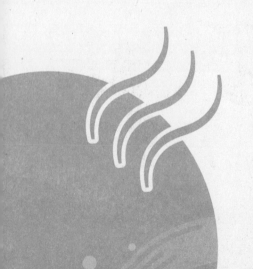

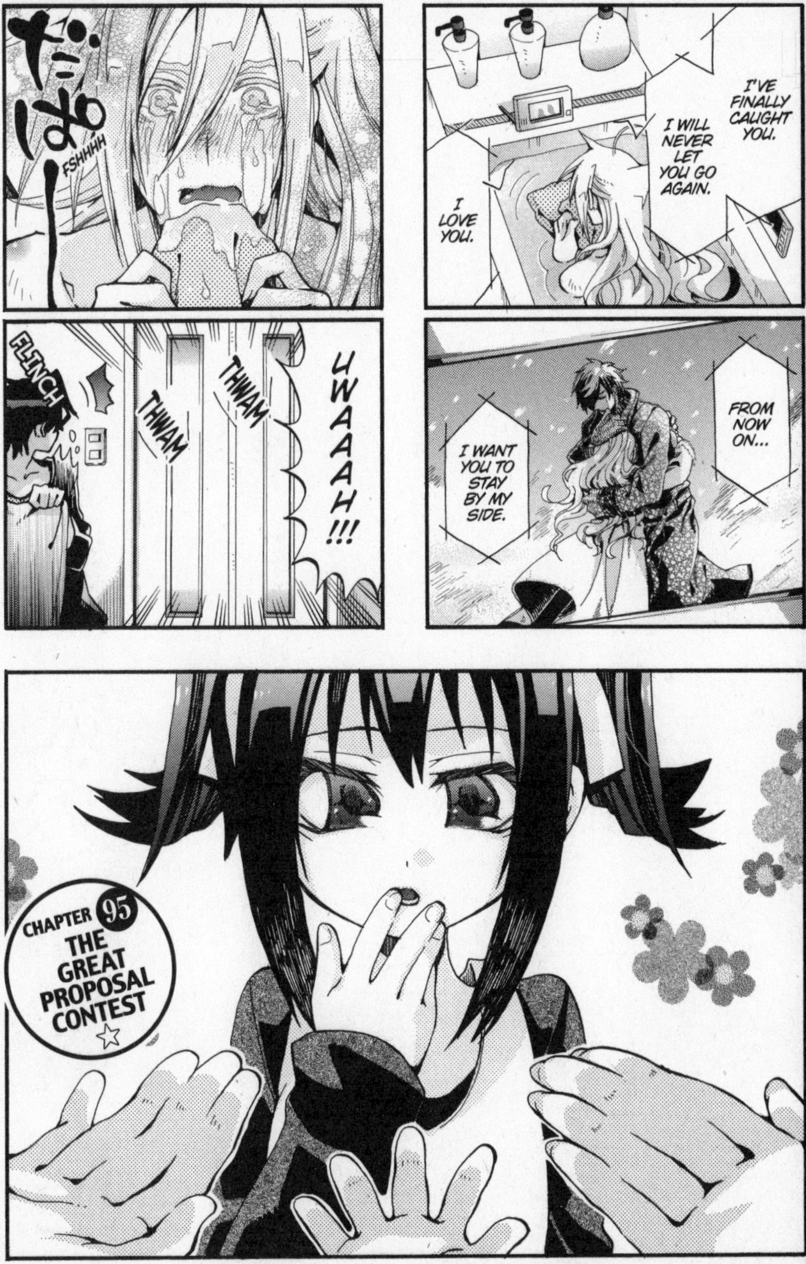
I'VE FINALLY CAUGHT YOU.
I WILL NEVER LET YOU GO AGAIN.
I LOVE YOU.
FSHHHH
FROM NOW ON...
I WANT YOU TO STAY BY MY SIDE.
UWAAAAH!!!
THWAM
THWAM
FLINCH
CHAPTER 95 THE GREAT PROPOSAL CONTEST ☆

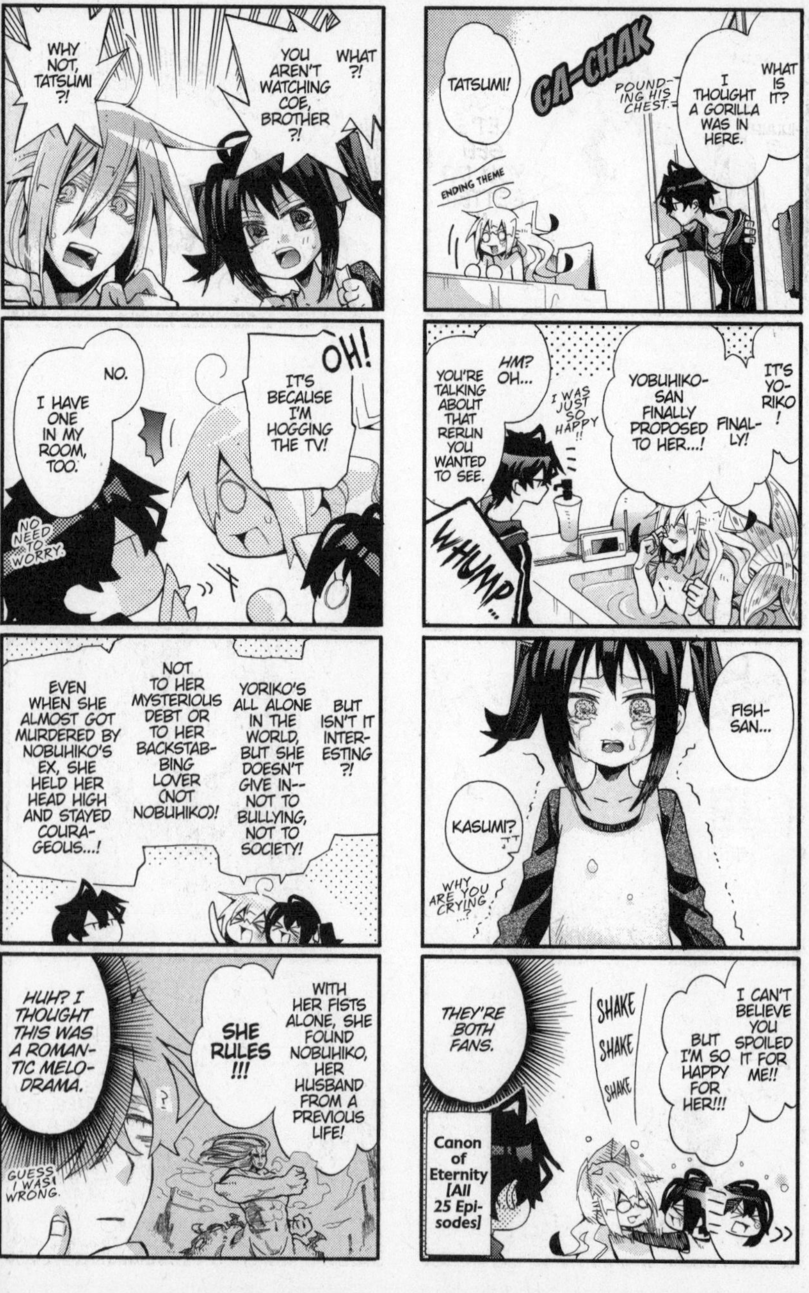
WHAT IS IT?
I THOUGHT A GORILLA WAS IN HERE.
POUNDING HIS CHEST.
GA-CHAK
TATSUMI!
ENDING THEME
IT'S YORIKO!
FINALLY!
YOBUHIKO-SAN FINALLY PROPOSED TO HER...!
I WAS JUST SO HAPPY!!
HM? OH...
YOU'RE TALKING ABOUT THAT RERUN YOU WANTED TO SEE.
WHUMP...
FISH-SAN...
KASUMI?
WHY ARE YOU CRYING...?
I CAN'T BELIEVE YOU SPOILED IT FOR ME!!
BUT I'M SO HAPPY FOR HER!!!
SHAKE
SHAKE
SHAKE
THEY'RE BOTH FANS.
Canon of Eternity [All 25 Episodes]
WHAT?!
YOU AREN'T WATCHING COE, BROTHER?!
WHY NOT, TATSUMI?!
OH!
IT'S BECAUSE I'M HOGGING THE TV!
NO.
I HAVE ONE IN MY ROOM, TOO.
NO NEED TO WORRY.
BUT ISN'T IT INTERESTING?!
YORIKO'S ALL ALONE IN THE WORLD, BUT SHE DOESN'T GIVE IN--NOT TO BULLYING, NOT TO SOCIETY!
NOT TO HER MYSTERIOUS DEBT OR TO HER BACKSTABBING LOVER (NOT NOBUHIKO)!
EVEN WHEN SHE ALMOST GOT MURDERED BY NOBUHIKO'S EX, SHE HELD HER HEAD HIGH AND STAYED COURAGEOUS...!
WITH HER FISTS ALONE, SHE FOUND NOBUHIKO, HER HUSBAND FROM A PREVIOUS LIFE!
SHE RULES!!!
HUH? I THOUGHT THIS WAS A ROMANTIC MELODRAMA.
?
GUESS I WAS WRONG.

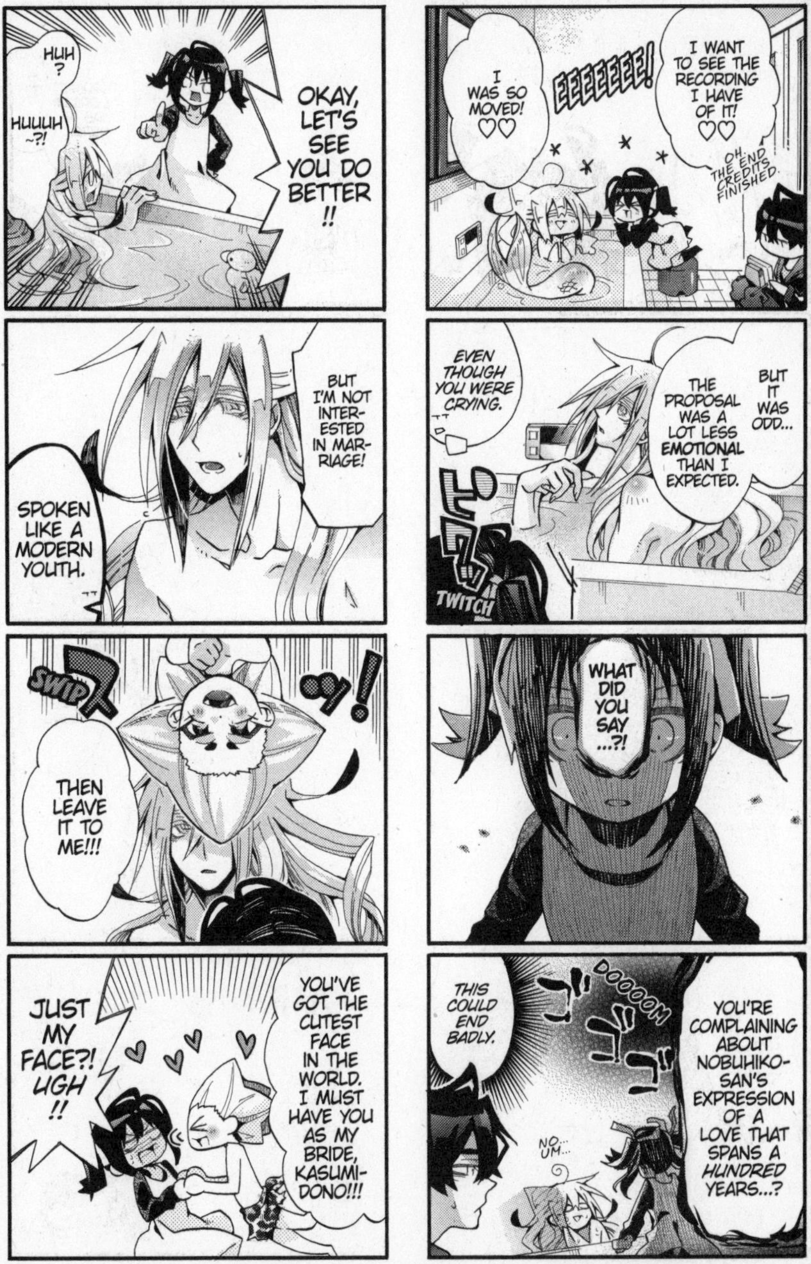
I WANT TO SEE THE RECORDING I HAVE OF IT!
EEEEEEE!
I WAS SO MOVED!
OH, THE END CREDITS FINISHED.
OKAY, LET'S SEE YOU DO BETTER!!
HUH?
HUUUH~?!
BUT IT WAS ODD...
THE PROPOSAL WAS A LOT LESS EMOTIONAL THAN I EXPECTED.
EVEN THOUGH YOU WERE CRYING.
TWITCH
BUT I'M NOT INTERESTED IN MARRIAGE!
SPOKEN LIKE A MODERN YOUTH.
WHAT DID YOU SAY...?!
SWIP
THEN LEAVE IT TO ME!!!
YOU'RE COMPLAINING ABOUT NOBUHIKO-SAN'S EXPRESSION OF A LOVE THAT SPANS A HUNDRED YEARS...?
DOOOOM
THIS COULD END BADLY.
NO... UM...
YOU'VE GOT THE CUTEST FACE IN THE WORLD. I MUST HAVE YOU AS MY BRIDE, KASUMI-DONO!!!
JUST MY FACE?! UGH!!

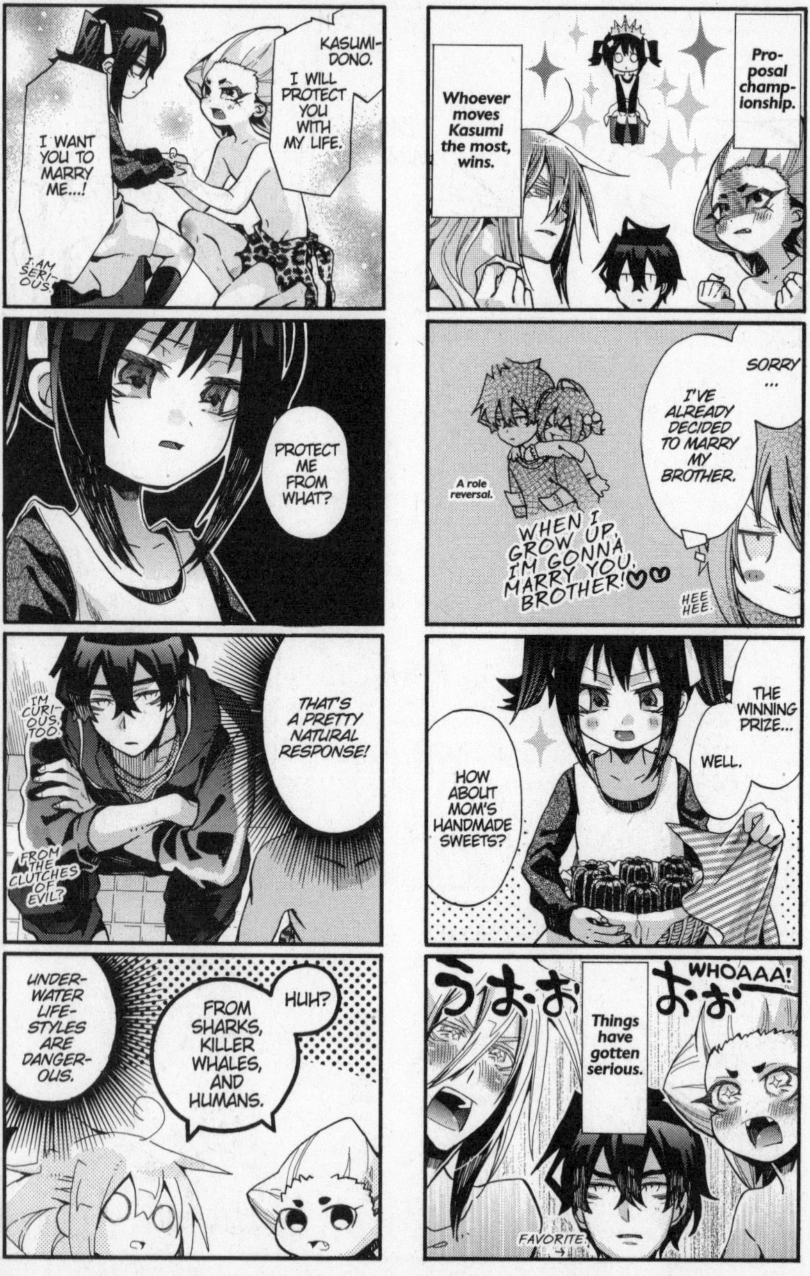
Proposal championship.
Whoever moves Kasumi the most, wins.
SORRY ...
I'VE ALREADY DECIDED TO MARRY MY BROTHER.
A role reversal.
WHEN I GROW UP, I'M GONNA MARRY YOU, BROTHER!
HEE HEE.
THE WINNING PRIZE...
WELL.
HOW ABOUT MOM'S HANDMADE SWEETS?
WHOAAA!
おぉー
Things have gotten serious.
うおぉ
FAVORITE.
KASUMI-DONO.
I WILL PROTECT YOU WITH MY LIFE.
I WANT YOU TO MARRY ME...!
I AM SERIOUS.
PROTECT ME FROM WHAT?
THAT'S A PRETTY NATURAL RESPONSE!
I'M CURIOUS, TOO.
FROM THE CLUTCHES OF EVIL?
HUH?
FROM SHARKS, KILLER WHALES, AND HUMANS.
UNDERWATER LIFESTYLES ARE DANGEROUS.

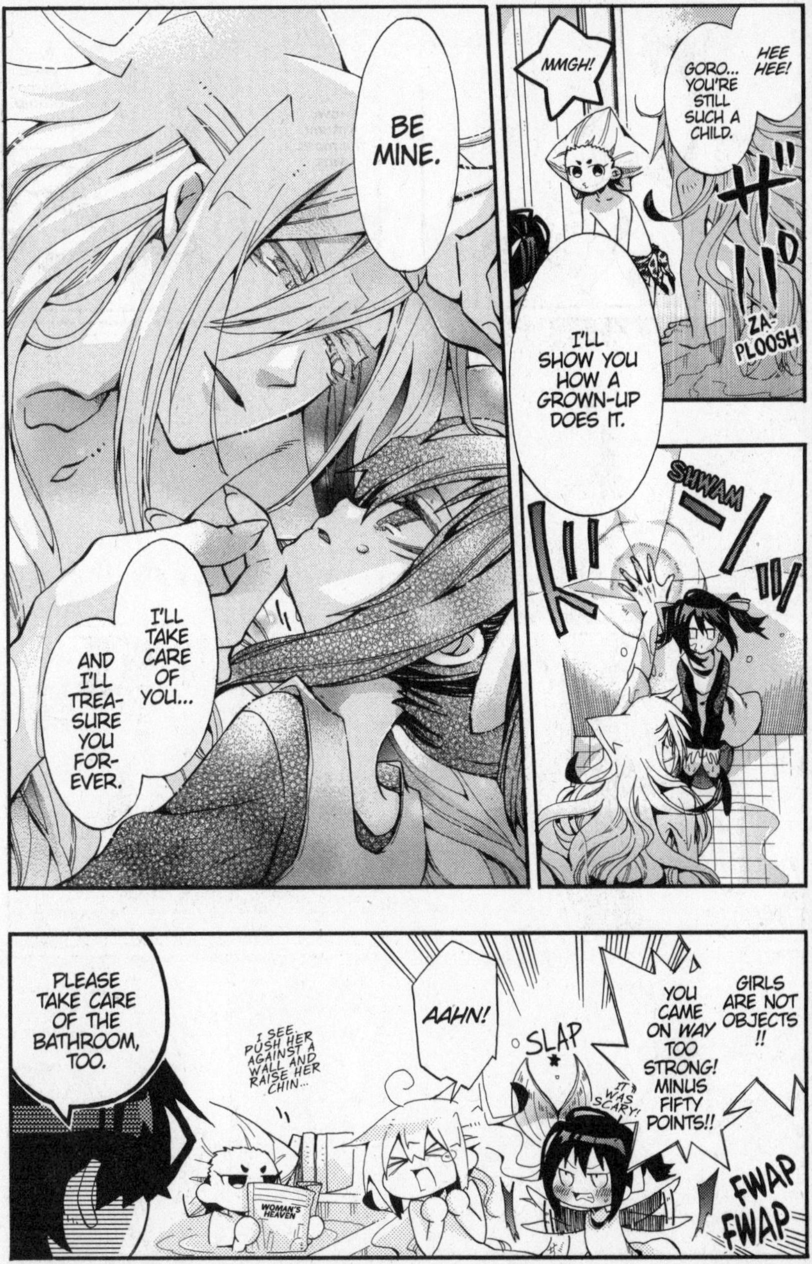
HEE HEE!
GORO... YOU'RE STILL SUCH A CHILD.
MMGH!
ZA-PLOOSH
I'LL SHOW YOU HOW A GROWN-UP DOES IT.
SHWAM
BE MINE.
I'LL TAKE CARE OF YOU...
AND I'LL TREASURE YOU FOREVER.
GIRLS ARE NOT OBJECTS!!
YOU CAME ON WAY TOO STRONG! MINUS FIFTY POINTS!!
FWAP FWAP
IT WAS SCARY!
SLAP
AAHN!
I SEE. PUSH HER AGAINST A WALL AND RAISE HER CHIN...
WOMAN'S HEAVEN
PLEASE TAKE CARE OF THE BATHROOM, TOO.

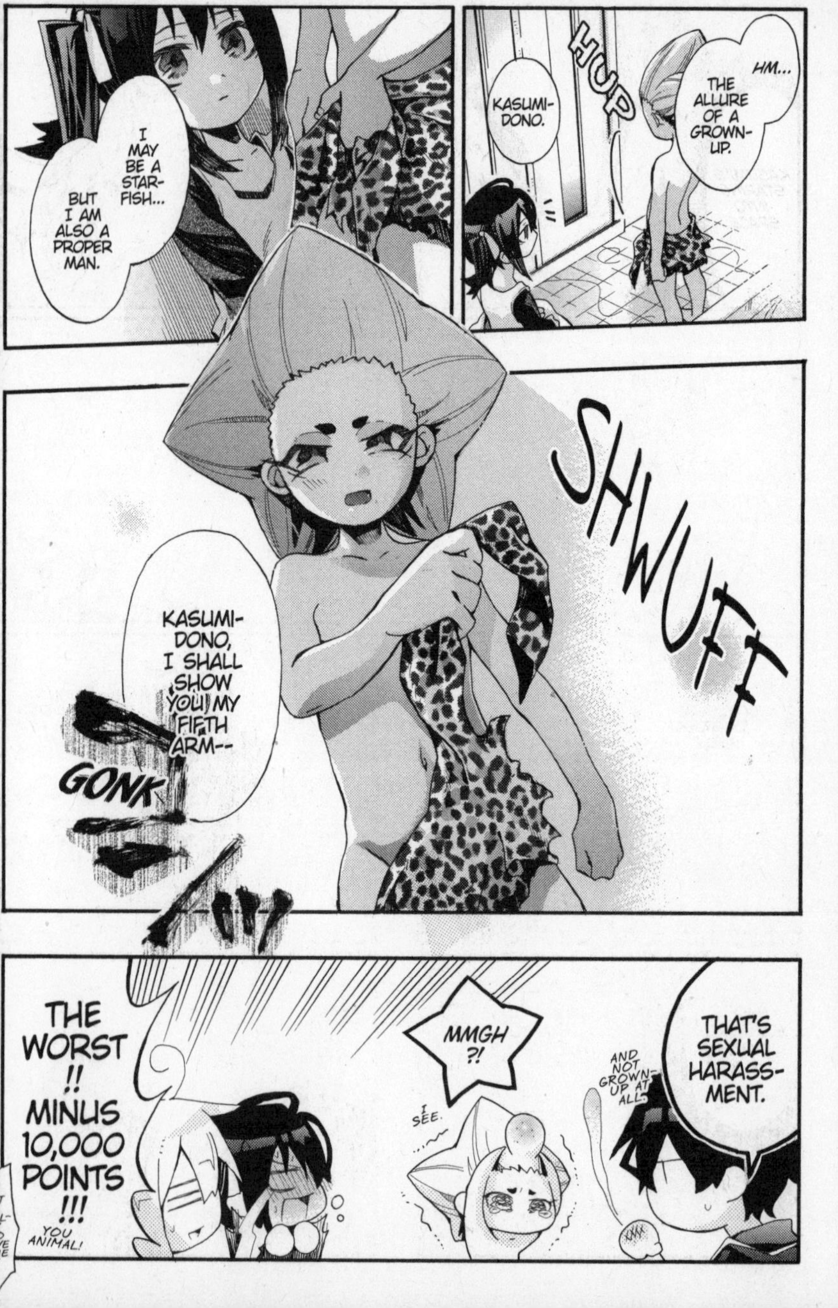
HM... THE ALLURE OF A GROWN-UP.
HUP
KASUMI-DONO.
I MAY BE A STAR-FISH...
BUT I AM ALSO A PROPER MAN.
SHWUFF
KASUMI-DONO, I SHALL SHOW YOU MY FIFTH ARM--
GONK
THAT'S SEXUAL HARASS-MENT.
AND NOT GROWN-UP AT ALL.
MMGH ?!
I SEE.
THE WORST !! MINUS 10,000 POINTS !!!
YOU ANIMAL!

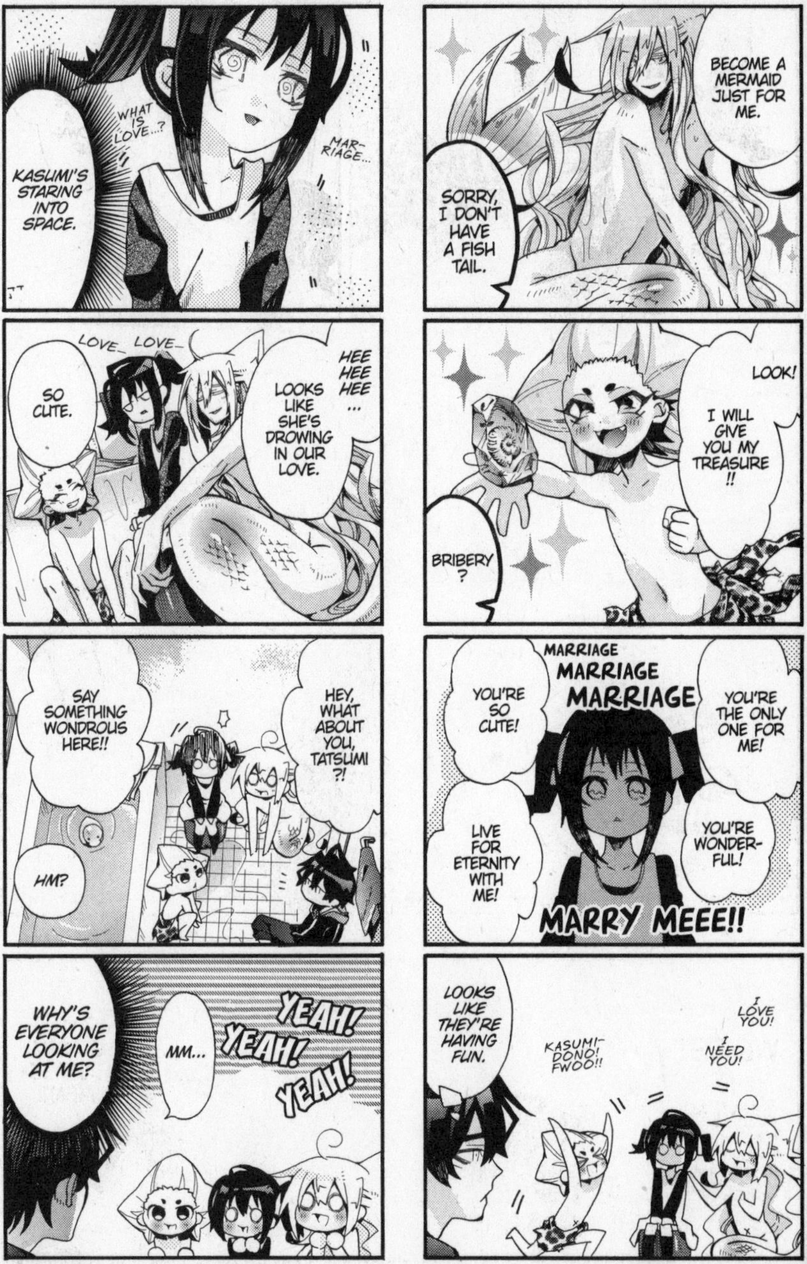
BECOME A MERMAID JUST FOR ME.
SORRY, I DON'T HAVE A FISH TAIL.
LOOK!
I WILL GIVE YOU MY TREASURE !!
BRIBERY ?
MARRIAGE
MARRIAGE
MARRIAGE
YOU'RE THE ONLY ONE FOR ME!
YOU'RE SO CUTE!
YOU'RE WONDER-FUL!
LIVE FOR ETERNITY WITH ME!
MARRY MEEE!!
I LOVE YOU!
I NEED YOU!
KASUMI-DONO! FWOO!!
LOOKS LIKE THEY"RE HAVING FUN.
MAR-RIAGE...
WHAT IS LOVE...?
KASUMI'S STARING INTO SPACE.
HEE HEE HEE ...
LOOKS LIKE SHE'S DROWING IN OUR LOVE.
LOVE_ LOVE_
SO CUTE.
HEY, WHAT ABOUT YOU, TATSUMI ?!
SAY SOMETHING WONDROUS HERE!!
HM?
YEAH!
YEAH!
YEAH!
MM...
WHY'S EVERYONE LOOKING AT ME?

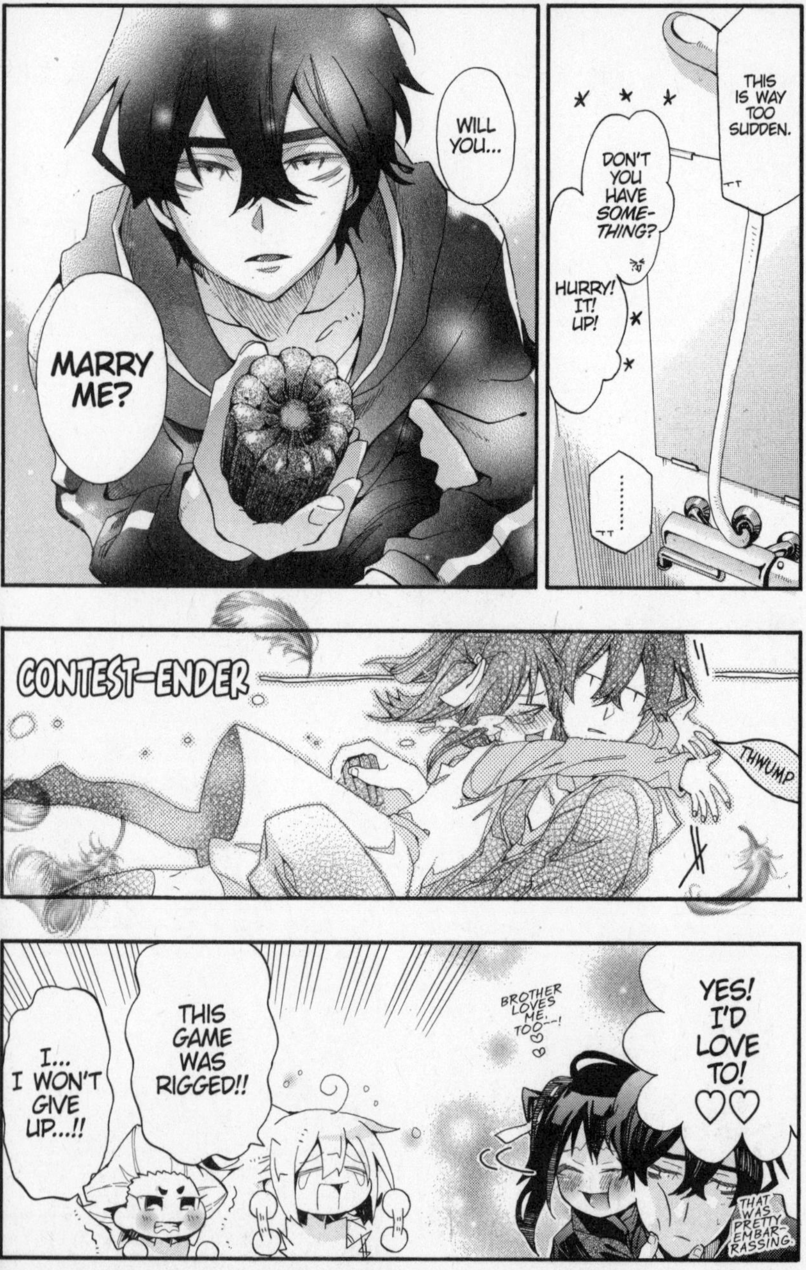
THIS IS WAY TOO SUDDEN.
DON'T YOU HAVE SOME-THING?
HURRY! IT! UP!
......
WILL YOU...
MARRY ME?
CONTEST-ENDER
THWUMP
YES! I'D LOVE TO! ♡♡
BROTHER LOVES ME, TOO--! ♡
THAT WAS PRETTY EMBAR-RASSING.
THIS GAME WAS RIGGED!!
I... I WON'T GIVE UP...!!

Merman in My Tub

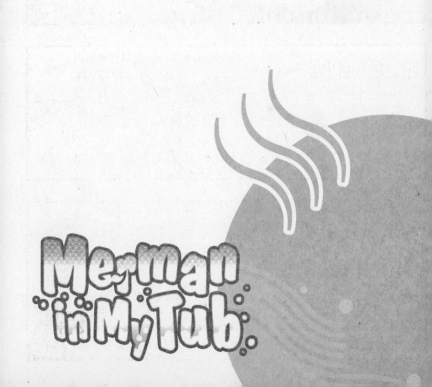

オレん家のフロ事情

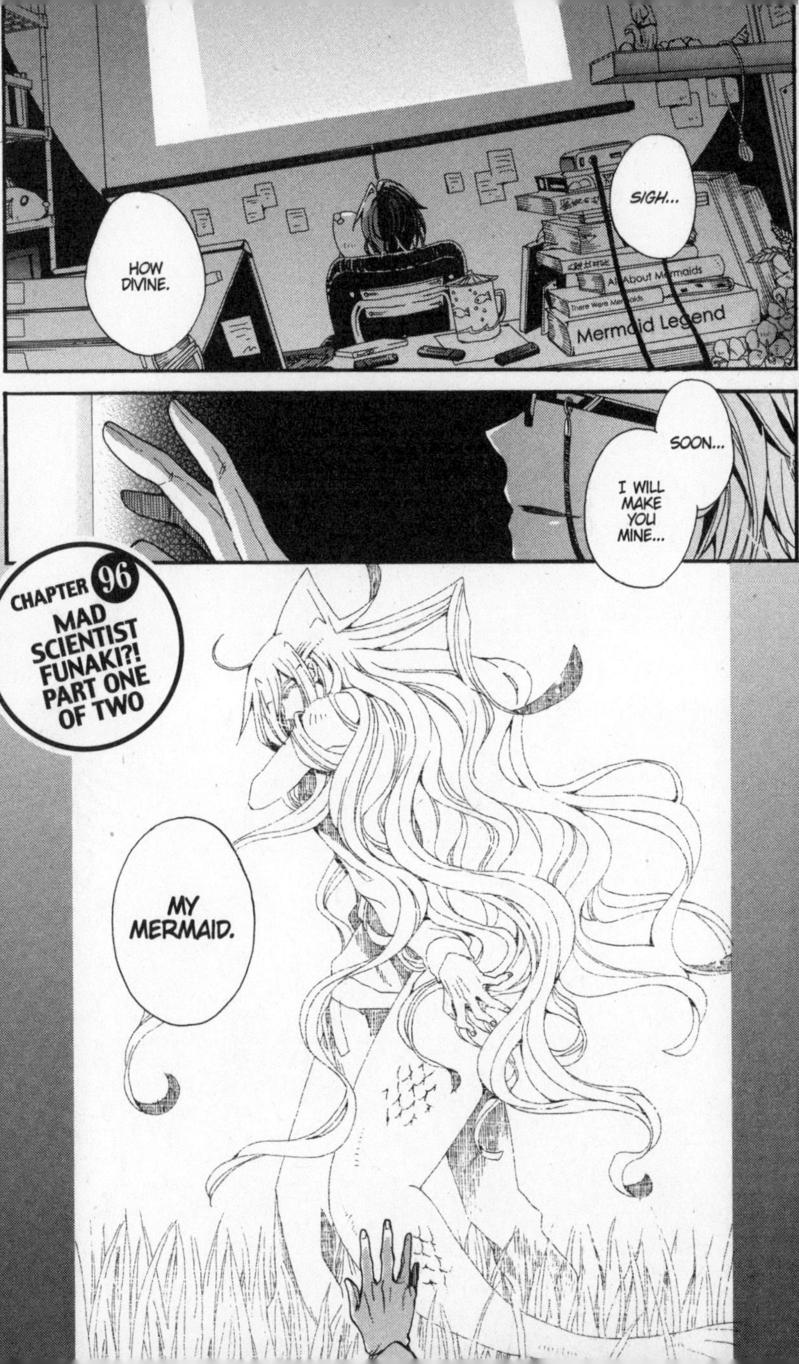
SIGH...
HOW DIVINE.
All About Mermaids
There Were Mermaids
Mermaid Legend
SOON...
I WILL MAKE YOU MINE...
CHAPTER 96
MAD SCIENTIST FUNAKI?! PART ONE OF TWO
MY MERMAID.

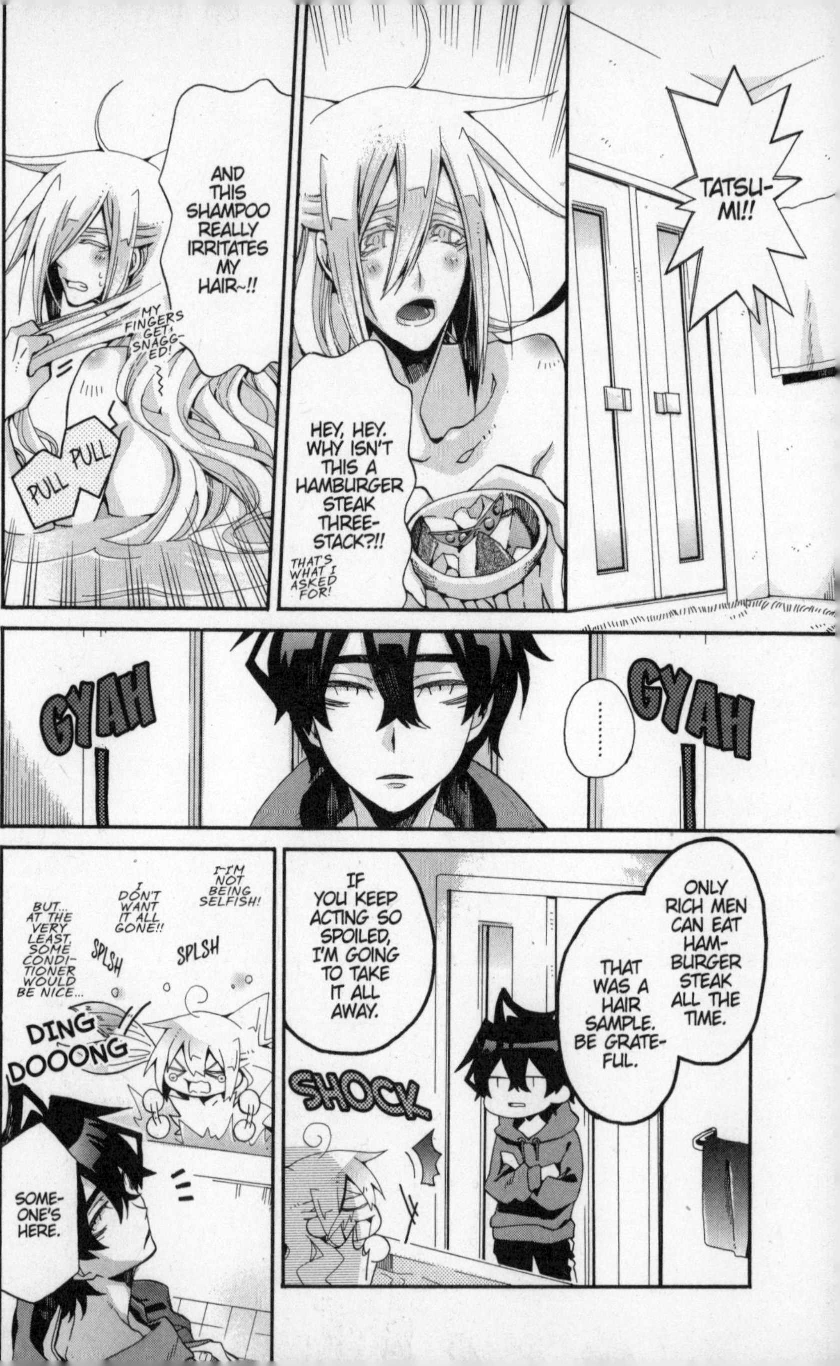
TATSU-MI!!
HEY, HEY. WHY ISN'T THIS A HAMBURGER STEAK THREE-STACK?!!
THAT'S WHAT I ASKED FOR!
AND THIS SHAMPOO REALLY IRRITATES MY HAIR~!!
MY FINGERS GET SNAGG-ED!
PULL PULL
GYAH
......
GYAH
ONLY RICH MEN CAN EAT HAM-BURGER STEAK ALL THE TIME.
THAT WAS A HAIR SAMPLE. BE GRATE-FUL.
IF YOU KEEP ACTING SO SPOILED, I'M GOING TO TAKE IT ALL AWAY.
SHOCK
I-I'M NOT BEING SELFISH!
I DON'T WANT IT ALL GONE!!
BUT... AT THE VERY LEAST, SOME CONDI-TIONER WOULD BE NICE...
SPLSH
SPLSH
DING DOOONG
SOME-ONE'S HERE.

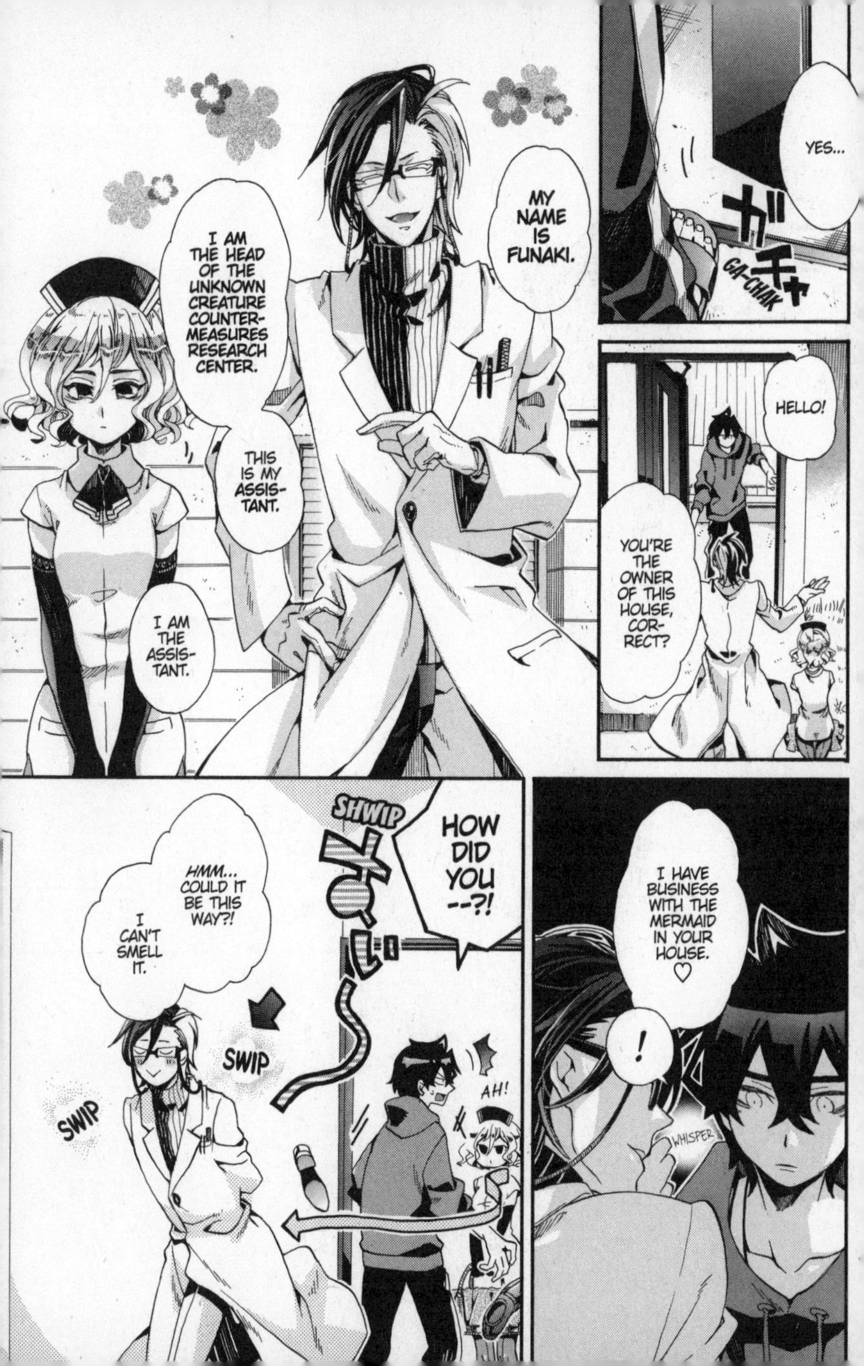
YES...
ガチャ
GA-CHAK
HELLO!
YOU'RE THE OWNER OF THIS HOUSE, CORRECT?
MY NAME IS FUNAKI.
I AM THE HEAD OF THE UNKNOWN CREATURE COUNTER-MEASURES RESEARCH CENTER.
THIS IS MY ASSISTANT.
I AM THE ASSISTANT.
I HAVE BUSINESS WITH THE MERMAID IN YOUR HOUSE. ♡
!
WHISPER
HOW DID YOU--?!
SHWIP
AH!
HMM... COULD IT BE THIS WAY?!
I CAN'T SMELL IT.
SWIP
SWIP

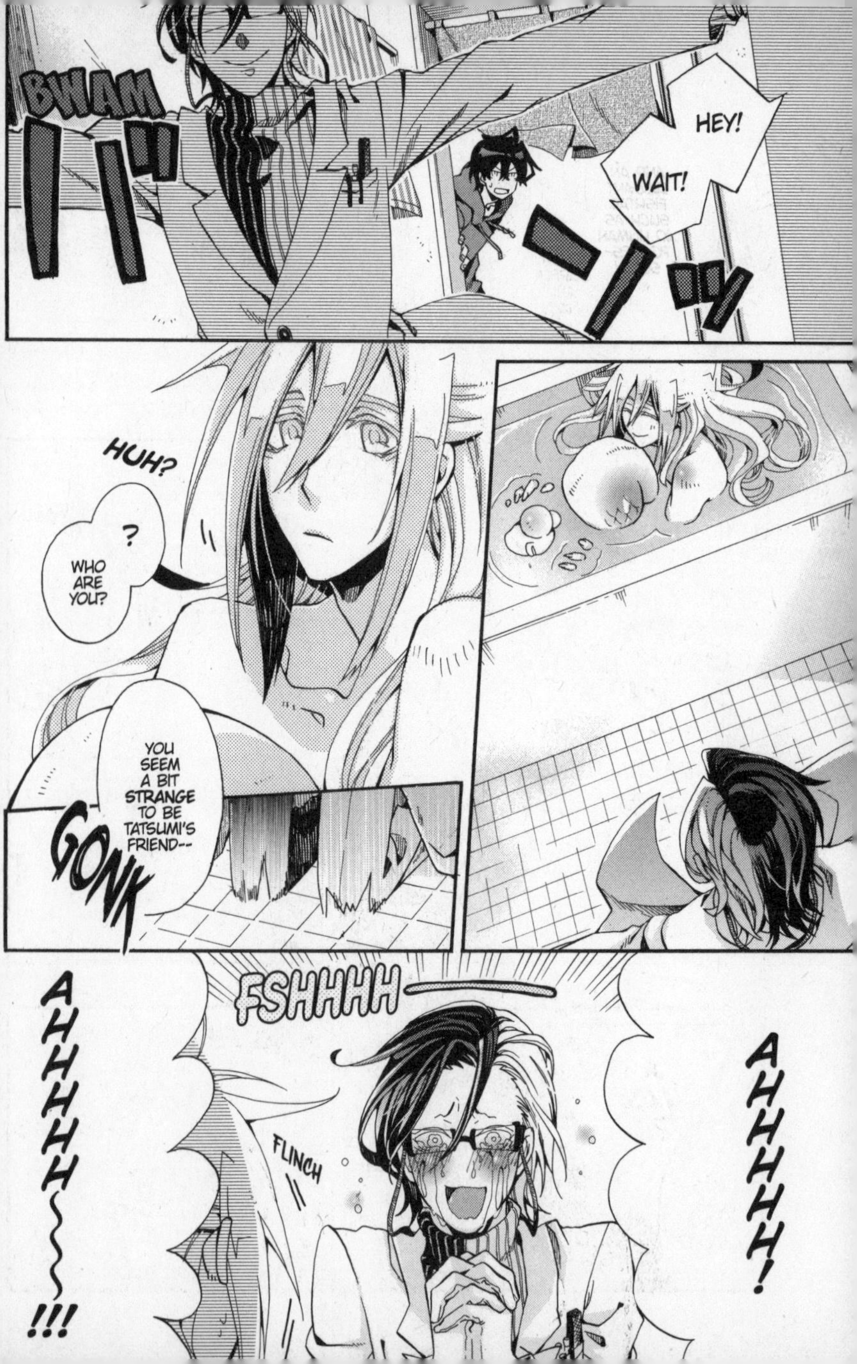

HEY!
WAIT!
BWAM
HUH?
?
WHO ARE YOU?
YOU SEEM A BIT STRANGE TO BE TATSUMI'S FRIEND--
GONK
FSHHHH
AHHHHH!
FLINCH
AHHHHH~~~!!!

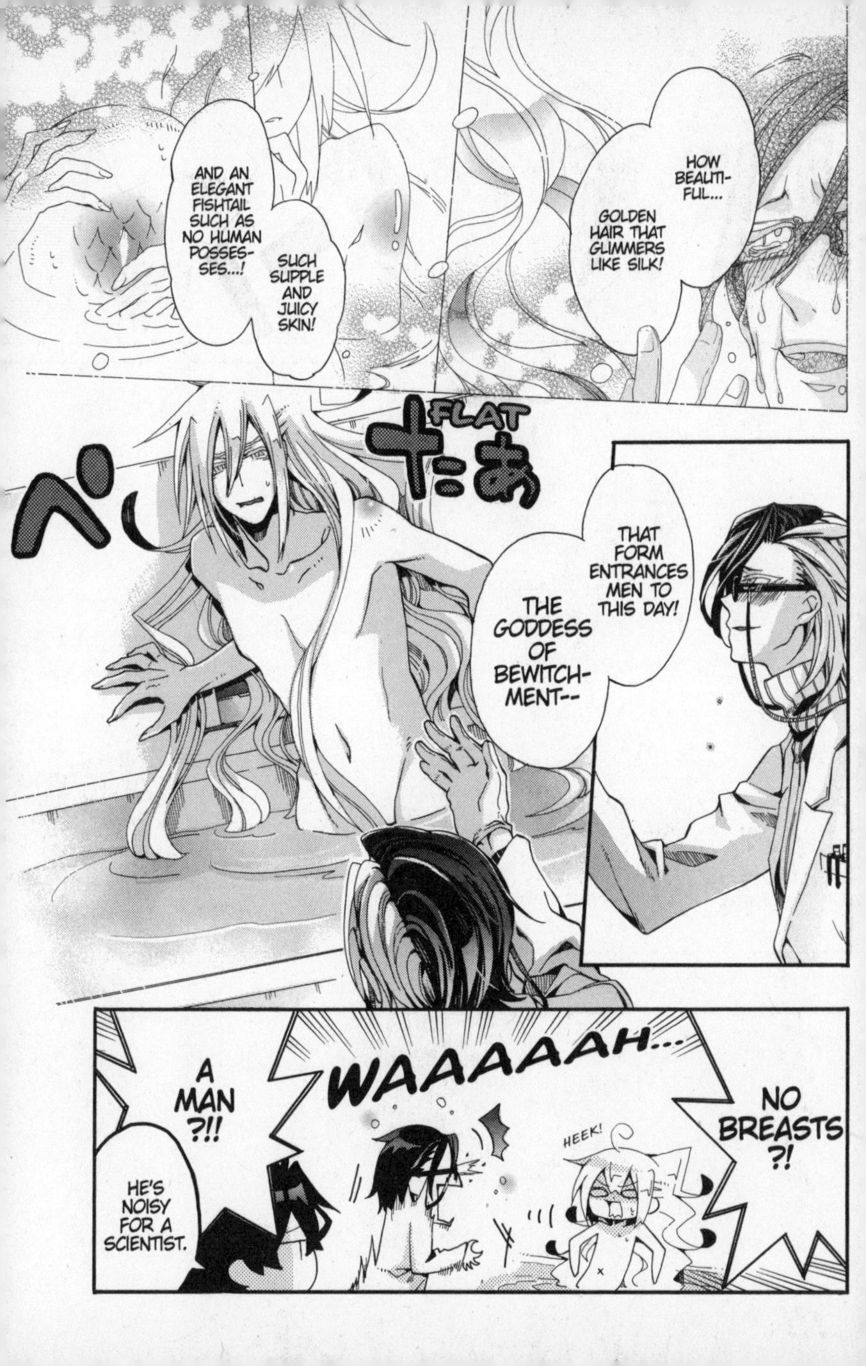

HOW BEAUTIFUL...
GOLDEN HAIR THAT GLIMMERS LIKE SILK!
SUCH SUPPLE AND JUICY SKIN!
AND AN ELEGANT FISHTAIL SUCH AS NO HUMAN POSSESSES...!
THAT FORM ENTRANCES MEN TO THIS DAY!
THE GODDESS OF BEWITCHMENT--
FLAT
ぺたぁ
NO BREASTS?!
HEEK!
WAAAAAH...
A MAN?!!
HE'S NOISY FOR A SCIENTIST.

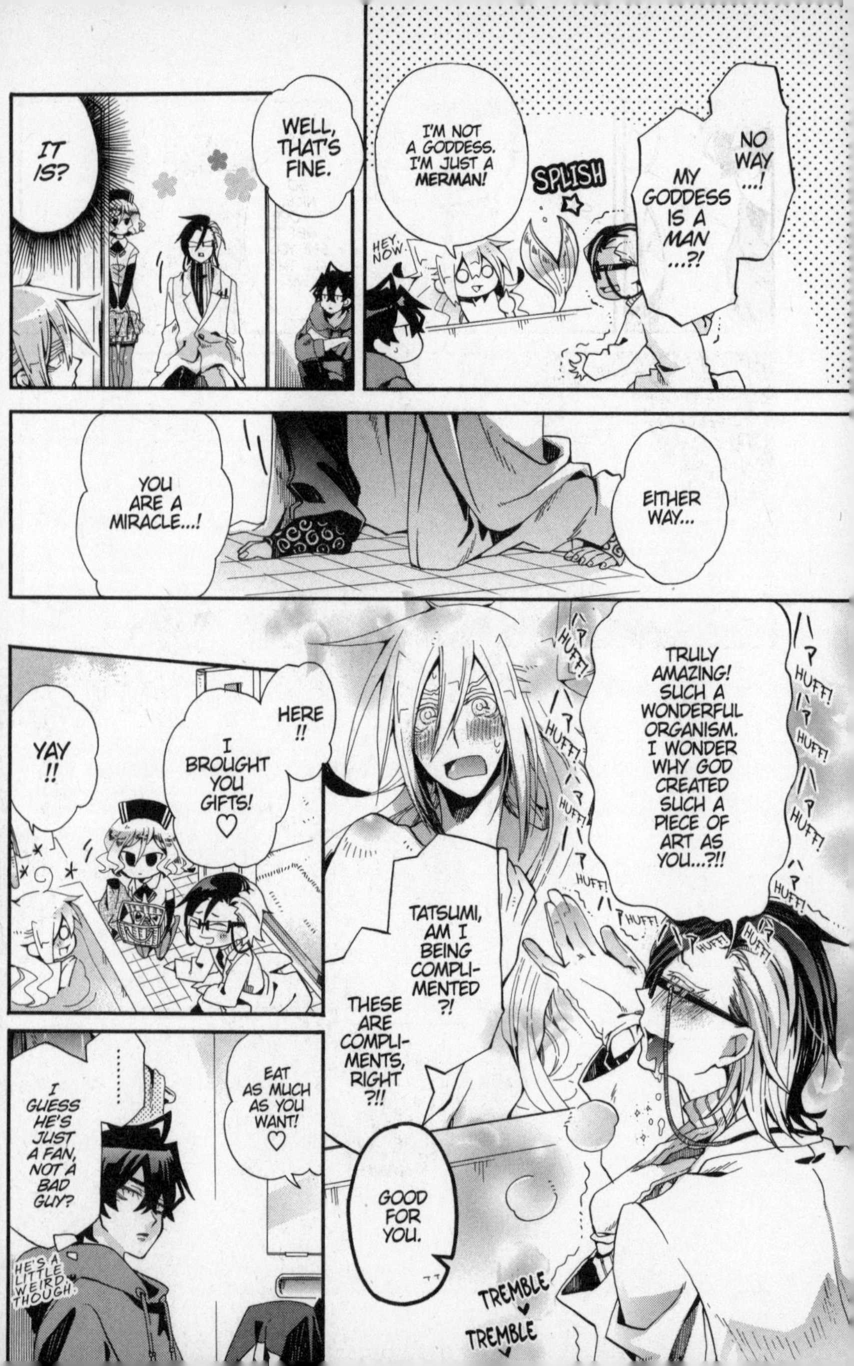
NO WAY ...!
MY GODDESS IS A MAN ...?!
SPLISH
I'M NOT A GODDESS. I'M JUST A MERMAN!
HEY, NOW.
WELL, THAT'S FINE.
IT IS?
EITHER WAY...
YOU ARE A MIRACLE...!
HUFF! HUFF! HUFF! HUFF!
TRULY AMAZING! SUCH A WONDERFUL ORGANISM. I WONDER WHY GOD CREATED SUCH A PIECE OF ART AS YOU...?!!
HUFF! HUFF! HUFF! HUFF! HUFF! HUFF! HUFF!
TATSUMI, AM I BEING COMPLI- MENTED ?!
THESE ARE COMPLI- MENTS, RIGHT ?!!
GOOD FOR YOU.
TREMBLE TREMBLE
HERE !!
I BROUGHT YOU GIFTS! ♡
YAY !!
EAT AS MUCH AS YOU WANT! ♡
......
I GUESS HE'S JUST A FAN, NOT A BAD GUY?
HE'S A LITTLE WEIRD THOUGH.

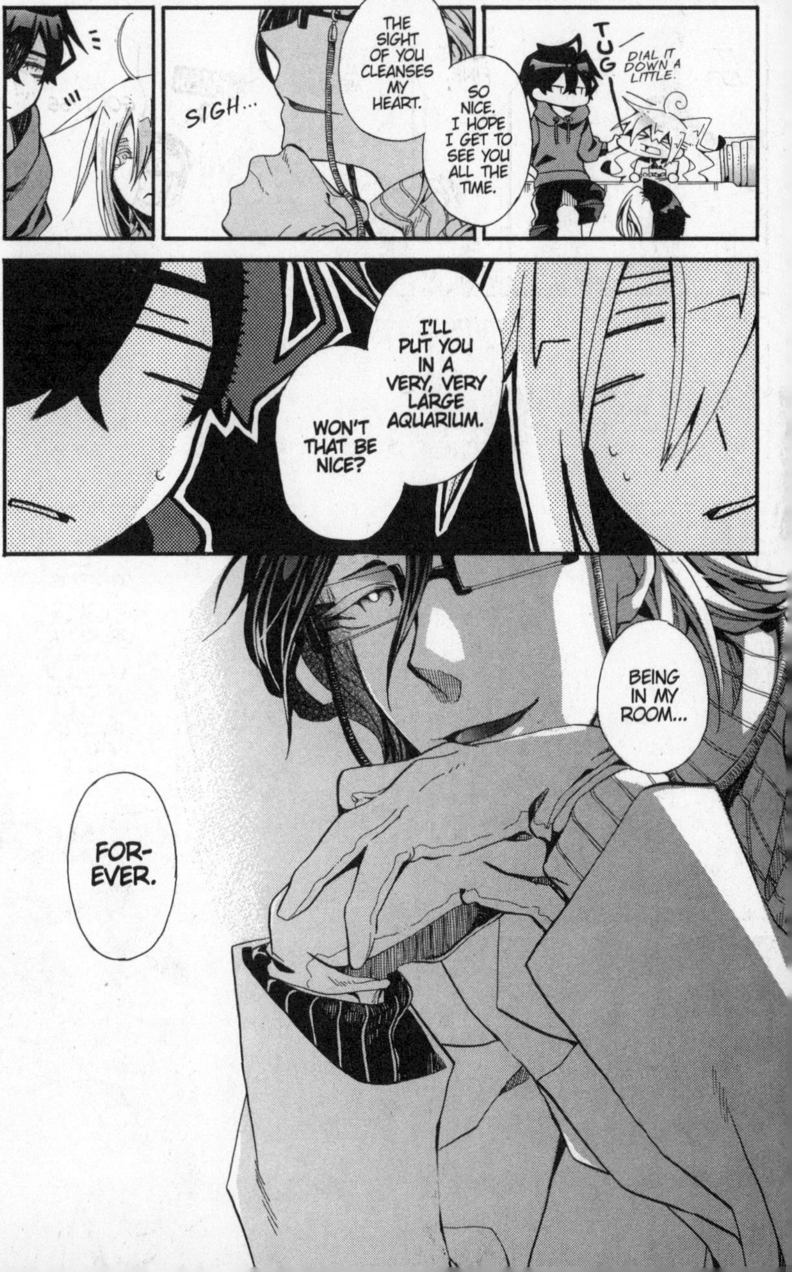
TUG
DIAL IT DOWN A LITTLE.
THE SIGHT OF YOU CLEANSES MY HEART.
SO NICE. I HOPE I GET TO SEE YOU ALL THE TIME.
SIGH...
I'LL PUT YOU IN A VERY, VERY LARGE AQUARIUM.
WON'T THAT BE NICE?
BEING IN MY ROOM...
FOR-EVER.

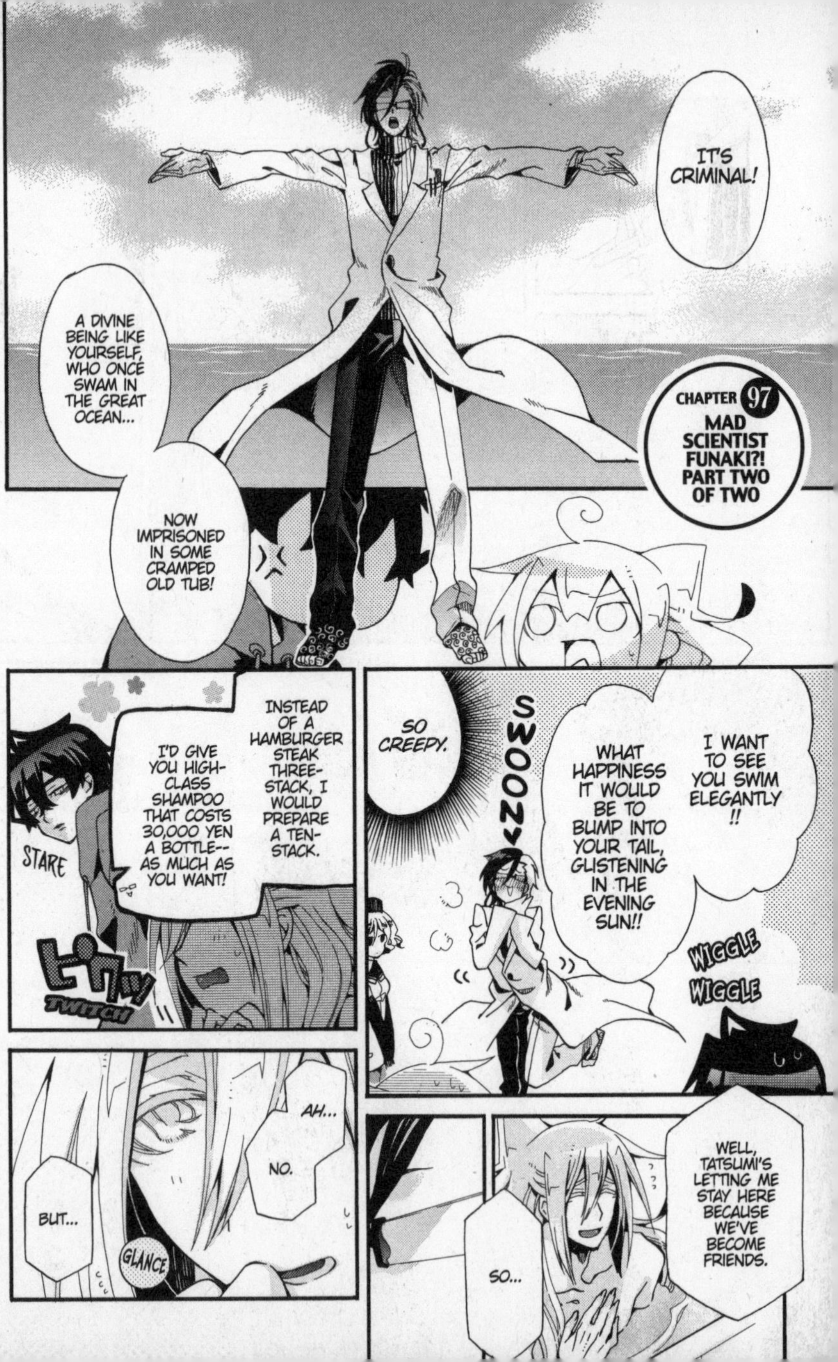
IT'S CRIMINAL!
CHAPTER 97
MAD SCIENTIST FUNAKI?! PART TWO OF TWO
A DIVINE BEING LIKE YOURSELF, WHO ONCE SWAM IN THE GREAT OCEAN...
NOW IMPRISONED IN SOME CRAMPED OLD TUB!
I WANT TO SEE YOU SWIM ELEGANTLY!!
WHAT HAPPINESS IT WOULD BE TO BUMP INTO YOUR TAIL, GLISTENING IN THE EVENING SUN!!
SWOON
SO CREEPY.
WIGGLE
WIGGLE
INSTEAD OF A HAMBURGER STEAK THREE-STACK, I WOULD PREPARE A TEN-STACK.
I'D GIVE YOU HIGH-CLASS SHAMPOO THAT COSTS 30,000 YEN A BOTTLE-- AS MUCH AS YOU WANT!
STARE
TWITCH
WELL, TATSUMI'S LETTING ME STAY HERE BECAUSE WE'VE BECOME FRIENDS.
SO...
AH...
NO.
BUT...
GLANCE

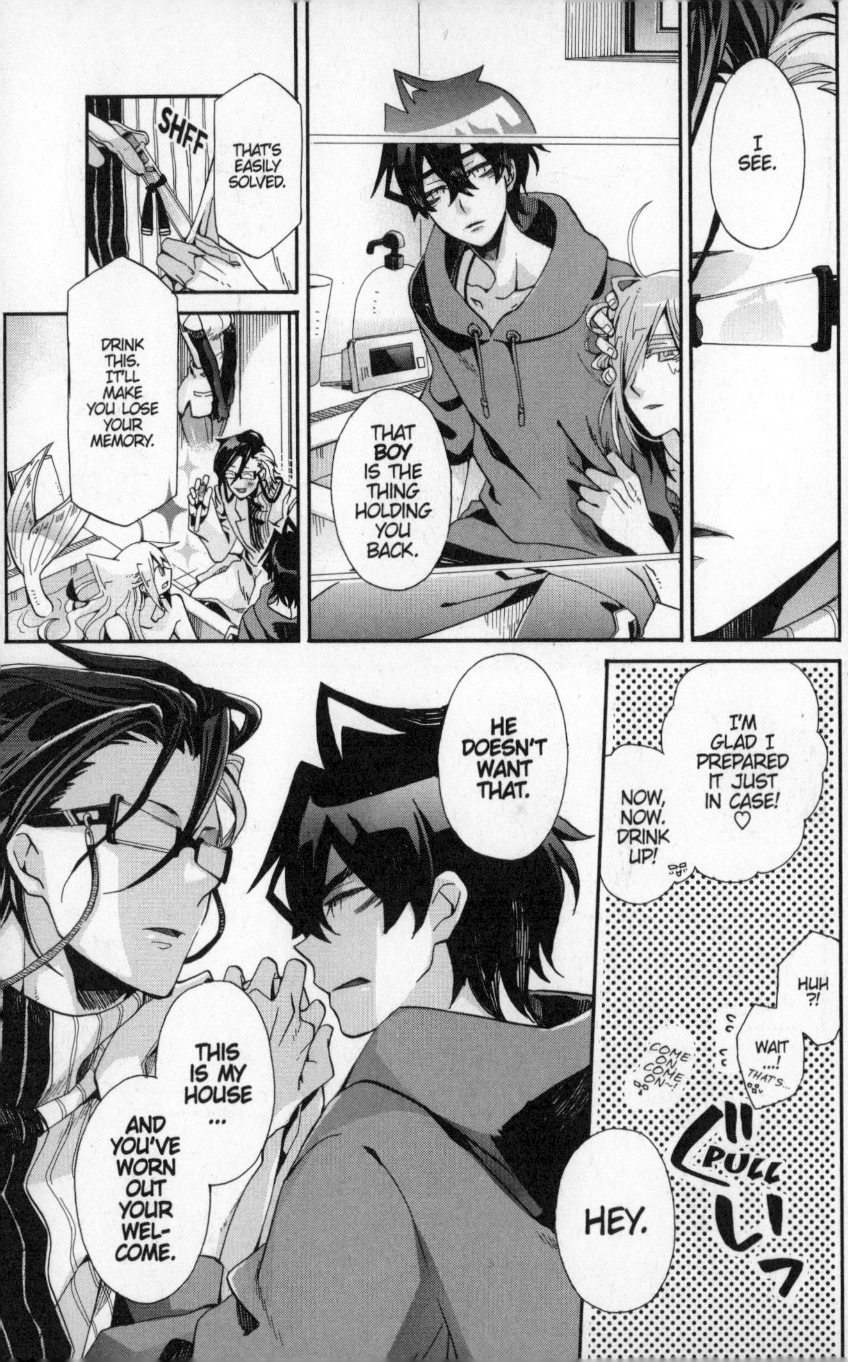
I SEE.
THAT BOY IS THE THING HOLDING YOU BACK.
THAT'S EASILY SOLVED.
SHFF
DRINK THIS. IT'LL MAKE YOU LOSE YOUR MEMORY.
I'M GLAD I PREPARED IT JUST IN CASE! ♡
NOW, NOW. DRINK UP!
HUH ?!
WAIT ...! THAT'S...
COME ON COME ON~!
PULL
HEY.
HE DOESN'T WANT THAT.
THIS IS MY HOUSE ...
AND YOU'VE WORN OUT YOUR WEL-COME.

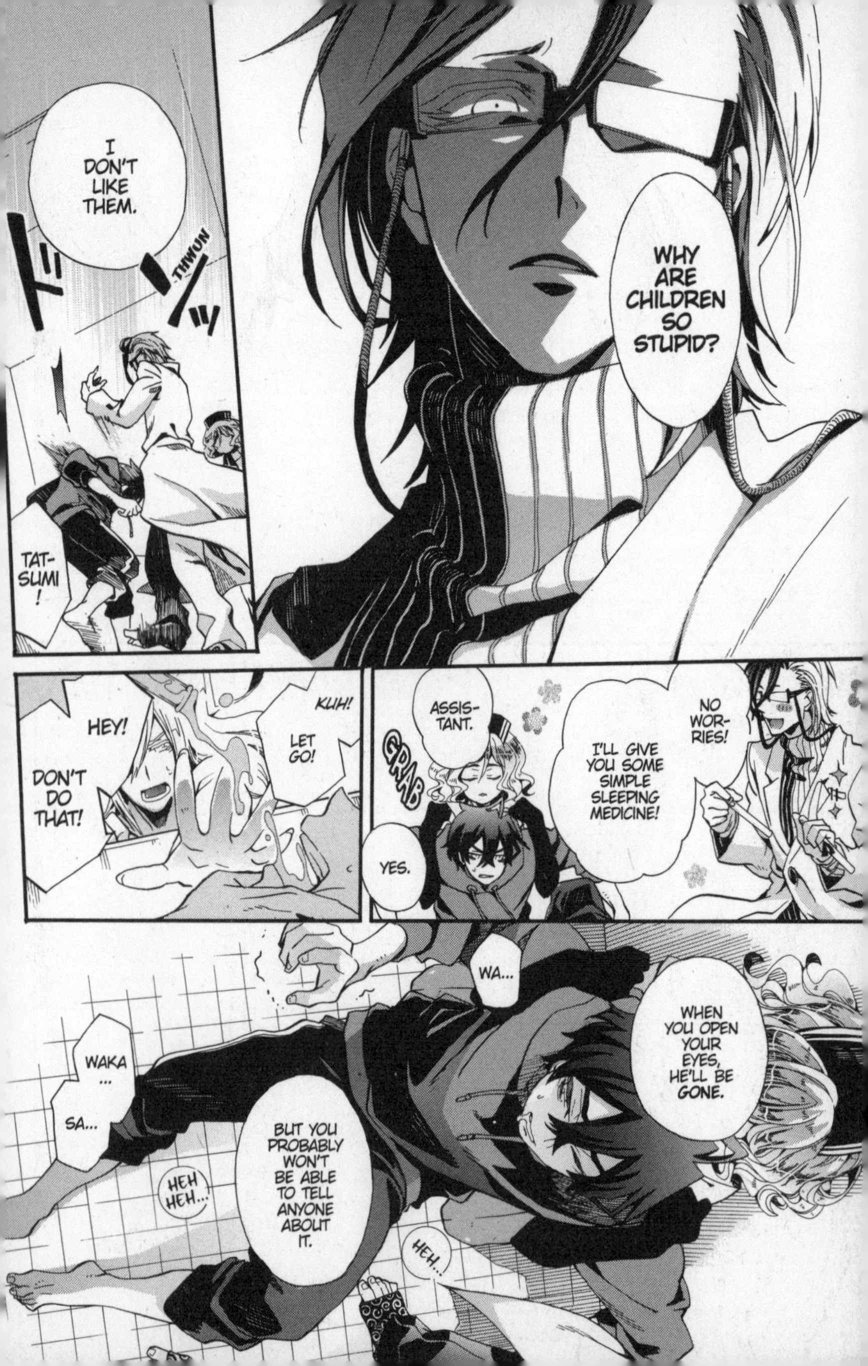
WHY ARE CHILDREN SO STUPID?
I DON'T LIKE THEM.
THWUN
TATSUMI!
NO WORRIES!
I'LL GIVE YOU SOME SIMPLE SLEEPING MEDICINE!
ASSISTANT.
GRAB
YES.
KUH!
LET GO!
HEY!
DON'T DO THAT!
WHEN YOU OPEN YOUR EYES, HE'LL BE GONE.
WA...
BUT YOU PROBABLY WON'T BE ABLE TO TELL ANYONE ABOUT IT.
HEH...
HEH HEH...
WAKA...
SA...

ALL YOU'LL BE ABLE TO DO IS WISH FOR HIS HAPPINESS.

DROOP

RUN...

AWAY.

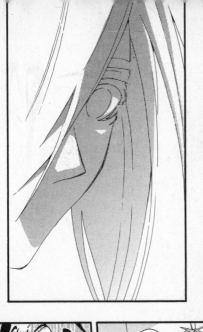

GWA-PLOOSH!

HM?

HMM?

PONK!

PONK

PONK

FUNAKI-SAMA!

!

SHUDDER

SHUDDER

SHUDDER

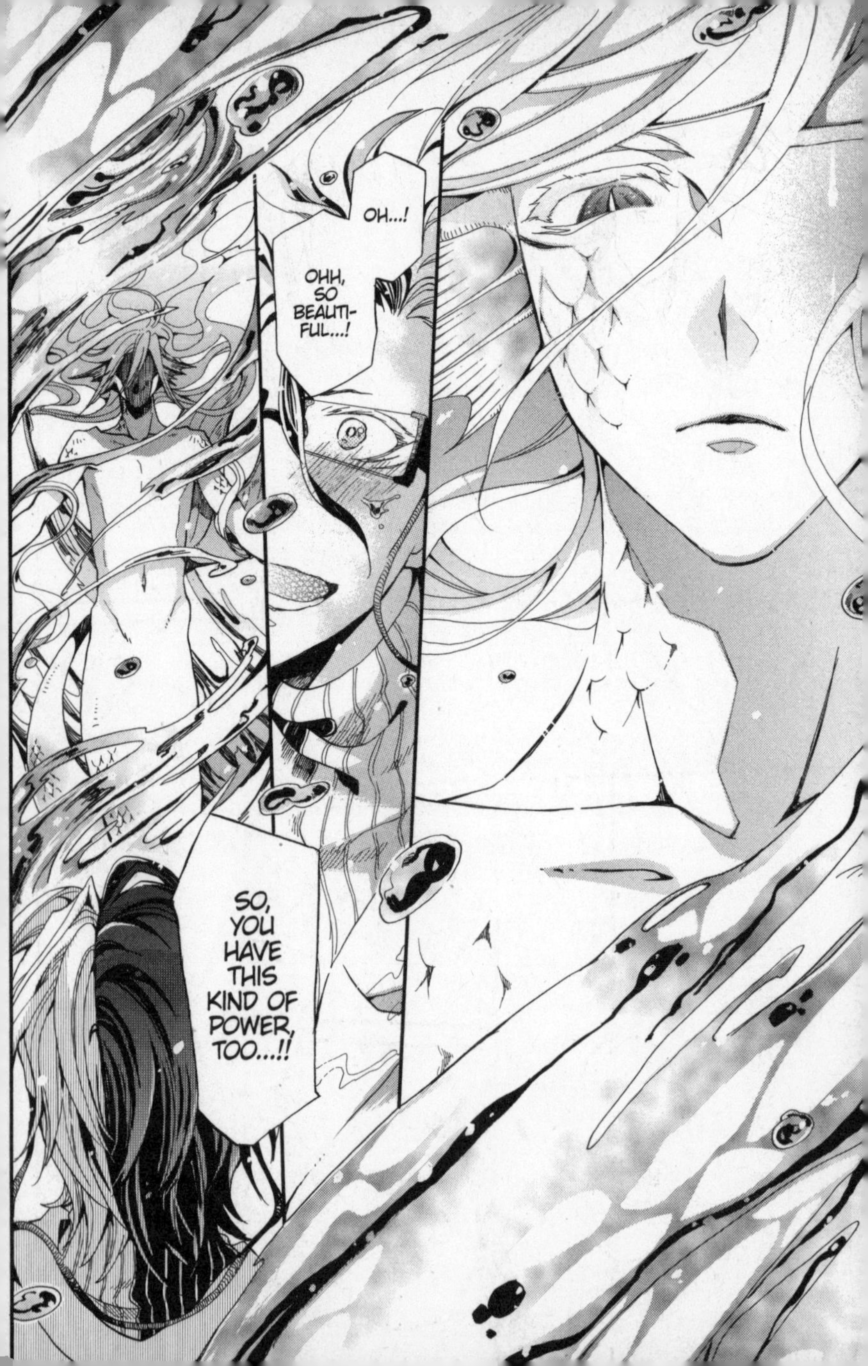
OH...!
OHH, SO BEAUTI-FUL...!
SO, YOU HAVE THIS KIND OF POWER, TOO...!!

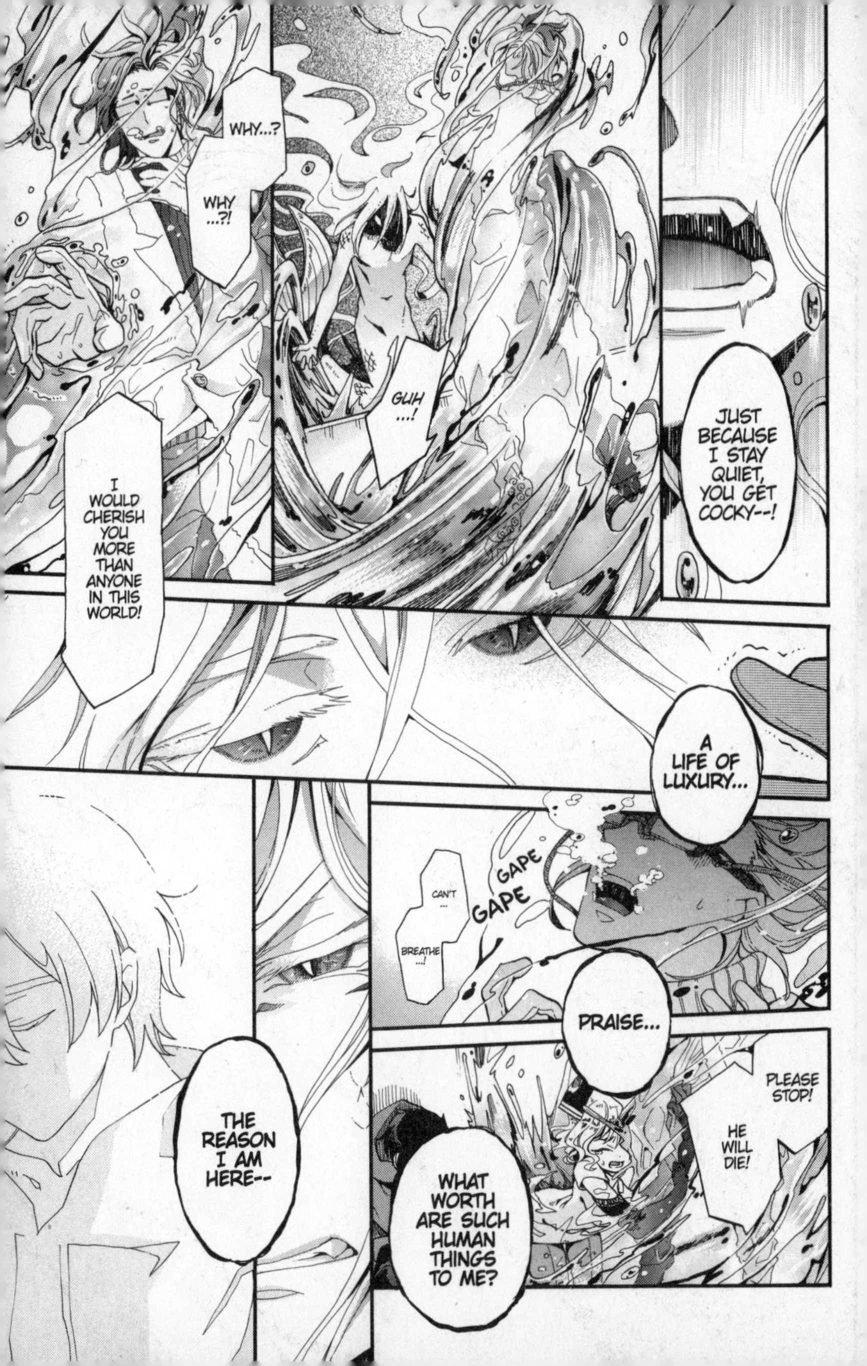
JUST BECAUSE I STAY QUIET, YOU GET COCKY--!
GUH...!
WHY...?
WHY...?!
I WOULD CHERISH YOU MORE THAN ANYONE IN THIS WORLD!
A LIFE OF LUXURY...
GAPE
GAPE
CAN'T... BREATHE...!
PRAISE...
PLEASE STOP!
HE WILL DIE!
WHAT WORTH ARE SUCH HUMAN THINGS TO ME?
THE REASON I AM HERE--

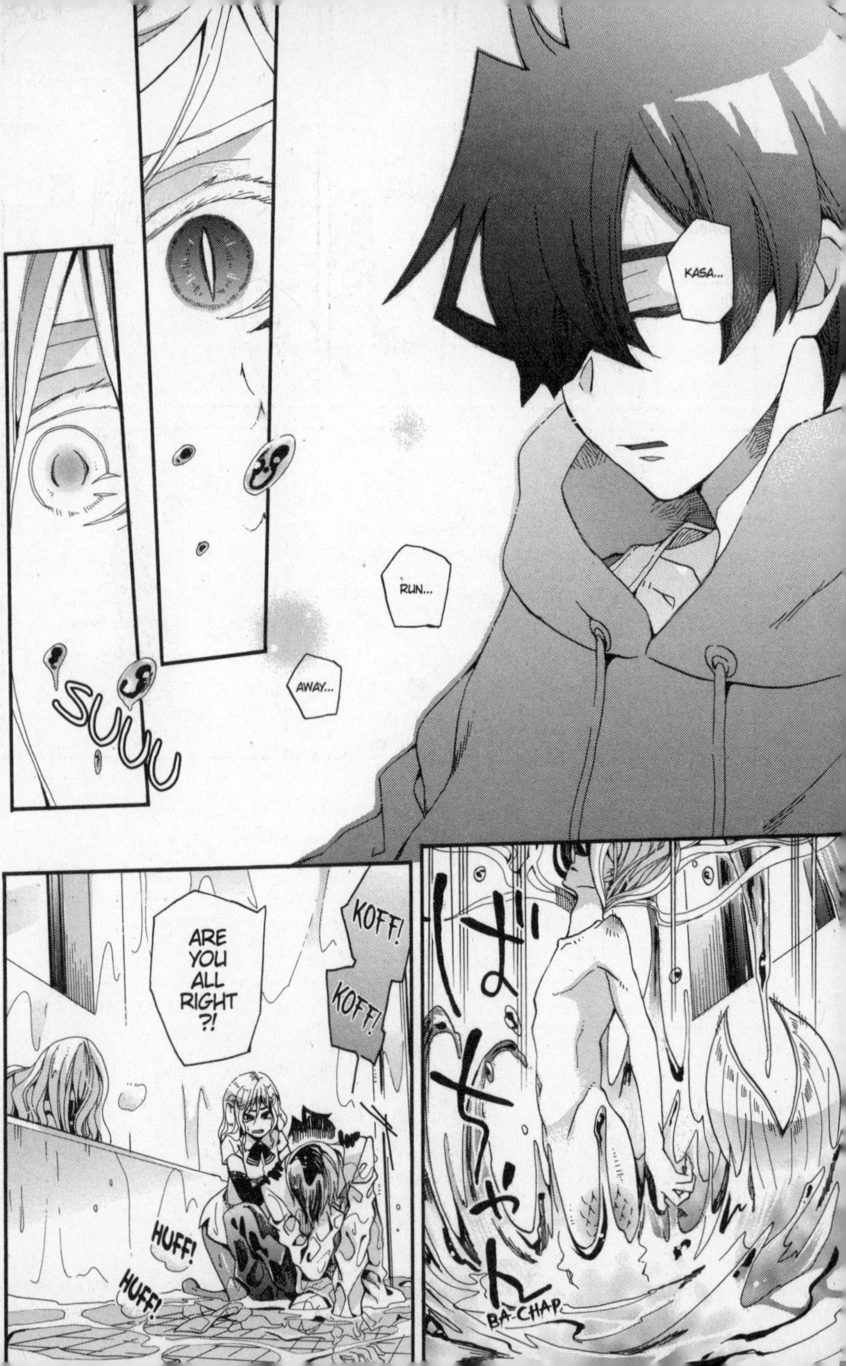
KASA...
RUN...
AWAY...
SUUU
BA-CHAP
KOFF!
KOFF!
ARE YOU ALL RIGHT?!
HUFF!
HUFF!

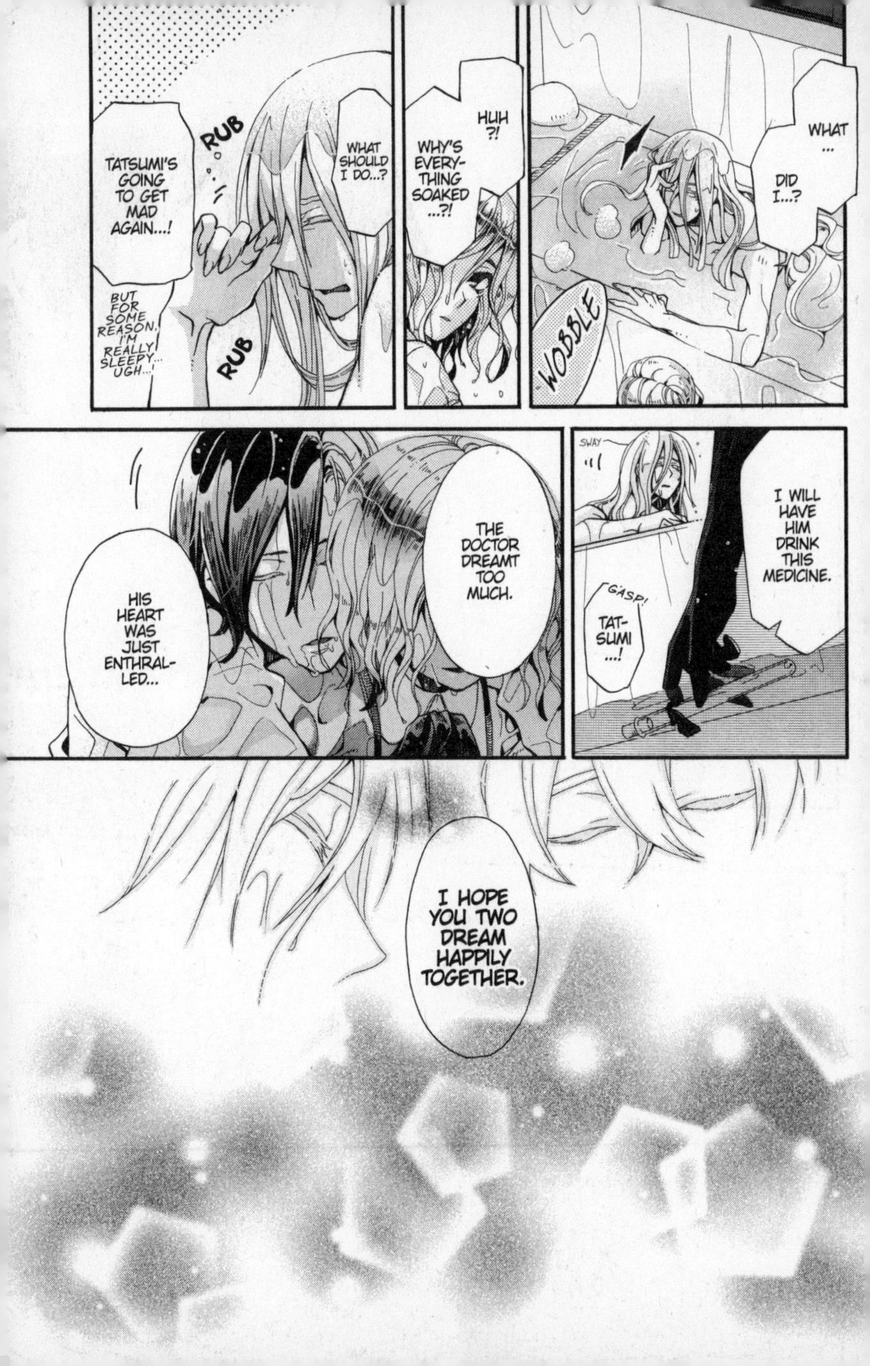
WHAT ... DID I...?
WOBBLE
HUH ?!
WHY'S EVERY-THING SOAKED ...?!
WHAT SHOULD I DO...?
RUB
TATSUMI'S GOING TO GET MAD AGAIN...!
BUT FOR SOME REASON, I'M REALLY SLEEPY... UGH...!
RUB
SWAY
I WILL HAVE HIM DRINK THIS MEDICINE.
GASP!
TAT-SUMI ...!
THE DOCTOR DREAMT TOO MUCH.
HIS HEART WAS JUST ENTHRAL-LED...
I HOPE YOU TWO DREAM HAPPILY TOGETHER.

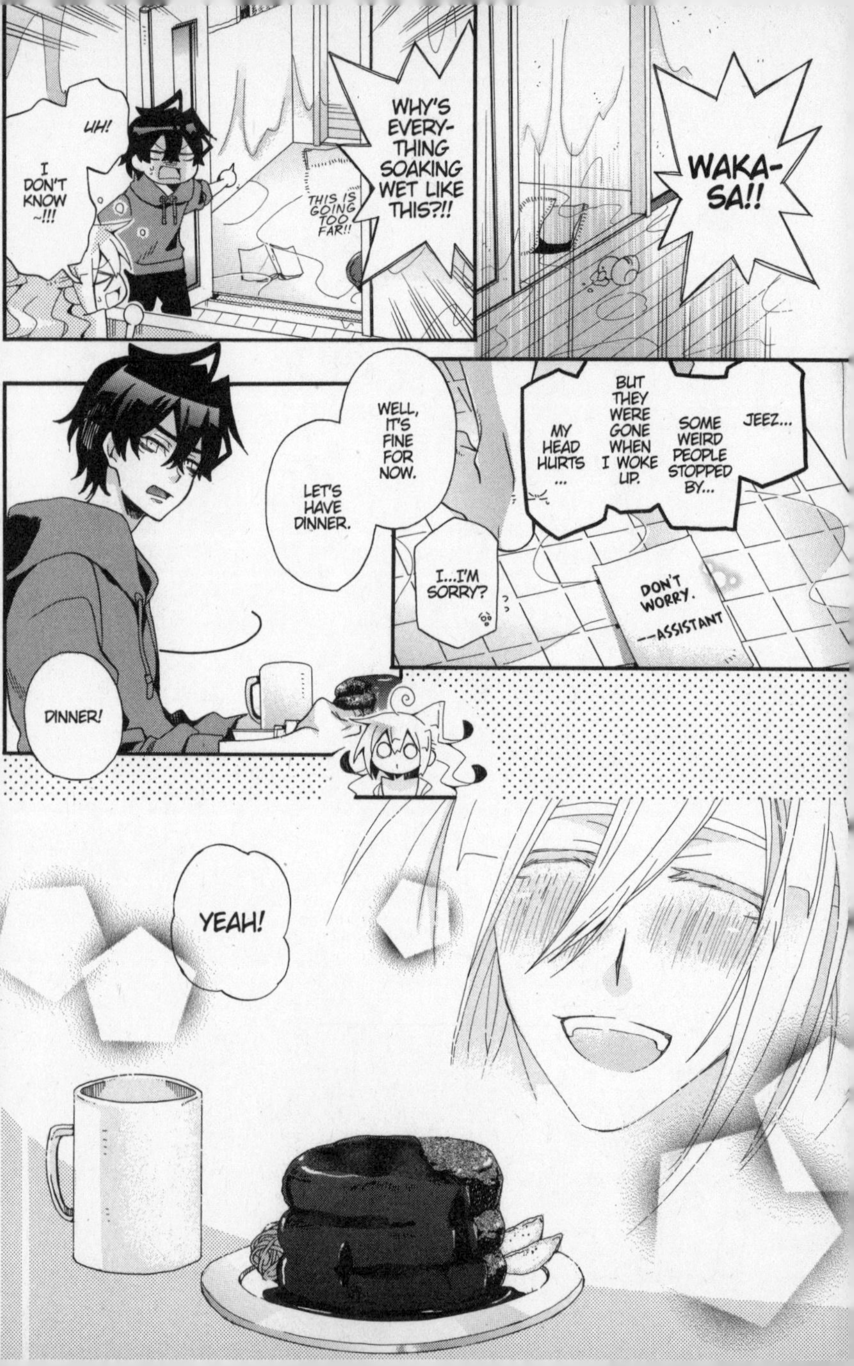
WAKA-SA!!
WHY'S EVERY-THING SOAKING WET LIKE THIS?!!
THIS IS GOING TOO FAR!!
UH!
I DON'T KNOW ~!!!
JEEZ...
SOME WEIRD PEOPLE STOPPED BY...
BUT THEY WERE GONE WHEN I WOKE UP.
MY HEAD HURTS...
I...I'M SORRY?
DON'T WORRY. --ASSISTANT
WELL, IT'S FINE FOR NOW.
LET'S HAVE DINNER.
DINNER!
YEAH!

Merman in My Tub

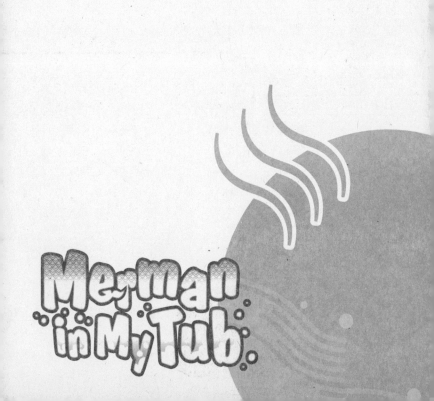

オレん家のフロ事情

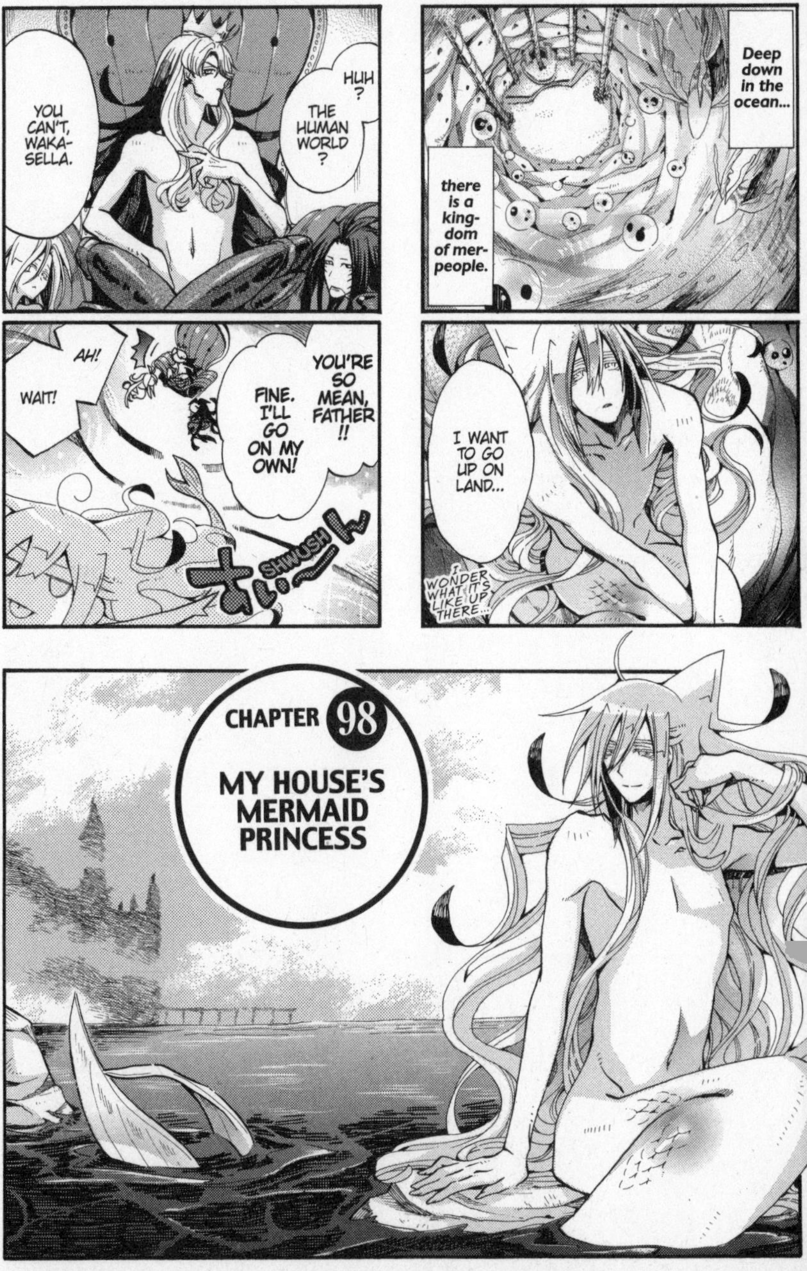
Deep down in the ocean...
there is a kingdom of merpeople.
HUH? THE HUMAN WORLD?
YOU CAN'T, WAKASELLA.
I WANT TO GO UP ON LAND...
I WONDER WHAT IT'S LIKE UP THERE...
YOU'RE SO MEAN, FATHER!!
FINE. I'LL GO ON MY OWN!
AH!
WAIT!
SHWUSH
CHAPTER 98
MY HOUSE'S MERMAID PRINCESS

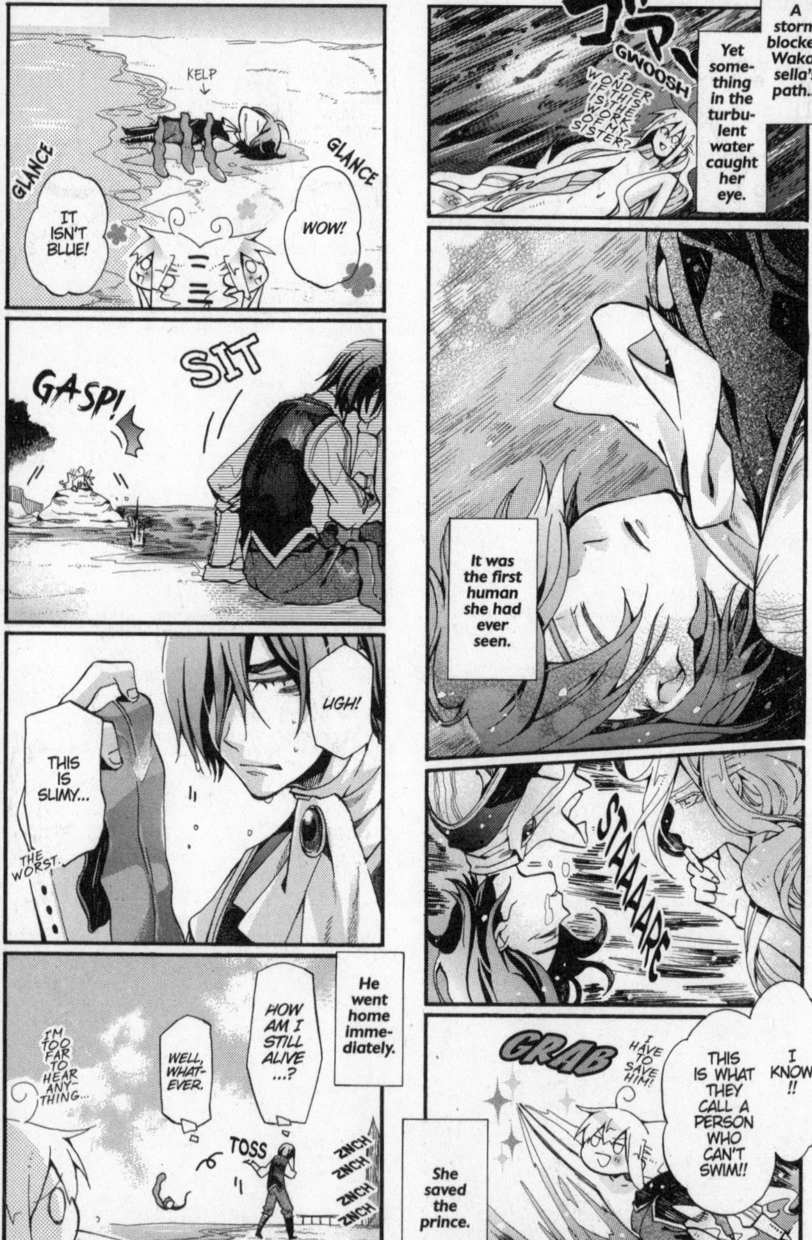
A storm blocked Waka-sella's path...
Yet some-thing in the turbu-lent water caught her eye.
GWOOSH
I WONDER IF THIS IS THE WORK OF MY SISTER?
It was the first human she had ever seen.
STAAAARE
I KNOW!!
THIS IS WHAT THEY CALL A PERSON WHO CAN'T SWIM!!
I HAVE TO SAVE HIM!
GRAB
She saved the prince.
KELP
GLANCE
GLANCE
WOW!
IT ISN'T BLUE!
SIT
GASP!
UGH!
THIS IS SLIMY...
THE WORST.
He went home imme-diately.
HOW AM I STILL ALIVE ...?
WELL, WHAT-EVER.
I'M TOO FAR TO HEAR ANY-THING...
TOSS
ZNCH ZNCH ZNCH ZNCH

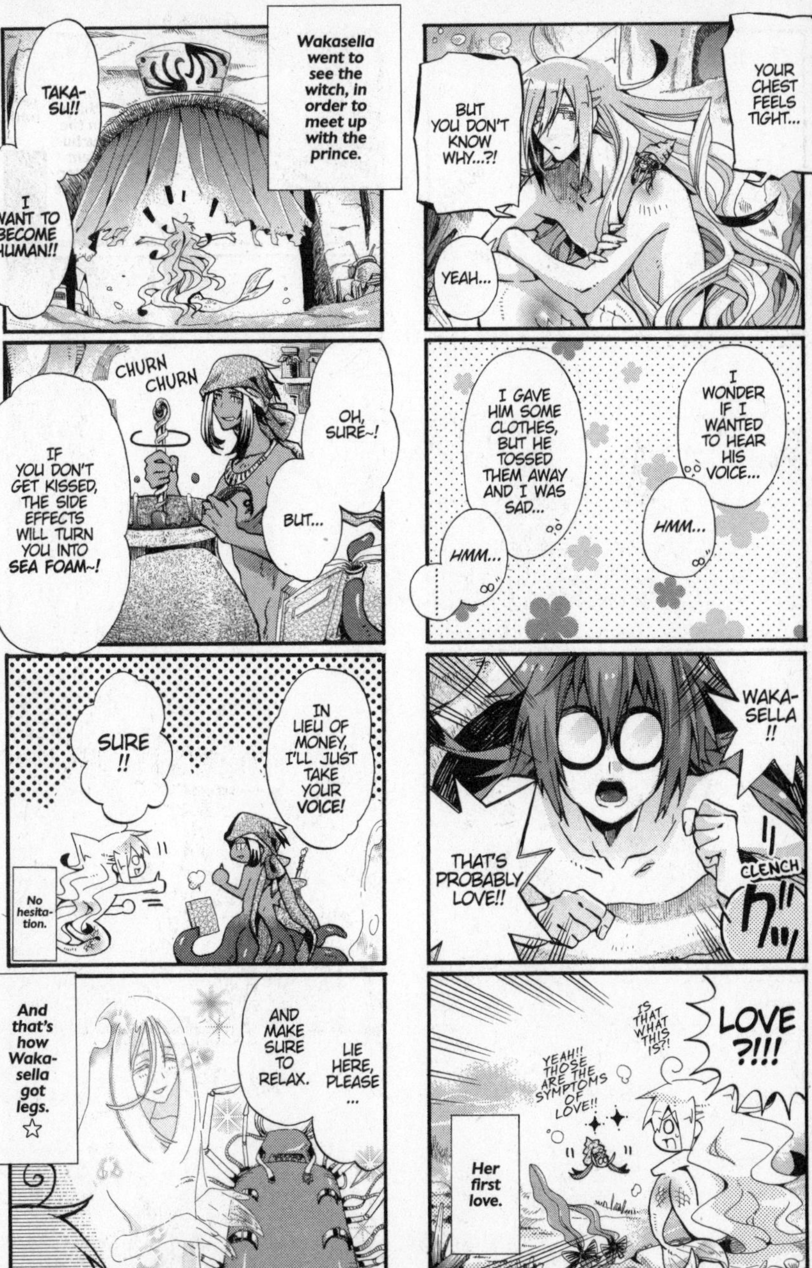
YOUR CHEST FEELS TIGHT...
BUT YOU DON'T KNOW WHY...?!
YEAH...
I WONDER IF I WANTED TO HEAR HIS VOICE...
HMM...
I GAVE HIM SOME CLOTHES, BUT HE TOSSED THEM AWAY AND I WAS SAD...
HMM...
WAKA-SELLA!!
THAT'S PROBABLY LOVE!!
CLENCH
LOVE?!!!
IS THAT WHAT THIS IS?!
YEAH!! THOSE ARE THE SYMPTOMS OF LOVE!!
Her first love.
Wakasella went to see the witch, in order to meet up with the prince.
TAKA-SU!!
I WANT TO BECOME HUMAN!!
OH, SURE~!
BUT...
CHURN CHURN
IF YOU DON'T GET KISSED, THE SIDE EFFECTS WILL TURN YOU INTO SEA FOAM~!
IN LIEU OF MONEY, I'LL JUST TAKE YOUR VOICE!
SURE!!
No hesita-tion.
LIE HERE, PLEASE...
AND MAKE SURE TO RELAX.
And that's how Waka-sella got legs. ☆

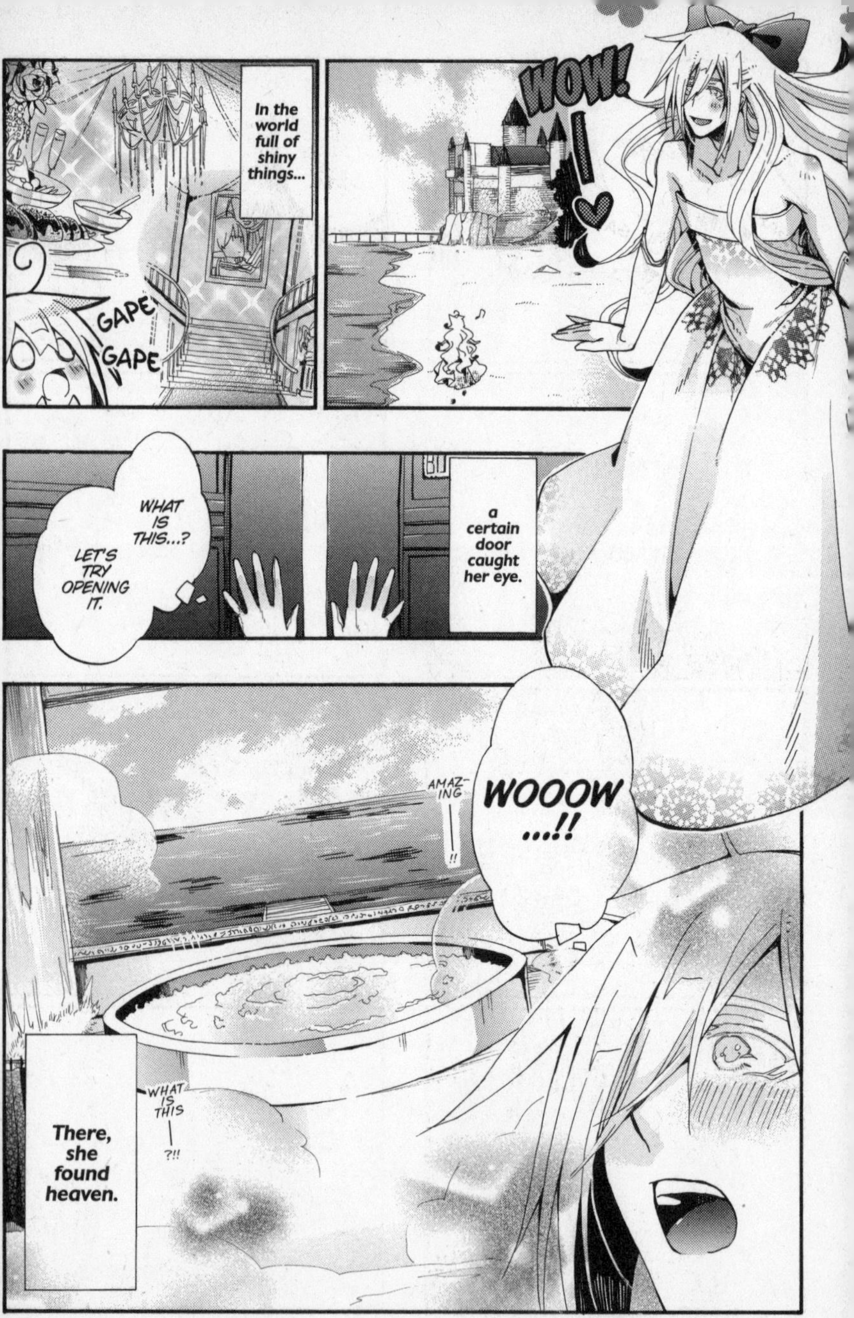
WOW!!
In the world full of shiny things...
GAPE GAPE
a certain door caught her eye.
WHAT IS THIS...?
LET'S TRY OPENING IT.
WOOOW ...!!
AMAZING—!!
WHAT IS THIS—?!!
There, she found heaven.

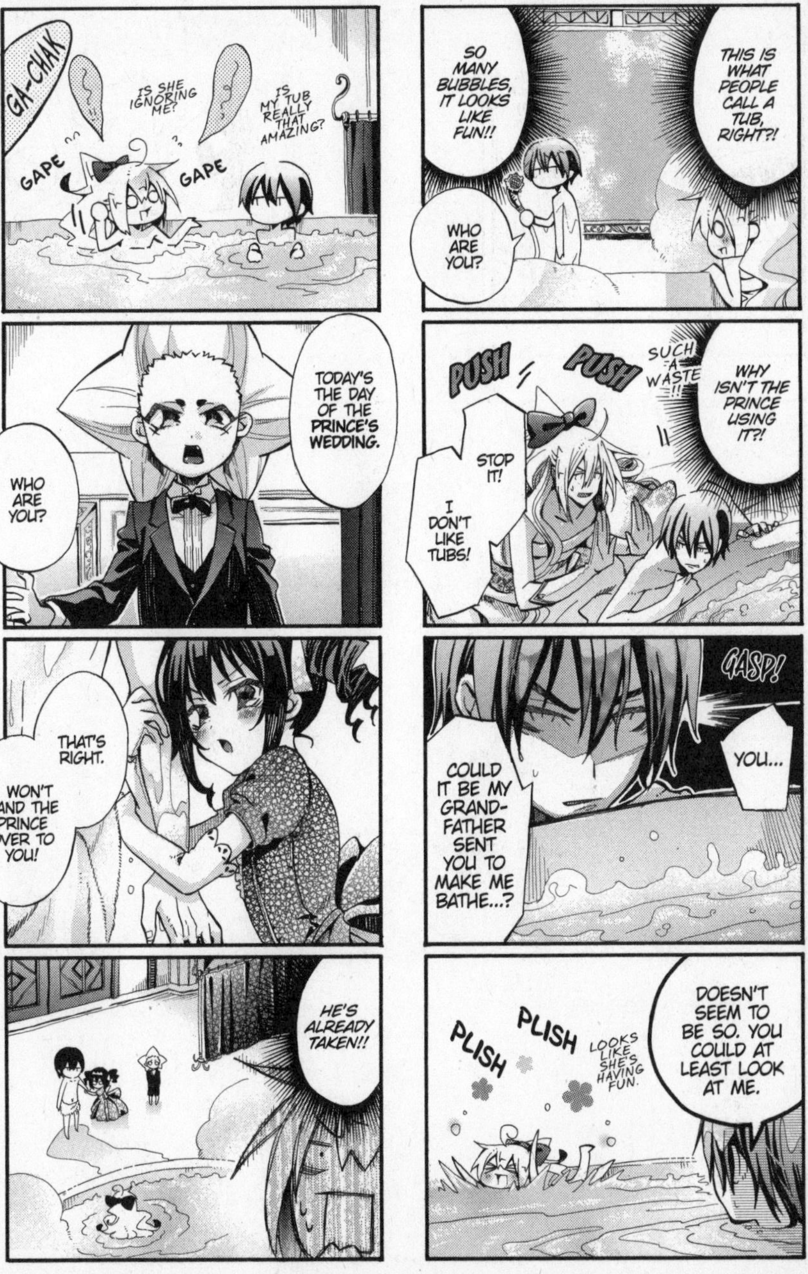
THIS IS WHAT PEOPLE CALL A TUB, RIGHT?!
SO MANY BUBBLES, IT LOOKS LIKE FUN!!
WHO ARE YOU?
WHY ISN'T THE PRINCE USING IT?!
SUCH A WASTE!!
PUSH
PUSH
STOP IT!
I DON'T LIKE TUBS!
GASP!
YOU...
COULD IT BE MY GRANDFATHER SENT YOU TO MAKE ME BATHE...?
DOESN'T SEEM TO BE SO. YOU COULD AT LEAST LOOK AT ME.
LOOKS LIKE SHE'S HAVING FUN.
PLISH
PLISH
IS MY TUB REALLY THAT AMAZING?
IS SHE IGNORING ME?
GA-CHAK
GAPE
GAPE
TODAY'S THE DAY OF THE PRINCE'S WEDDING.
WHO ARE YOU?
THAT'S RIGHT.
I WON'T HAND THE PRINCE OVER TO YOU!
HE'S ALREADY TAKEN!!

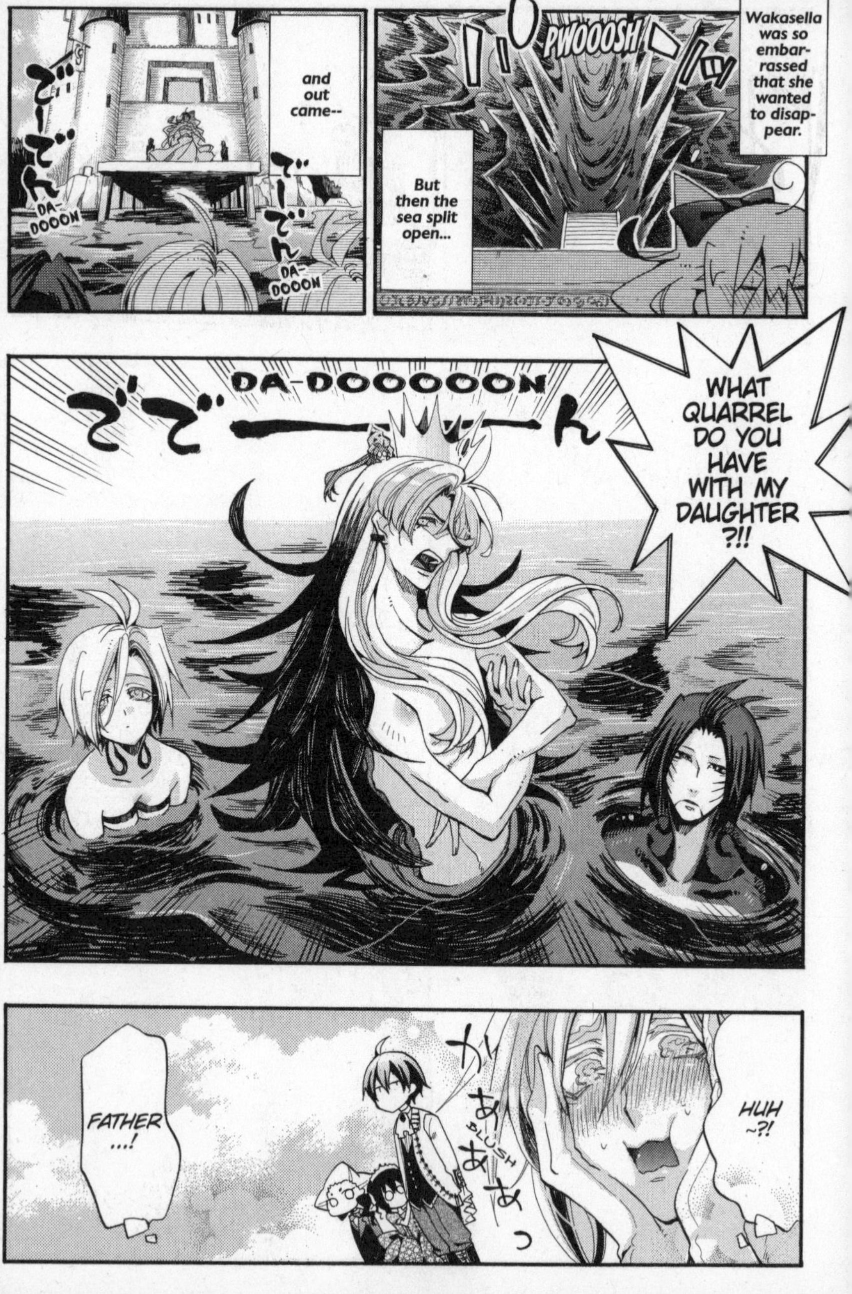
Wakasella was so embarrassed that she wanted to disappear.
PWOOOSH
But then the sea split open...
and out came--
DA-DOOON
DA-DOOON
WHAT QUARREL DO YOU HAVE WITH MY DAUGHTER?!!
DA-DOOOOOON
HUH~?!
BLUSH
FATHER...!

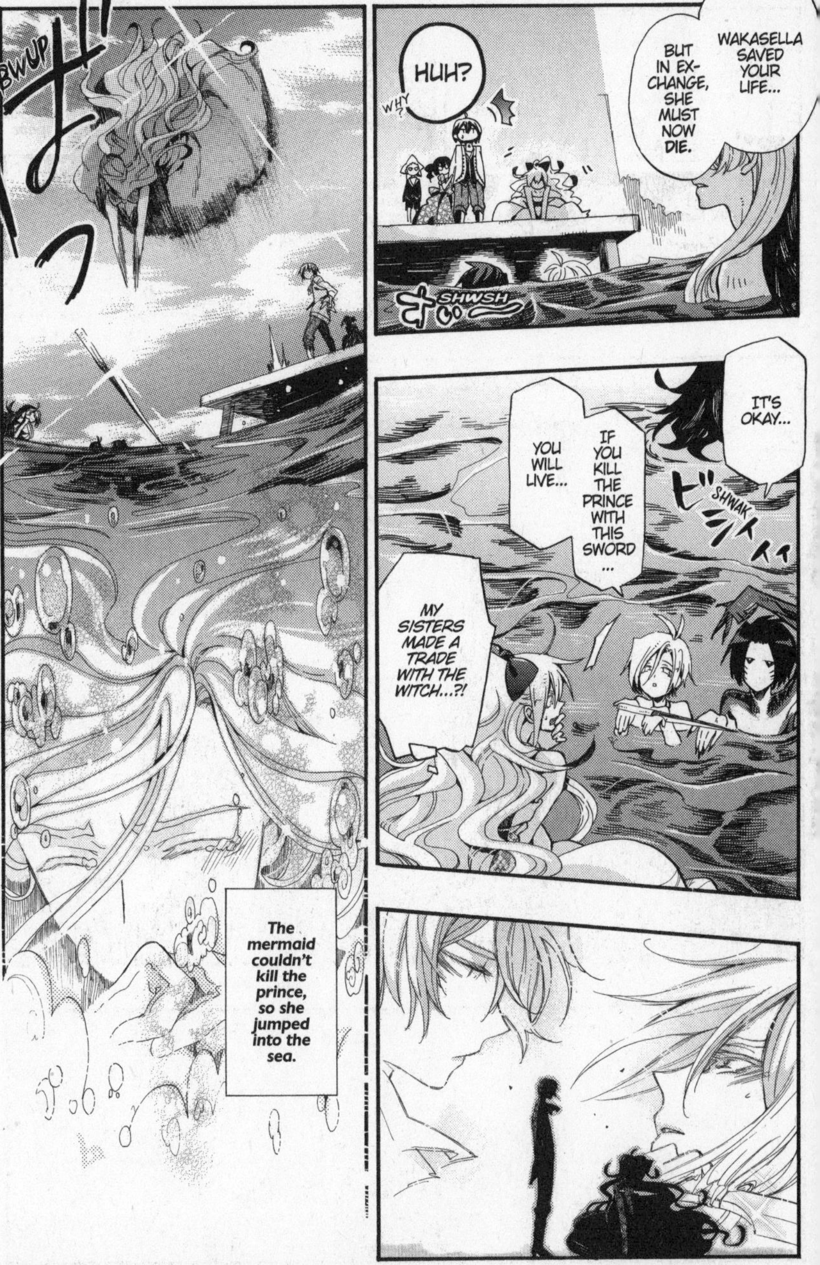
WAKASELLA SAVED YOUR LIFE...
BUT IN EXCHANGE, SHE MUST NOW DIE.
HUH?
WHY?
SHWSH
IT'S OKAY...
SHWAK
IF YOU KILL THE PRINCE WITH THIS SWORD...
YOU WILL LIVE...
MY SISTERS MADE A TRADE WITH THE WITCH...?!
BWUP
The mermaid couldn't kill the prince, so she jumped into the sea.

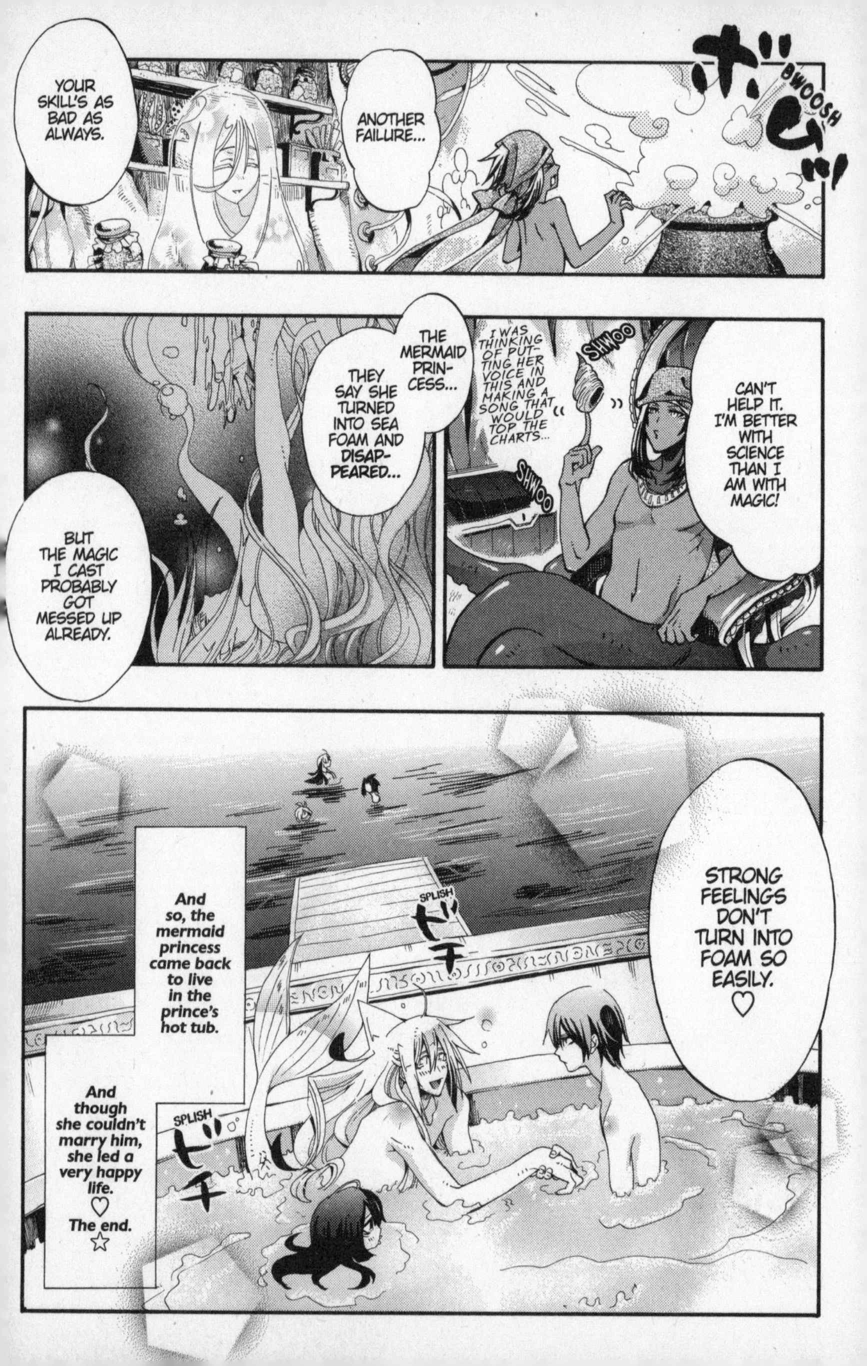
BWOOSH
ANOTHER FAILURE...
YOUR SKILL'S AS BAD AS ALWAYS.
CAN'T HELP IT. I'M BETTER WITH SCIENCE THAN I AM WITH MAGIC!
SHWOO
I WAS THINKING OF PUTTING HER VOICE IN THIS AND MAKING A SONG THAT WOULD TOP THE CHARTS...
SHWOO
THE MERMAID PRINCESS...
THEY SAY SHE TURNED INTO SEA FOAM AND DISAPPEARED...
BUT THE MAGIC I CAST PROBABLY GOT MESSED UP ALREADY.
STRONG FEELINGS DON'T TURN INTO FOAM SO EASILY. ♡
SPLISH
And so, the mermaid princess came back to live in the prince's hot tub.
SPLISH
And though she couldn't marry him, she led a very happy life. ♡ The end. ☆

Merman in My Tub

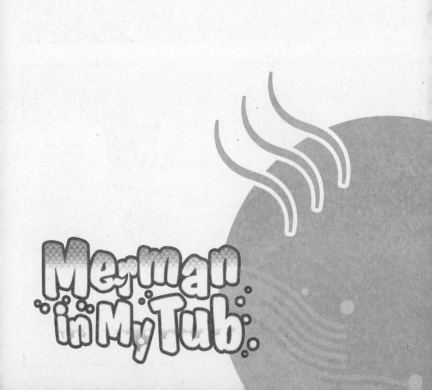

オレん家のフロ事情

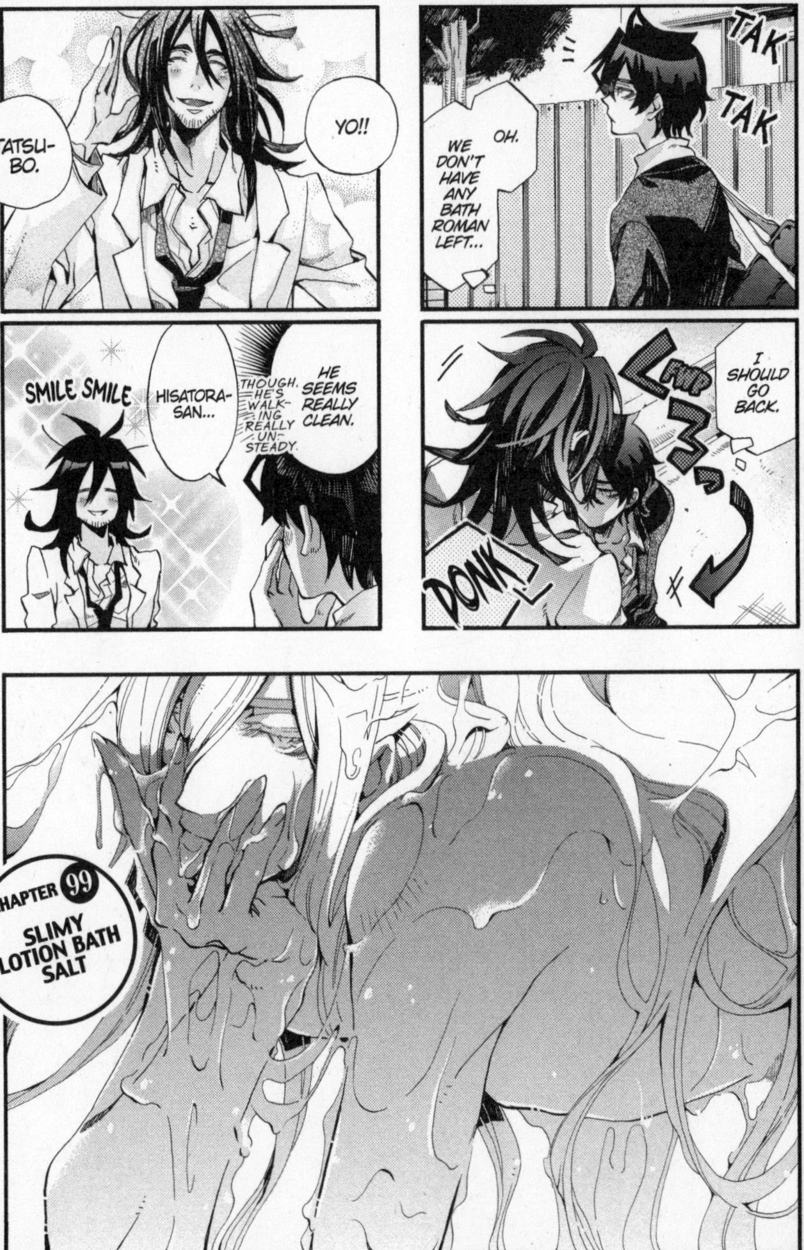
TAK
TAK
OH.
WE DON'T HAVE ANY BATH ROMAN LEFT...
YO!!
TATSU-BO.
I SHOULD GO BACK.
DONK
HE SEEMS REALLY CLEAN.
THOUGH. HE'S WALK-ING REALLY UN-STEADY.
HISATORA-SAN...
SMILE SMILE
CHAPTER 99
SLIMY LOTION BATH SALT

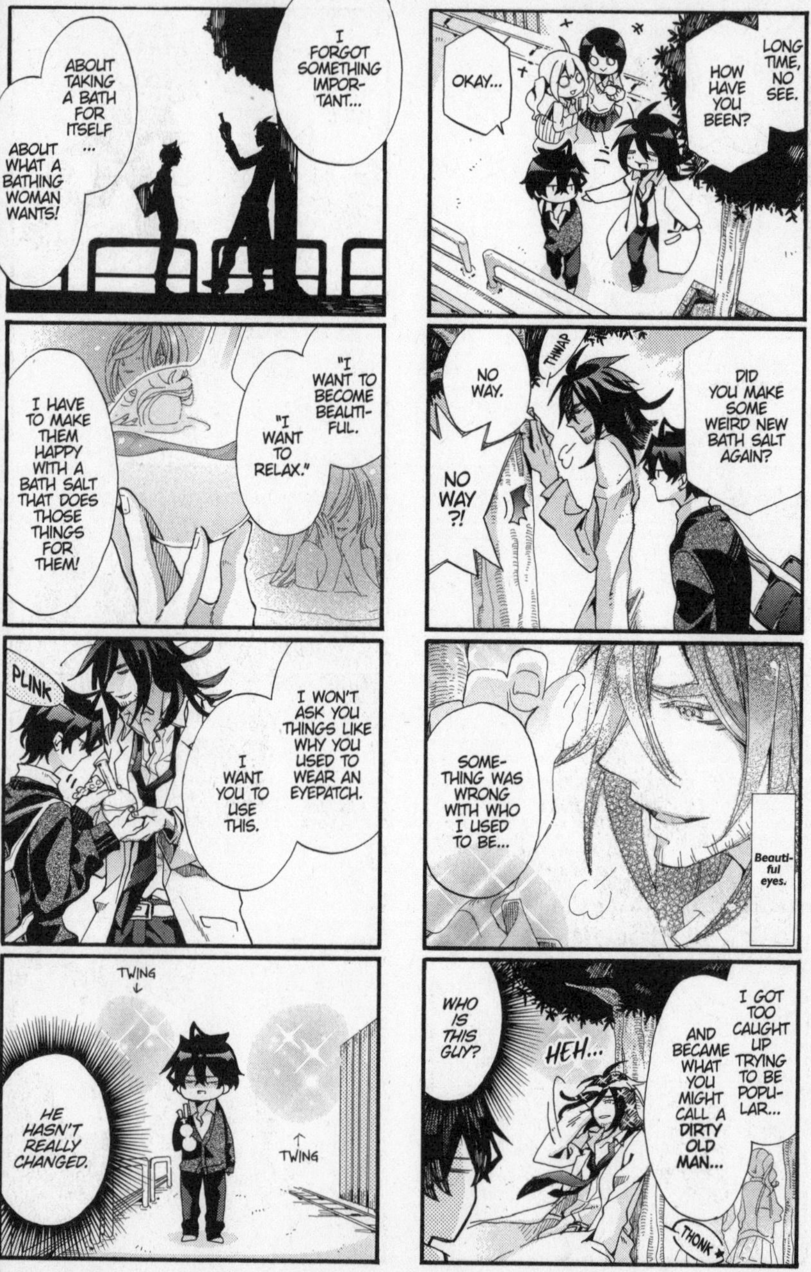
LONG TIME, NO SEE.
HOW HAVE YOU BEEN?
OKAY...
I FORGOT SOMETHING IMPORTANT...
ABOUT TAKING A BATH FOR ITSELF...
ABOUT WHAT A BATHING WOMAN WANTS!
DID YOU MAKE SOME WEIRD NEW BATH SALT AGAIN?
THWAP
NO WAY.
NO WAY?!
"I WANT TO BECOME BEAUTIFUL.
"I WANT TO RELAX."
I HAVE TO MAKE THEM HAPPY WITH A BATH SALT THAT DOES THOSE THINGS FOR THEM!
Beautiful eyes.
SOMETHING WAS WRONG WITH WHO I USED TO BE...
I WON'T ASK YOU THINGS LIKE WHY YOU USED TO WEAR AN EYEPATCH.
I WANT YOU TO USE THIS.
PLINK
I GOT TOO CAUGHT UP TRYING TO BE POPULAR...
AND BECAME WHAT YOU MIGHT CALL A DIRTY OLD MAN...
HEH...
WHO IS THIS GUY?
THONK
TWING
TWING
HE HASN'T REALLY CHANGED.

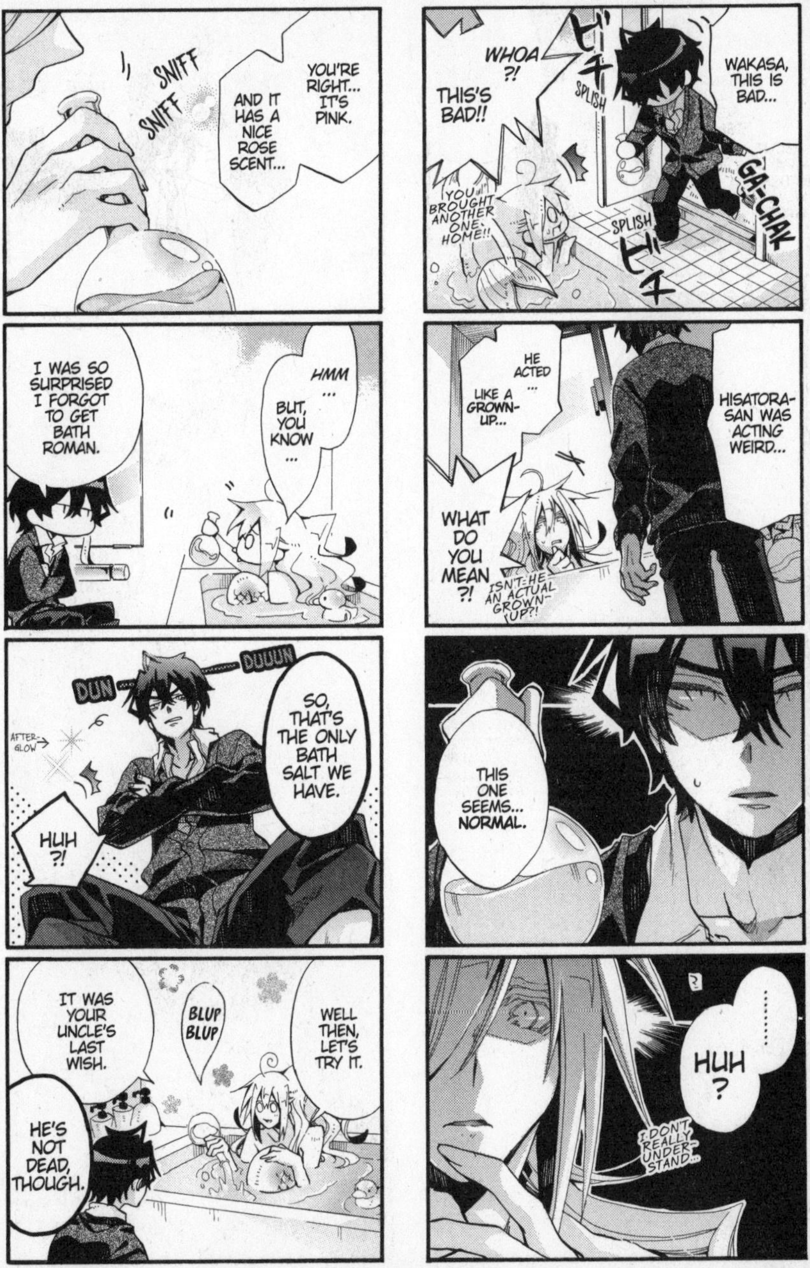
WAKASA, THIS IS BAD...
GA-CHAK
WHOA ?!
THIS'S BAD!!
SPLISH
SPLISH
YOU BROUGHT ANOTHER ONE HOME!!
YOU'RE RIGHT... IT'S PINK.
AND IT HAS A NICE ROSE SCENT...
SNIFF
SNIFF
HISATORA-SAN WAS ACTING WEIRD...
HE ACTED ...
LIKE A GROWN-UP...
WHAT DO YOU MEAN ?!
ISN'T HE AN ACTUAL GROWN-UP?!
HMM ...
BUT, YOU KNOW ...
I WAS SO SURPRISED I FORGOT TO GET BATH ROMAN.
THIS ONE SEEMS... NORMAL.
DUUUN
DUN
SO, THAT'S THE ONLY BATH SALT WE HAVE.
AFTER-GLOW
HUH ?!
......
?
HUH ?
I DON'T REALLY UNDER-STAND...
WELL THEN, LET'S TRY IT.
BLUP BLUP
IT WAS YOUR UNCLE'S LAST WISH.
HE'S NOT DEAD, THOUGH.

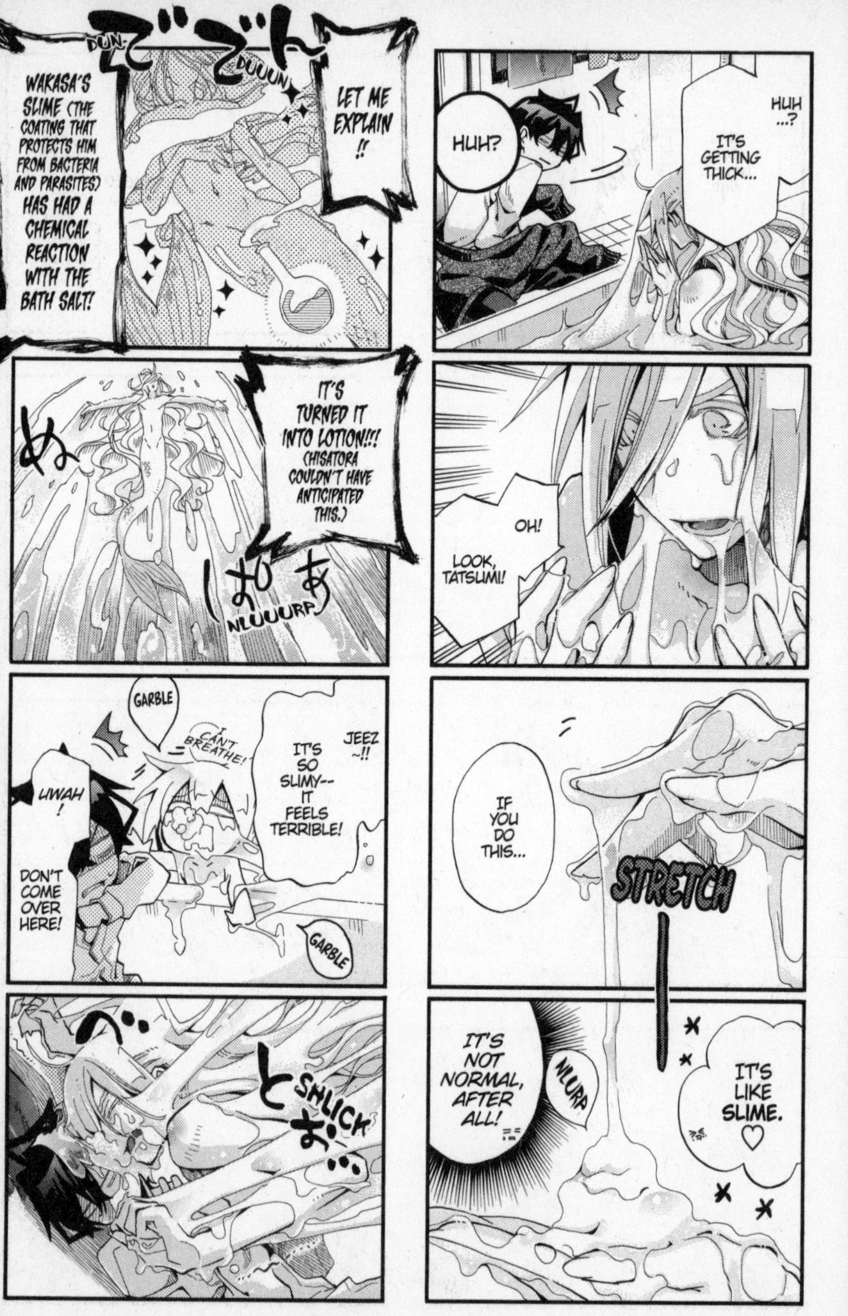
HUH ...?
IT'S GETTING THICK...
HUH?
DUN-
DUUUN
LET ME EXPLAIN!!
WAKASA'S SLIME (THE COATING THAT PROTECTS HIM FROM BACTERIA AND PARASITES) HAS HAD A CHEMICAL REACTION WITH THE BATH SALT!
OH!
LOOK, TATSUMI!
IT'S TURNED IT INTO LOTION!!! (HISATORA COULDN'T HAVE ANTICIPATED THIS.)
NLUUURP
IF YOU DO THIS...
STRETCH
JEEZ~!!
IT'S SO SLIMY-- IT FEELS TERRIBLE!
I CAN'T BREATHE!
GARBLE
UWAH!
DON'T COME OVER HERE!
GARBLE
IT'S LIKE SLIME. ♡
NLURP
IT'S NOT NORMAL, AFTER ALL!
SHLICK

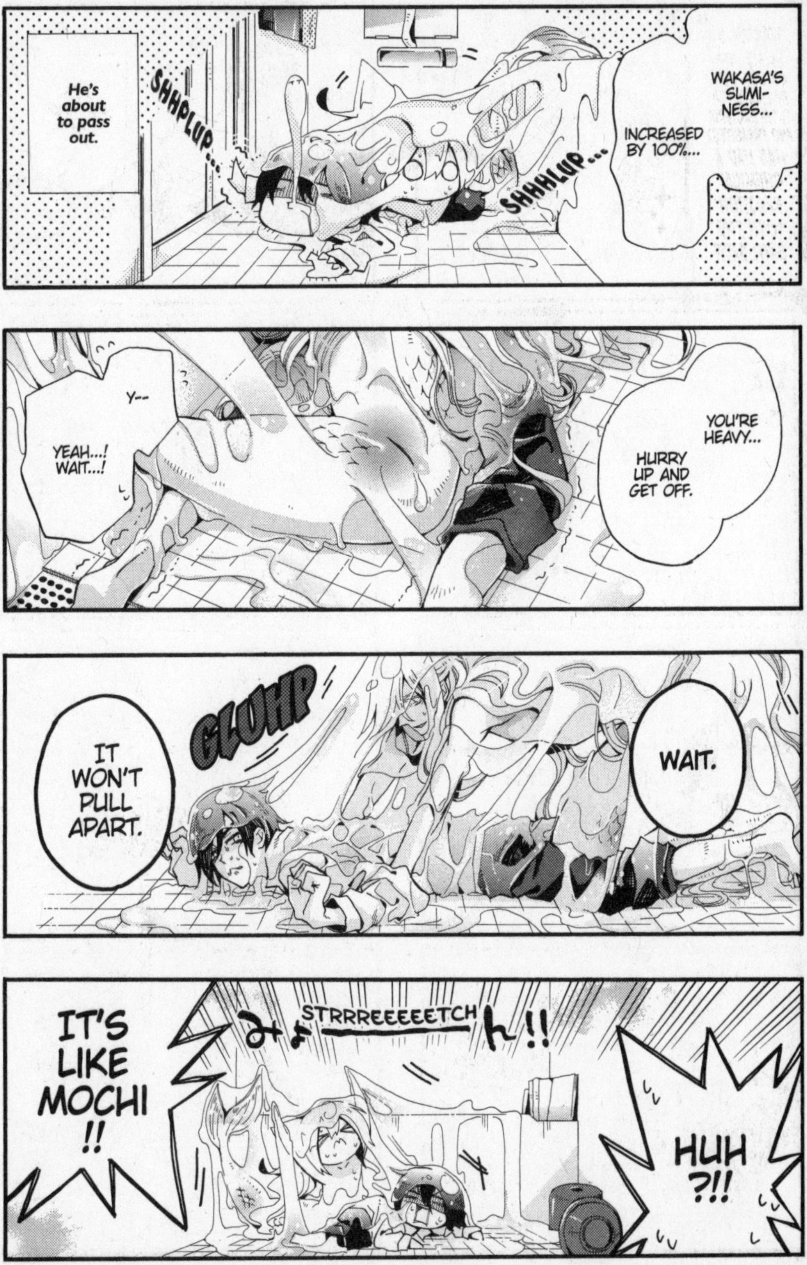
WAKASA'S SLIMI-NESS...
INCREASED BY 100%...
SHHHLUP...
SHHPLUP...
He's about to pass out.
YOU'RE HEAVY...
HURRY UP AND GET OFF.
Y--
YEAH...! WAIT...!
WAIT.
GLUHP
IT WON'T PULL APART.
HUH ?!!
みょ STRRREEEEEETCH ん!!
IT'S LIKE MOCHI !!

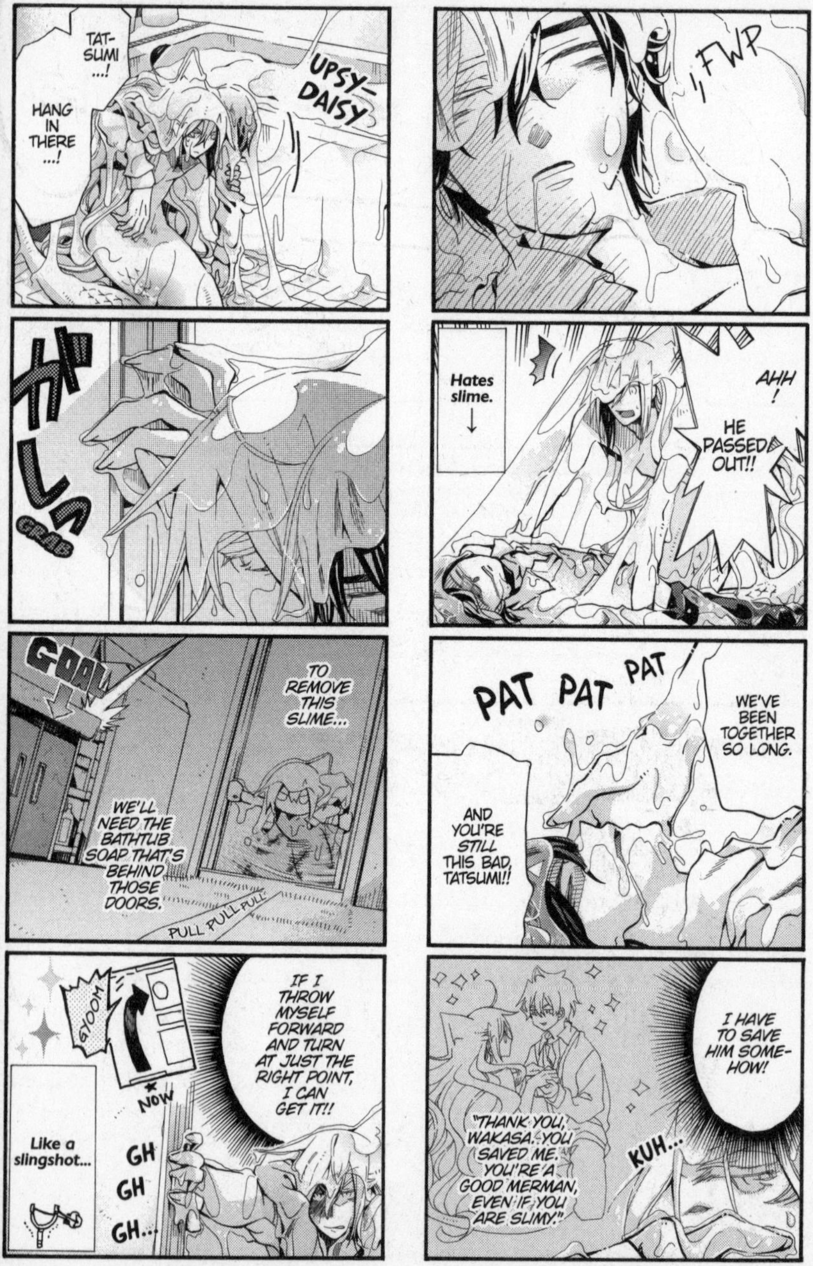

FWP
AHH!
HE PASSED OUT!!
Hates slime.
PAT PAT PAT
WE'VE BEEN TOGETHER SO LONG.
AND YOU'RE STILL THIS BAD, TATSUMI!!
I HAVE TO SAVE HIM SOME-HOW!
"THANK YOU, WAKASA. YOU SAVED ME. YOU'RE A GOOD MERMAN, EVEN IF YOU ARE SLIMY."
KUH...
TAT-SUMI...!
HANG IN THERE...!
UPSY-DAISY
GRAB
GOAL
TO REMOVE THIS SLIME...
WE'LL NEED THE BATHTUB SOAP THAT'S BEHIND THOSE DOORS.
PULL PULL PULL
IF I THROW MYSELF FORWARD AND TURN AT JUST THE RIGHT POINT, I CAN GET IT!!
GYOOM
NOW
Like a slingshot...
GH
GH
GH...

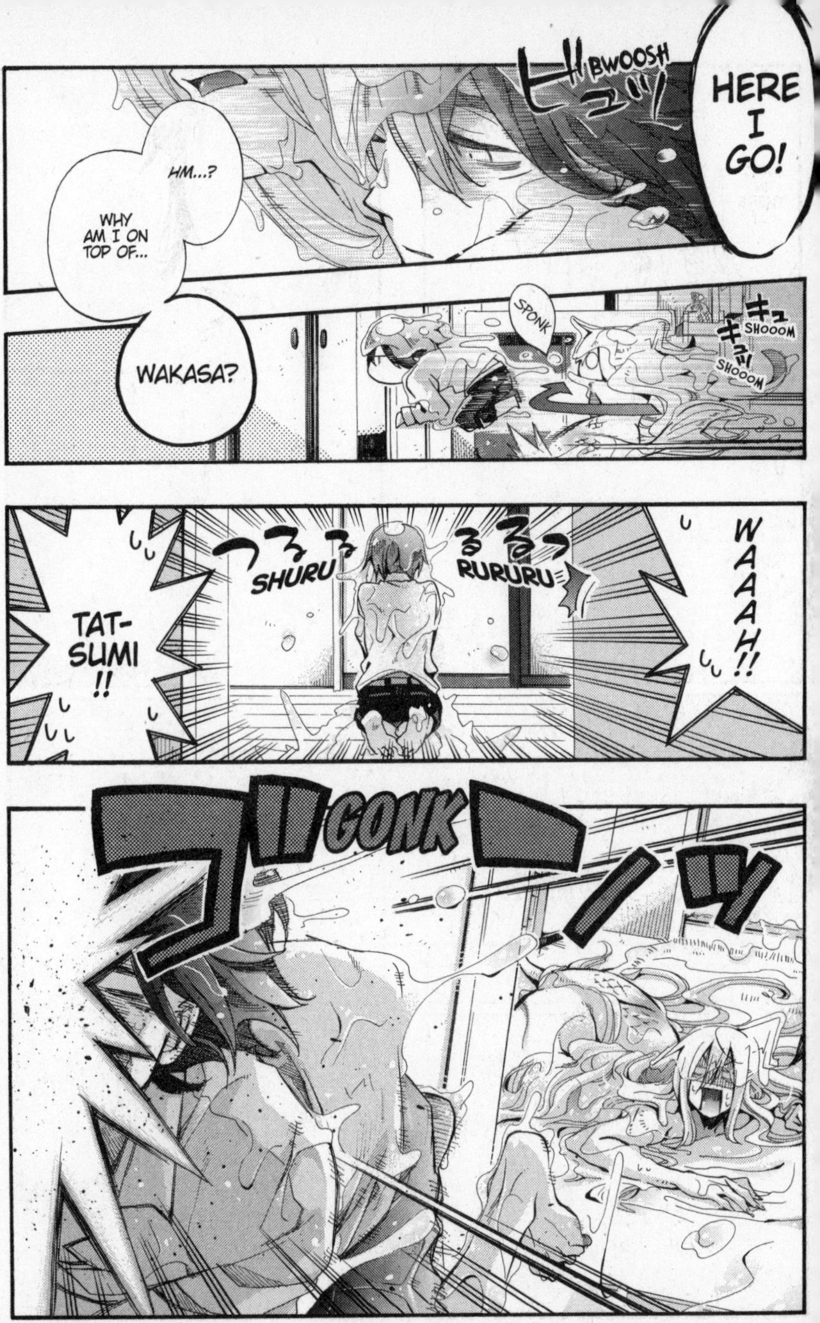
HERE I GO!
BWOOSH
HM...?
WHY AM I ON TOP OF...
WAKASA?
SHOOOM
SHOOOM
SPONK
WAAAAH!!
RURURU
SHURU
TAT-SUMI!!
GONK

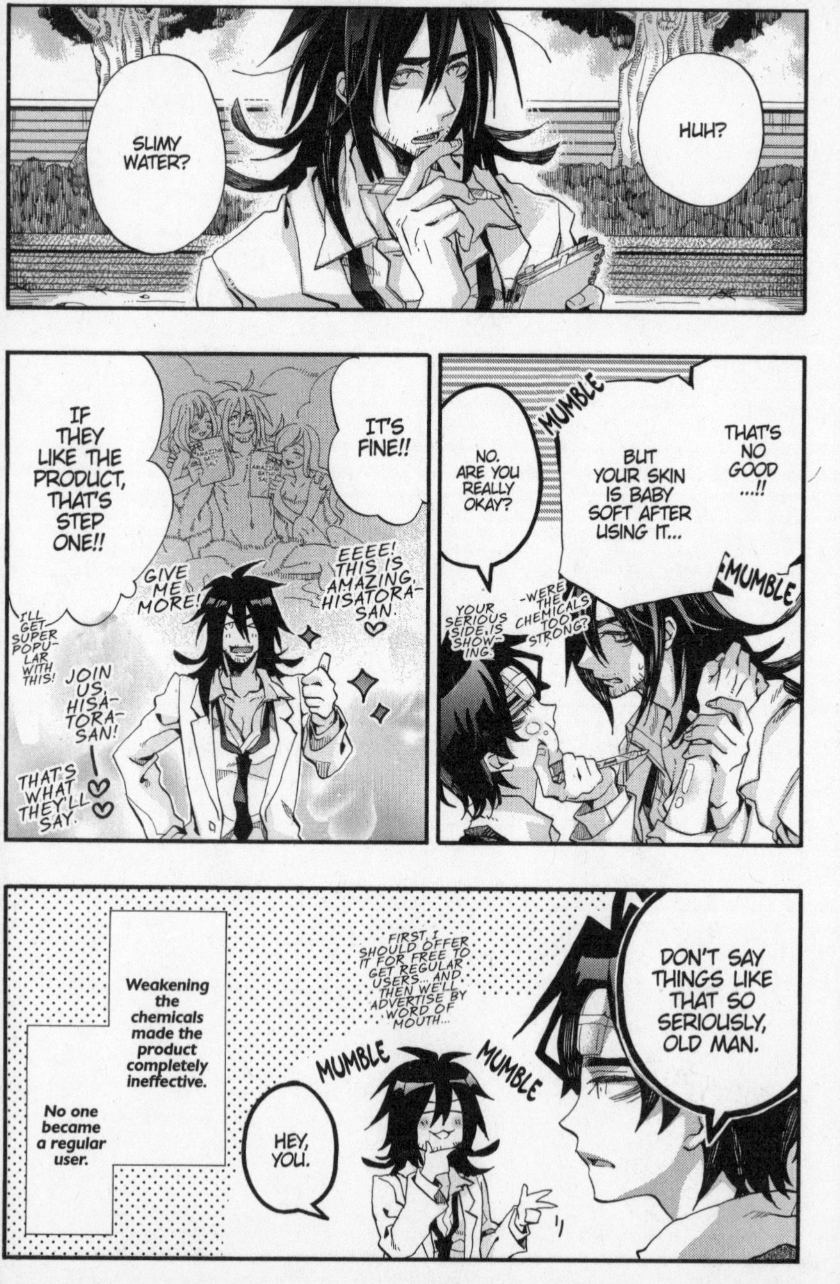
HUH?
SLIMY WATER?
THAT'S NO GOOD ...!!
MUMBLE
BUT YOUR SKIN IS BABY SOFT AFTER USING IT...
MUMBLE
NO. ARE YOU REALLY OKAY?
-WERE THE CHEMICALS TOO STRONG?
YOUR SERIOUS SIDE IS SHOWING.
IT'S FINE!!
IF THEY LIKE THE PRODUCT, THAT'S STEP ONE!!
EEEE! THIS IS AMAZING, HISATORA-SAN ♡
GIVE ME MORE!
I'LL GET SUPER POPULAR WITH THIS!
JOIN US, HISATORA-SAN!
THAT'S WHAT THEY'LL SAY.
DON'T SAY THINGS LIKE THAT SO SERIOUSLY, OLD MAN.
FIRST, I SHOULD OFFER IT FOR FREE TO GET REGULAR USERS... AND THEN WE'LL ADVERTISE BY WORD OF MOUTH...
MUMBLE
MUMBLE
HEY, YOU.
Weakening the chemicals made the product completely ineffective.
No one became a regular user.

To be continued
in Volume 8.

8

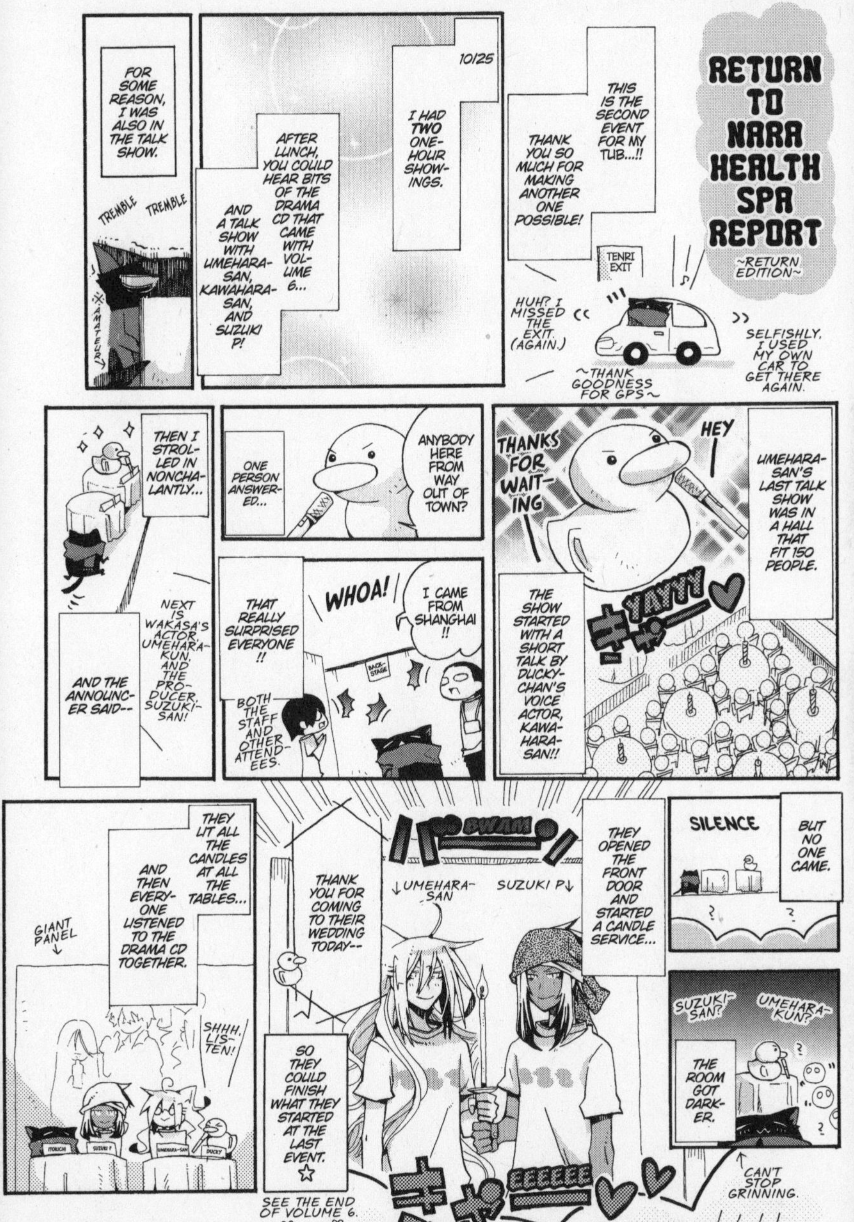
RETURN TO NARA HEALTH SPA REPORT
~RETURN EDITION~
THIS IS THE SECOND EVENT FOR MY TUB...!!
THANK YOU SO MUCH FOR MAKING ANOTHER ONE POSSIBLE!
TENRI EXIT
SELFISHLY, I USED MY OWN CAR TO GET THERE AGAIN.
HUH? I MISSED THE EXIT. (AGAIN.)
~THANK GOODNESS FOR GPS~
10/25
I HAD TWO ONE-HOUR SHOWINGS.
AFTER LUNCH, YOU COULD HEAR BITS OF THE DRAMA CD THAT CAME WITH VOLUME 6...
AND A TALK SHOW WITH UMEHARA-SAN, KAWAHARA-SAN, AND SUZUKI P!
FOR SOME REASON, I WAS ALSO IN THE TALK SHOW.
TREMBLE
TREMBLE
※AMATEUR
UMEHARA-SAN'S LAST TALK SHOW WAS IN A HALL THAT FIT 150 PEOPLE.
HEY
THANKS FOR WAITING
THE SHOW STARTED WITH A SHORT TALK BY DUCKY-CHAN'S VOICE ACTOR, KAWAHARA-SAN!!
YAYYY
ANYBODY HERE FROM WAY OUT OF TOWN?
ONE PERSON ANSWERED...
I CAME FROM SHANGHAI!!
WHOA!
THAT REALLY SURPRISED EVERYONE!!
BACK-STAGE
BOTH THE STAFF AND OTHER ATTENDEES.
THEN I STROLLED IN NONCHALANTLY...
NEXT IS WAKASA'S ACTOR, UMEHARA-KUN, AND THE PRODUCER, SUZUKI-SAN!
AND THE ANNOUNCER SAID--
BUT NO ONE CAME.
SILENCE
UMEHARA-KUN?
SUZUKI-SAN?
THE ROOM GOT DARKER.
CAN'T STOP GRINNING.
THEY OPENED THE FRONT DOOR AND STARTED A CANDLE SERVICE...
BWAM
SUZUKI P↓
↓UMEHARA-SAN
THANK YOU FOR COMING TO THEIR WEDDING TODAY--
SO THEY COULD FINISH WHAT THEY STARTED AT THE LAST EVENT. ☆
EEEEEE
SEE THE END OF VOLUME 6.
THEY LIT ALL THE CANDLES AT ALL THE TABLES...
AND THEN EVERYONE LISTENED TO THE DRAMA CD TOGETHER.
GIANT PANEL
SHHH, LISTEN!

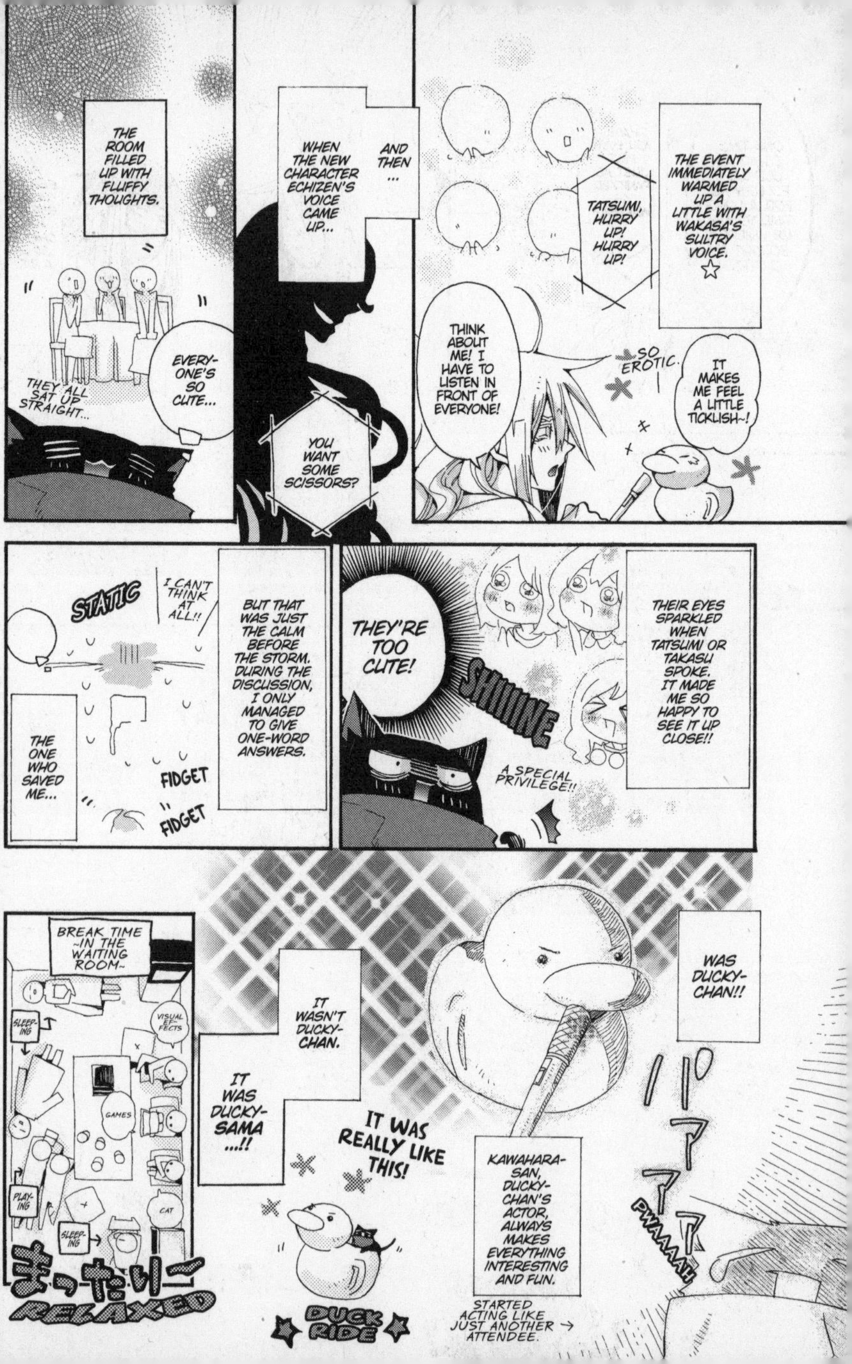
THE EVENT IMMEDIATELY WARMED UP A LITTLE WITH WAKASA'S SULTRY VOICE. ☆
TATSUMI, HURRY UP! HURRY UP!
THINK ABOUT ME! I HAVE TO LISTEN IN FRONT OF EVERYONE!
SO EROTIC.
IT MAKES ME FEEL A LITTLE TICKLISH~!
AND THEN ...
WHEN THE NEW CHARACTER ECHIZEN'S VOICE CAME UP...
YOU WANT SOME SCISSORS?
THE ROOM FILLED UP WITH FLUFFY THOUGHTS.
EVERYONE'S SO CUTE...
THEY ALL SAT UP STRAIGHT...
THEIR EYES SPARKLED WHEN TATSUMI OR TAKASU SPOKE. IT MADE ME SO HAPPY TO SEE IT UP CLOSE!!
THEY'RE TOO CUTE!
SHIIINE
A SPECIAL PRIVILEGE!!
BUT THAT WAS JUST THE CALM BEFORE THE STORM. DURING THE DISCUSSION, I ONLY MANAGED TO GIVE ONE-WORD ANSWERS.
I CAN'T THINK AT ALL!!
STATIC
THE ONE WHO SAVED ME...
FIDGET
FIDGET
WAS DUCKY-CHAN!!
PWAAAAH
KAWAHARA-SAN, DUCKY-CHAN'S ACTOR, ALWAYS MAKES EVERYTHING INTERESTING AND FUN.
STARTED ACTING LIKE JUST ANOTHER ATTENDEE. →
IT WASN'T DUCKY-CHAN.
IT WAS DUCKY-SAMA ...!!
IT WAS REALLY LIKE THIS!
DUCK RIDE
BREAK TIME ~IN THE WAITING ROOM~
SLEEP-ING
VISUAL EF-FECTS
GAMES
PLAY-ING
CAT
SLEEP-ING
まったりー
RELAXED

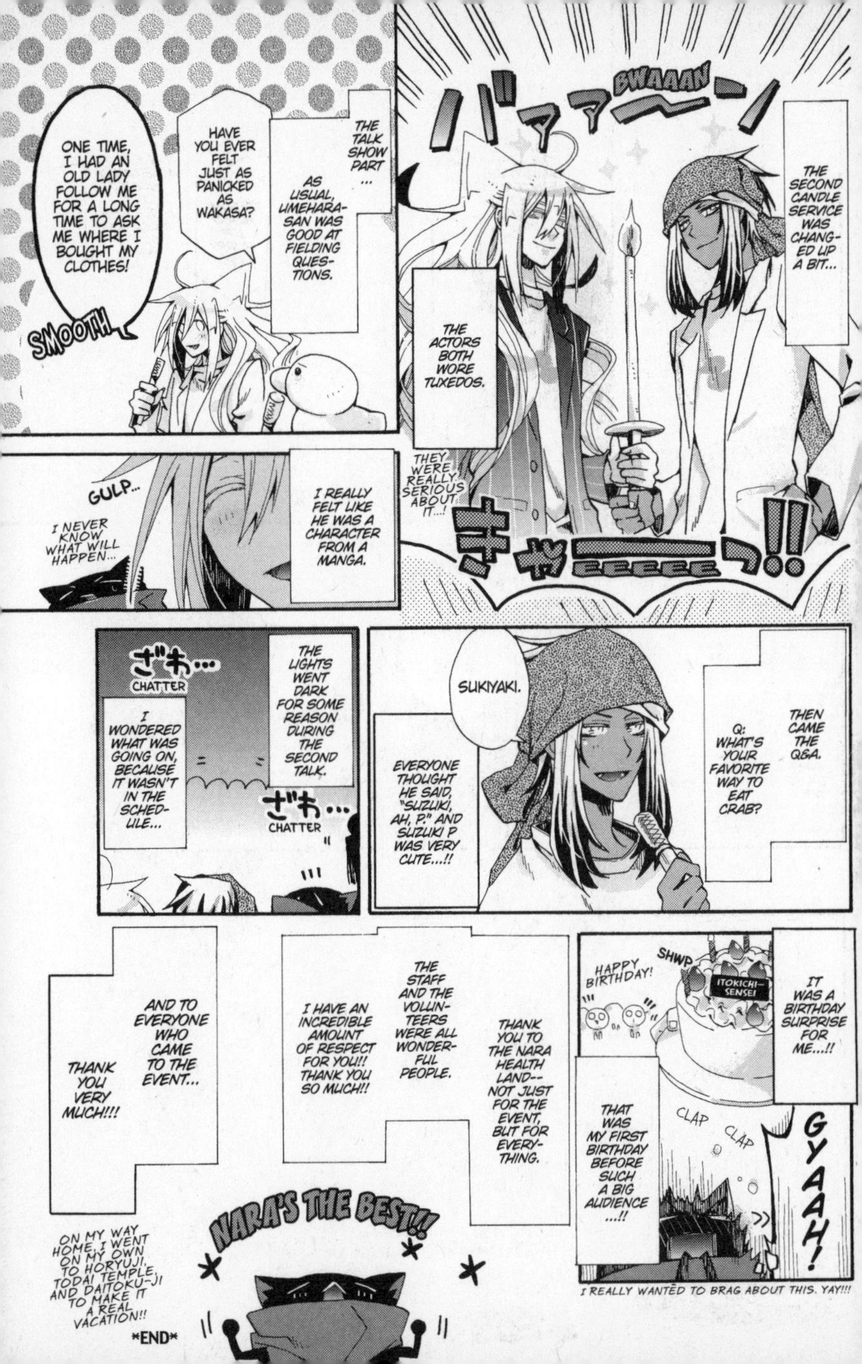

THE SECOND CANDLE SERVICE WAS CHANGED UP A BIT...
BWAAAN
THE ACTORS BOTH WORE TUXEDOS.
THEY WERE REALLY SERIOUS ABOUT IT...!
EEEEE
THE TALK SHOW PART...
AS USUAL, UMEHARA-SAN WAS GOOD AT FIELDING QUESTIONS.
HAVE YOU EVER FELT JUST AS PANICKED AS WAKASA?
ONE TIME, I HAD AN OLD LADY FOLLOW ME FOR A LONG TIME TO ASK ME WHERE I BOUGHT MY CLOTHES!
SMOOTH
I REALLY FELT LIKE HE WAS A CHARACTER FROM A MANGA.
GULP...
I NEVER KNOW WHAT WILL HAPPEN...
THEN CAME THE Q&A.
Q: WHAT'S YOUR FAVORITE WAY TO EAT CRAB?
SUKIYAKI.
EVERYONE THOUGHT HE SAID, "SUZUKI, AH, P." AND SUZUKI P WAS VERY CUTE...!!
THE LIGHTS WENT DARK FOR SOME REASON DURING THE SECOND TALK.
ざわ…
CHATTER
I WONDERED WHAT WAS GOING ON, BECAUSE IT WASN'T IN THE SCHEDULE...
ざわ…
CHATTER
IT WAS A BIRTHDAY SURPRISE FOR ME...!!
SHWP
HAPPY BIRTHDAY!
ITOKICHI-SENSEI
CLAP
CLAP
GYAAH!
THAT WAS MY FIRST BIRTHDAY BEFORE SUCH A BIG AUDIENCE...!!
I REALLY WANTED TO BRAG ABOUT THIS. YAY!!!
THANK YOU TO THE NARA HEALTH LAND-- NOT JUST FOR THE EVENT, BUT FOR EVERYTHING.
THE STAFF AND THE VOLUNTEERS WERE ALL WONDERFUL PEOPLE.
I HAVE AN INCREDIBLE AMOUNT OF RESPECT FOR YOU!! THANK YOU SO MUCH!!
AND TO EVERYONE WHO CAME TO THE EVENT...
THANK YOU VERY MUCH!!!
NARA'S THE BEST!!
ON MY WAY HOME, I WENT ON MY OWN TO HORYUJI, TODAI TEMPLE AND DAITOKU-JI TO MAKE IT A REAL VACATION!!
END

THE BACKGROUND CIRCUMSTANCES OF MY HOUSE SPECIAL

HERE WE WILL SHOW YOU VARIOUS ILLUSTRATIONS AND QUESTIONS WE'VE RECEIVED AFTER ASKING FOR THEM IN VOLUME 6!!

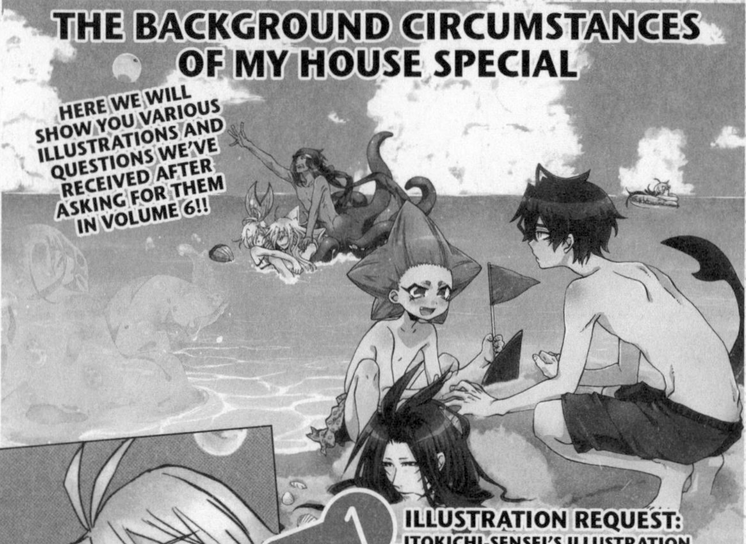

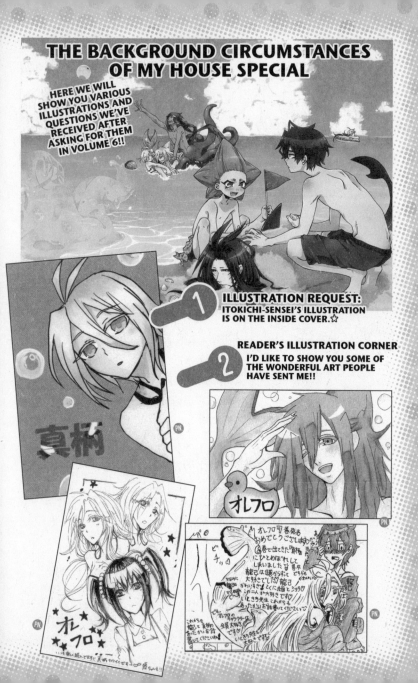

1 ILLUSTRATION REQUEST:
ITOKICHI-SENSEI'S ILLUSTRATION IS ON THE INSIDE COVER.☆

2 READER'S ILLUSTRATION CORNER
I'D LIKE TO SHOW YOU SOME OF THE WONDERFUL ART PEOPLE HAVE SENT ME!!

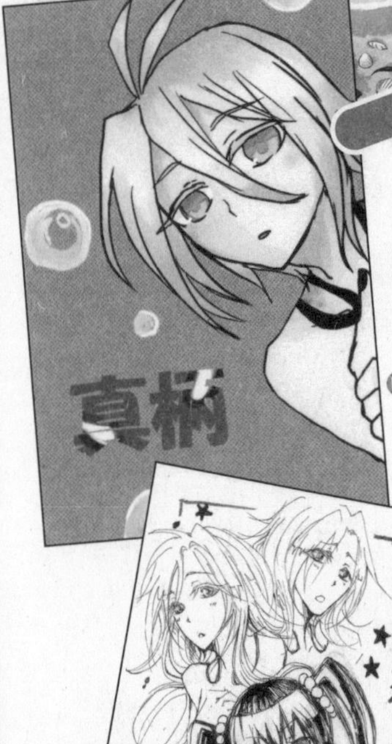
真柄
PN.

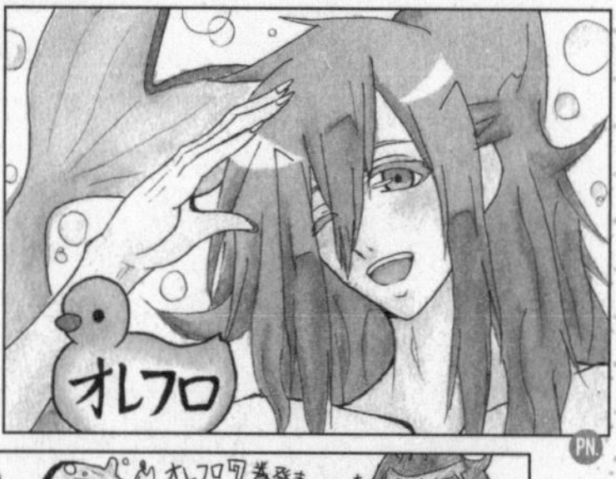
オレフロ
PN.

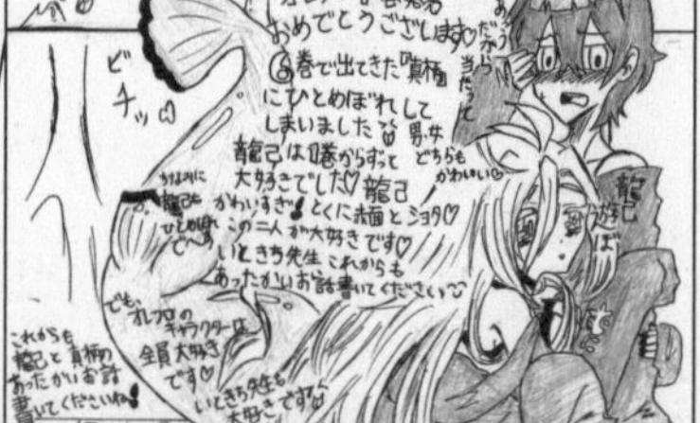
オレフロ7巻発売おめでとうございます♡
6巻で出てきた『真柄』にひとめぼれしてしまいました
龍己は1巻からずっと大好きでした♡
ビチッ
PN.

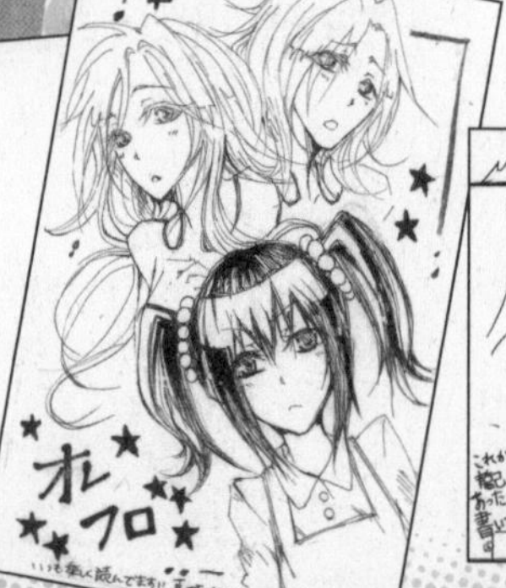
オレフロ
PN.

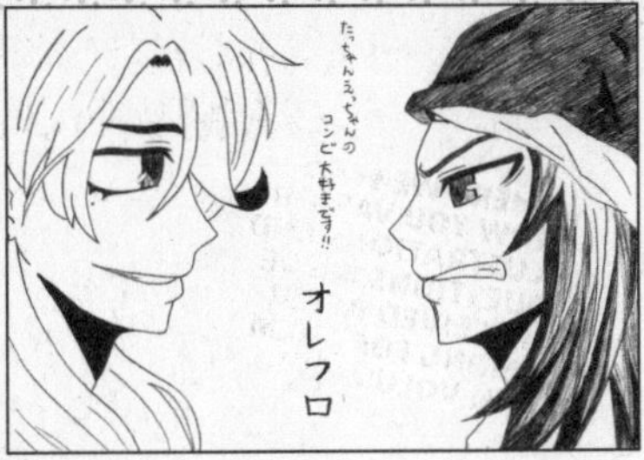
たっちゃんえっちゃんの
コンビ大好きです!!
オレフロ

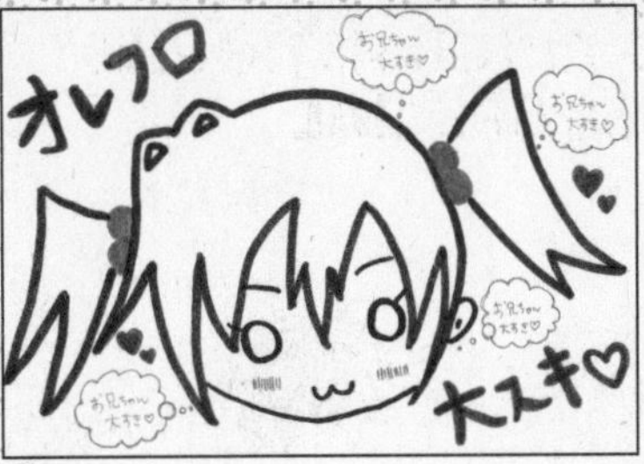
オレフロ
お兄ちゃん大好き♡
お兄ちゃん大好き♡
お兄ちゃん大好き♡
お兄ちゃん大好き♡
大スキ♡

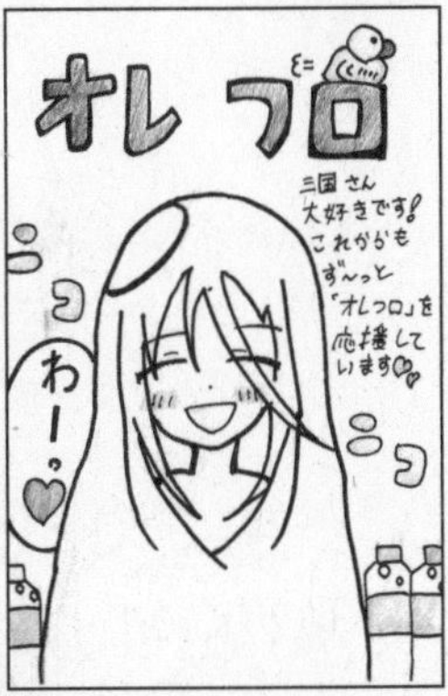
オレ フロ
三国さん
大好きです!
これからも
ず～っと
「オレフロ」を
応援して
います♡
わー!

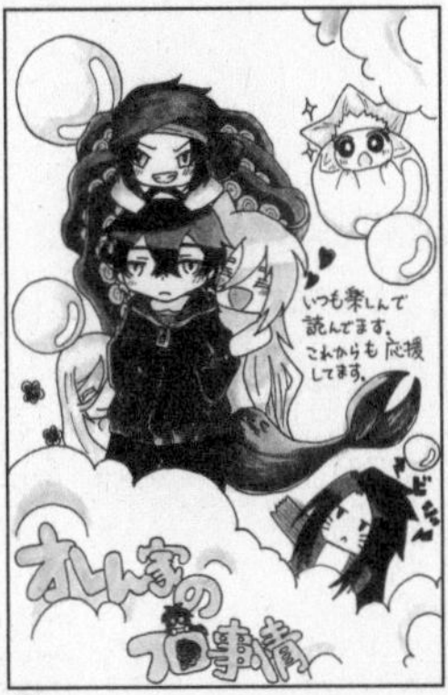
いつも楽しんで
読んでます。
これからも応援
してます。
オレん家のフロ事情

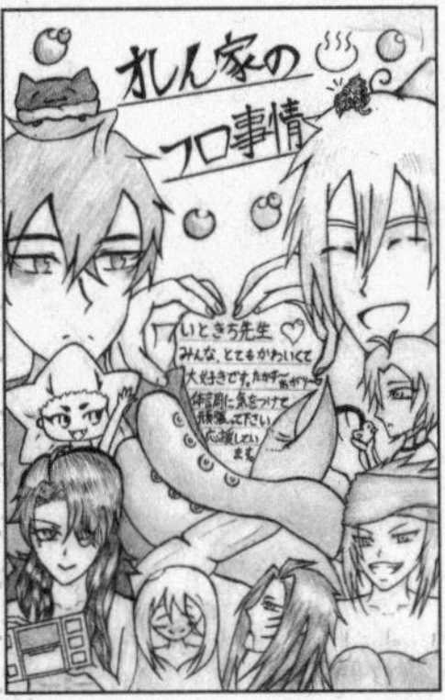
オレん家の
フロ事情
いときち先生♡
みんな、とてもかわいくて
大好きです。
体調に気をつけて
頑張って下さい
応援しています。

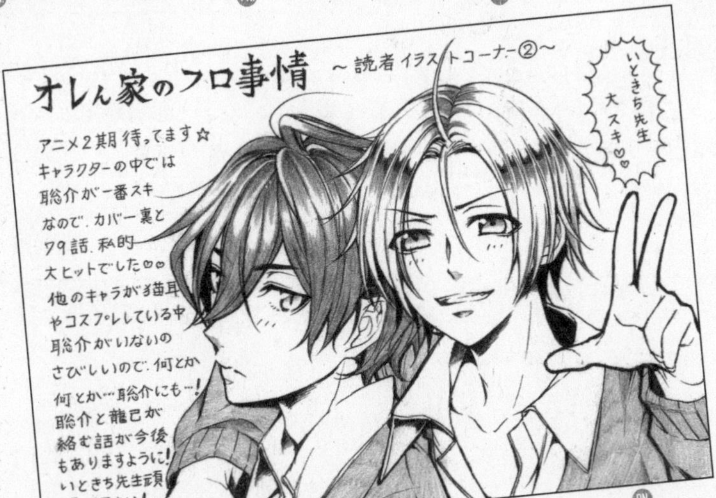
オレん家のフロ事情
～読者イラストコーナー②～
いときち先生
大スキ♡
アニメ2期待ってます☆
キャラクターの中では
聡介が一番スキ
なので、カバー裏と
79話、私的
大ヒットでした♡
他のキャラが猫耳
やコスプレしている中
聡介がいないの
さびしいので、何とか
何とか…聡介にも…!
聡介と龍己が
絡む話が今後
もありますように!
いときち先生頑
張って下さい!

REQUEST 3

QUESTIONS CORNER

ITOKICHI-SENSEI WILL ANSWER EVERYONE'S QUESTIONS!♪

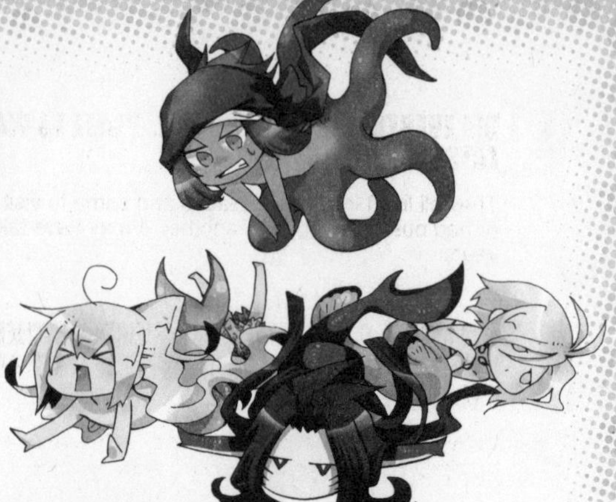

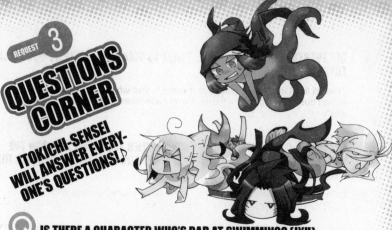

IS THERE A CHARACTER WHO'S BAD AT SWIMMING? (JYU)

Maki and Tatsumi. Maki looks like he's swimming, but he's just being pushed around by the current. He moves by attaching himself to something first. Tatsumi almost drowned that one time and doesn't like swimming.

WHO ARE THE EASIEST AND HARDEST CHARACTERS FOR YOU TO DRAW? (JYU)

Tatsumi's easy for me. Probably because of how much I draw him. The hardest for me is Makara. He's somewhere between a child and an adult. I feel like I end up being pulled one way or the other when I draw him.

MIKUNI-SAN'S A BOY, RIGHT...? WHEN I READ CHAPTER SIX I WENT, "HUH?" AND GOT A LITTLE CONFUSED. PLEASE TELL ME!! (ICHIHA)

Why were you confused...? His chest's completely flat. Though his crotch is flat as well. I can't really say "He's a guy!" definitively. He's technically neither sex. I-I mean, his voice was super cute in the anime. That's all.

DOES ECHIZEN'S NAME COME FROM "ECHIZEN CRAB"? PLEASE TELL ME HOW THE OTHER CHARACTERS GOT THEIR NAMES, AS WELL. (ICHIHA)

Echizen's name *does* come from the crab. Delicious, aren't they? "Wakasa" came from a land in the Yao Bikuni. "Takasu" came from the word "tacos." "Mikuni" came from a land that had a giant jellyfish problem, "Maki" came from spiral shells, "Agari" came from the word for "stage fright," and I chose "Goromaru" ["five"] because there are five points to a starfish. Makara is "Makara" because he has designs on his body... They're all puns! :-D By the way, Tatsumi's name comes from the Kuzuryu river, so he's not completely left out either.

DID EVERYONE LIVE IN THE SAME PLACE AS WAKASA BEFORE HE LIVED WITH TATSUMI? (ICHIHA)

They all lived in different places and came to visit when they wanted to play or had business with one another. It may have taken them a day or ten years.

IN VOLUME 6, TATSUMI AND WAKASA STUDIED TOGETHER, BUT CAN THE OTHER CHARACTERS NOT DO MATH, EITHER? OR IS IT THAT WAKASA'S JUST BAD AT IT? (ICHIHA)

Unfortunately, it's the former. It may be because everyone plays around too much. But they're just a little bad at it... A...little...

WHERE WERE WAKASA, TAKASU, AND MIKUNI-SAN BORN? HOW OLD ARE THEY? (ICHIHA)

Everyone was born in the sea. We don't know the exact dates. They aren't sure of their age themselves, so I can only give you the order...
Agari >> Wakasa >>> Mikuni > Takasu > Echizen >> Maki > Makara > Goromaru

WAKASA'S HEAVY, SO DOES THAT MEAN THAT TATSUMI'S REALLY STRONG SINCE HE CAN PIGGYBACK HIM AND CARRY HIM LIKE A PRINCESS? IS IT BECAUSE OF THE STRENGTH TRAINING HE DOES AT HIS PART-TIME JOB? (HYUGA)

You're right. Beer cases are really heavy, so he trains a lot and is really strong.

WILL THERE BE A SECOND SEASON OF THE ANIME? I WANT TO SEE AGARI-SENPAI MOVING!! I'D LIKE TO SEE SOUSUKE-KUN, AS WELL. (HYUGA)

I want to see them, too! But I really don't know the answer to this question! *Tee he*

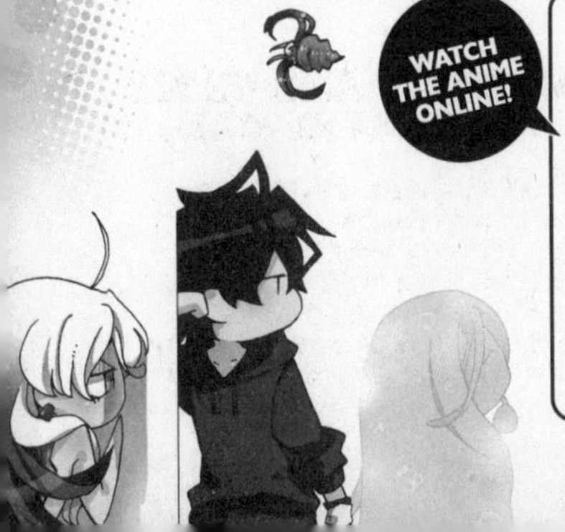
WATCH THE ANIME ONLINE!

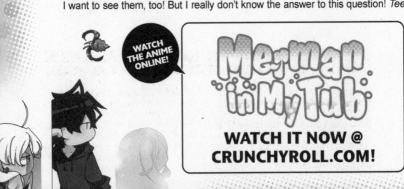

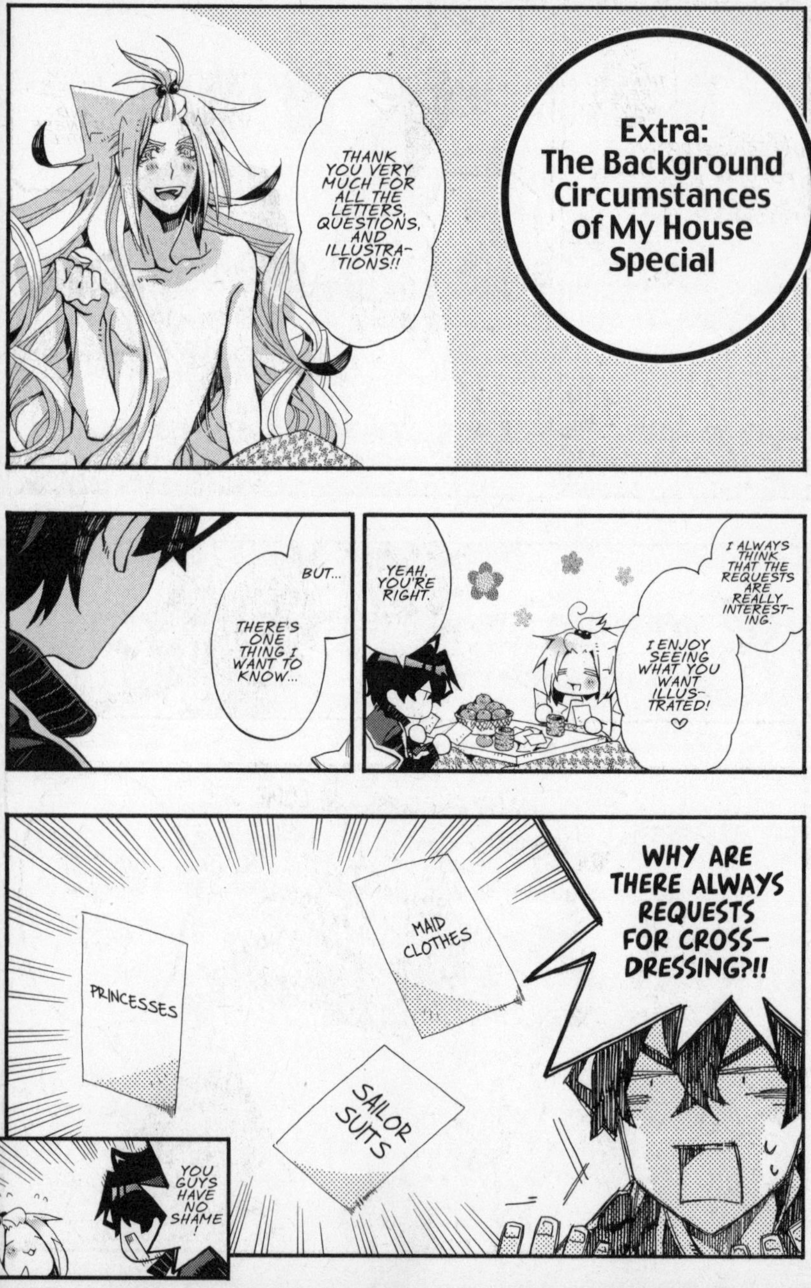
Extra: The Background Circumstances of My House Special
THANK YOU VERY MUCH FOR ALL THE LETTERS, QUESTIONS, AND ILLUSTRATIONS!!
I ALWAYS THINK THAT THE REQUESTS ARE REALLY INTERESTING.
I ENJOY SEEING WHAT YOU WANT ILLUSTRATED! ♡
YEAH, YOU'RE RIGHT.
BUT...
THERE'S ONE THING I WANT TO KNOW...
WHY ARE THERE ALWAYS REQUESTS FOR CROSS-DRESSING?!!
MAID CLOTHES
PRINCESSES
SAILOR SUITS
YOU GUYS HAVE NO SHAME!

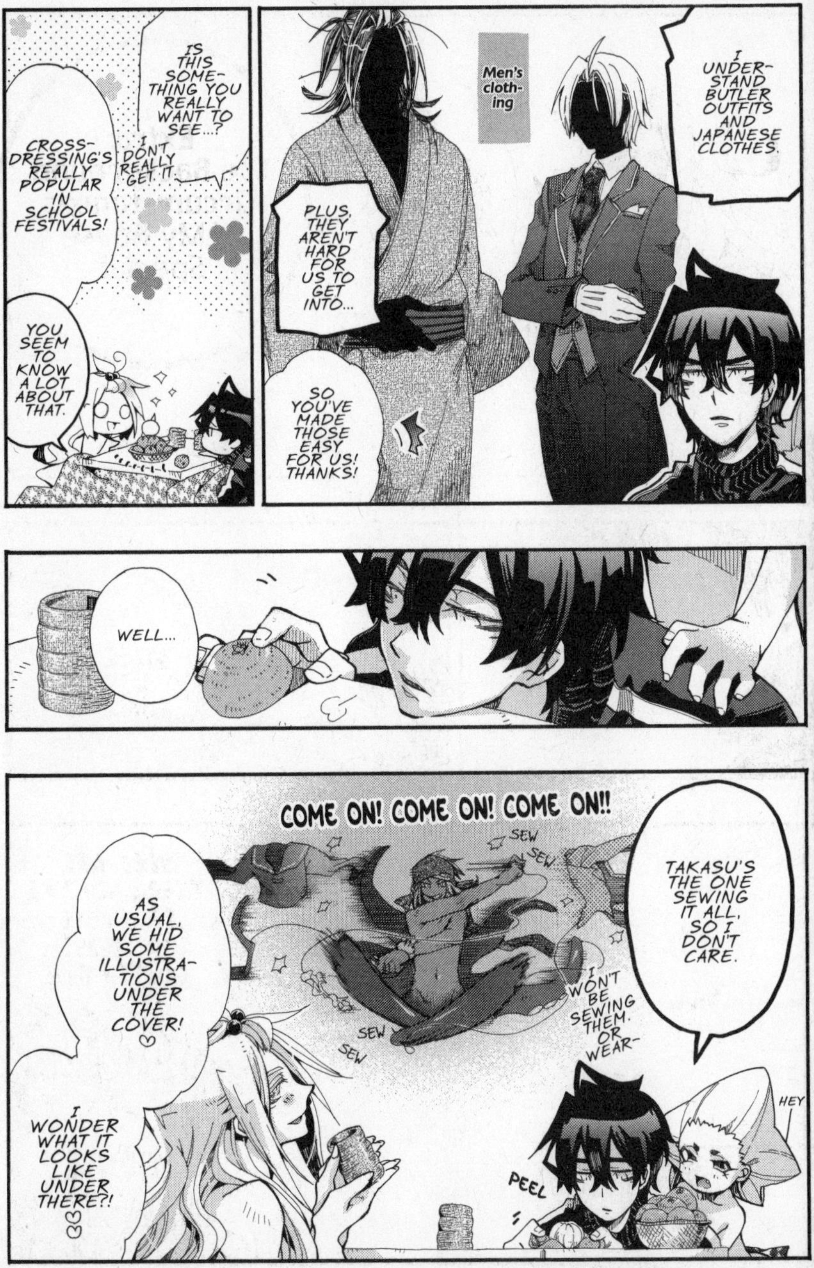
I UNDERSTAND BUTLER OUTFITS AND JAPANESE CLOTHES.
Men's clothing
PLUS, THEY AREN'T HARD FOR US TO GET INTO...
SO YOU'VE MADE THOSE EASY FOR US! THANKS!
IS THIS SOMETHING YOU REALLY WANT TO SEE...?
I DON'T REALLY GET IT.
CROSS-DRESSING'S REALLY POPULAR IN SCHOOL FESTIVALS!
YOU SEEM TO KNOW A LOT ABOUT THAT.
WELL...
COME ON! COME ON! COME ON!!
TAKASU'S THE ONE SEWING IT ALL, SO I DON'T CARE.
SEW SEW
I WON'T BE SEWING THEM. OR WEAR-
HEY
AS USUAL, WE HID SOME ILLUSTRATIONS UNDER THE COVER! ♡
SEW SEW
I WONDER WHAT IT LOOKS LIKE UNDER THERE?! ♡
PEEL

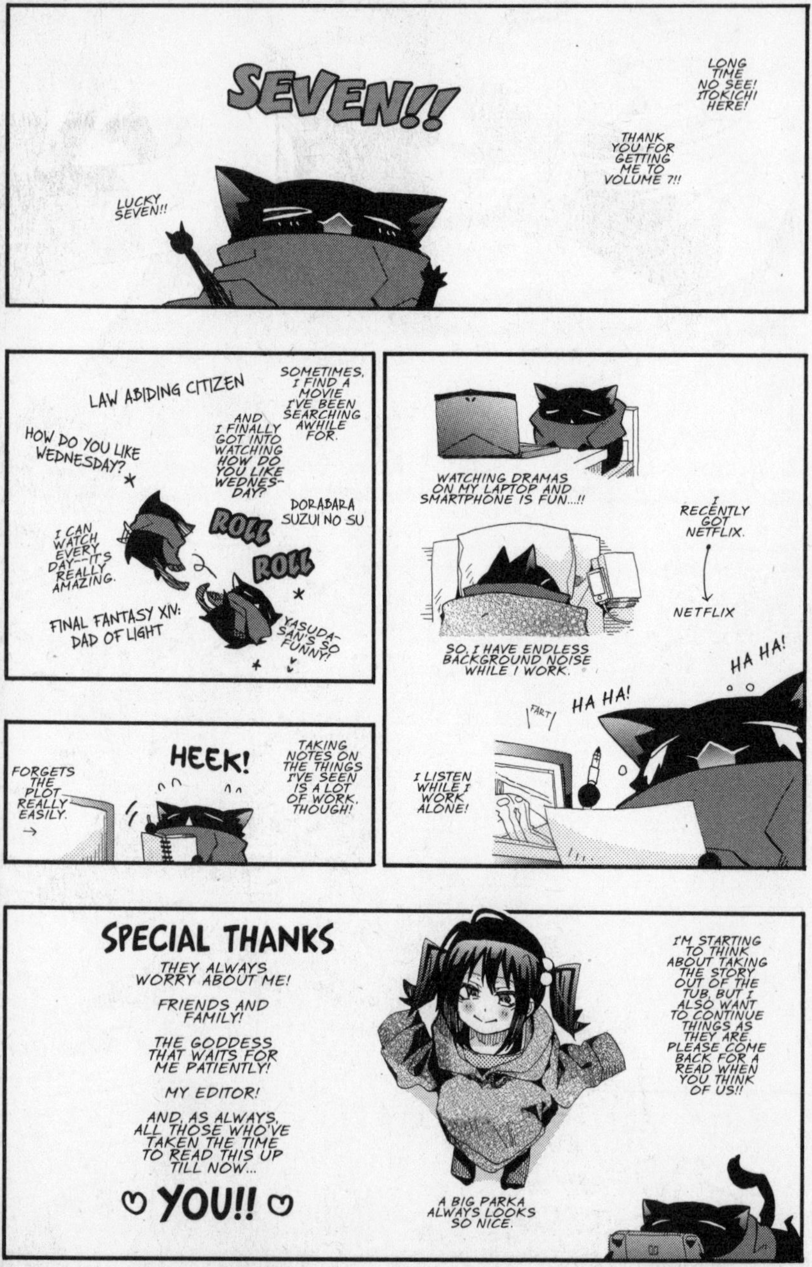
LONG TIME NO SEE! ITOKICHI HERE!
THANK YOU FOR GETTING ME TO VOLUME 7!!
SEVEN!!
LUCKY SEVEN!!
WATCHING DRAMAS ON MY LAPTOP AND SMARTPHONE IS FUN...!!
I RECENTLY GOT NETFLIX.
NETFLIX
SO, I HAVE ENDLESS BACKGROUND NOISE WHILE I WORK.
HA HA!
HA HA!
FART
I LISTEN WHILE I WORK ALONE!
SOMETIMES, I FIND A MOVIE I'VE BEEN SEARCHING AWHILE FOR.
LAW ABIDING CITIZEN
AND I FINALLY GOT INTO WATCHING HOW DO YOU LIKE WEDNES-DAY?
HOW DO YOU LIKE WEDNESDAY?
DORABARA SUZUI NO SU
ROLL
ROLL
I CAN WATCH EVERY DAY--IT'S REALLY AMAZING.
YASUDA-SAN'S SO FUNNY!
FINAL FANTASY XIV: DAD OF LIGHT
TAKING NOTES ON THE THINGS I'VE SEEN IS A LOT OF WORK, THOUGH!
HEEK!
FORGETS THE PLOT REALLY EASILY.
I'M STARTING TO THINK ABOUT TAKING THE STORY OUT OF THE TUB, BUT I ALSO WANT TO CONTINUE THINGS AS THEY ARE. PLEASE COME BACK FOR A READ WHEN YOU THINK OF US!!
SPECIAL THANKS
THEY ALWAYS WORRY ABOUT ME!
FRIENDS AND FAMILY!
THE GODDESS THAT WAITS FOR ME PATIENTLY!
MY EDITOR!
AND, AS ALWAYS, ALL THOSE WHO'VE TAKEN THE TIME TO READ THIS UP TILL NOW...
YOU!!
A BIG PARKA ALWAYS LOOKS SO NICE.

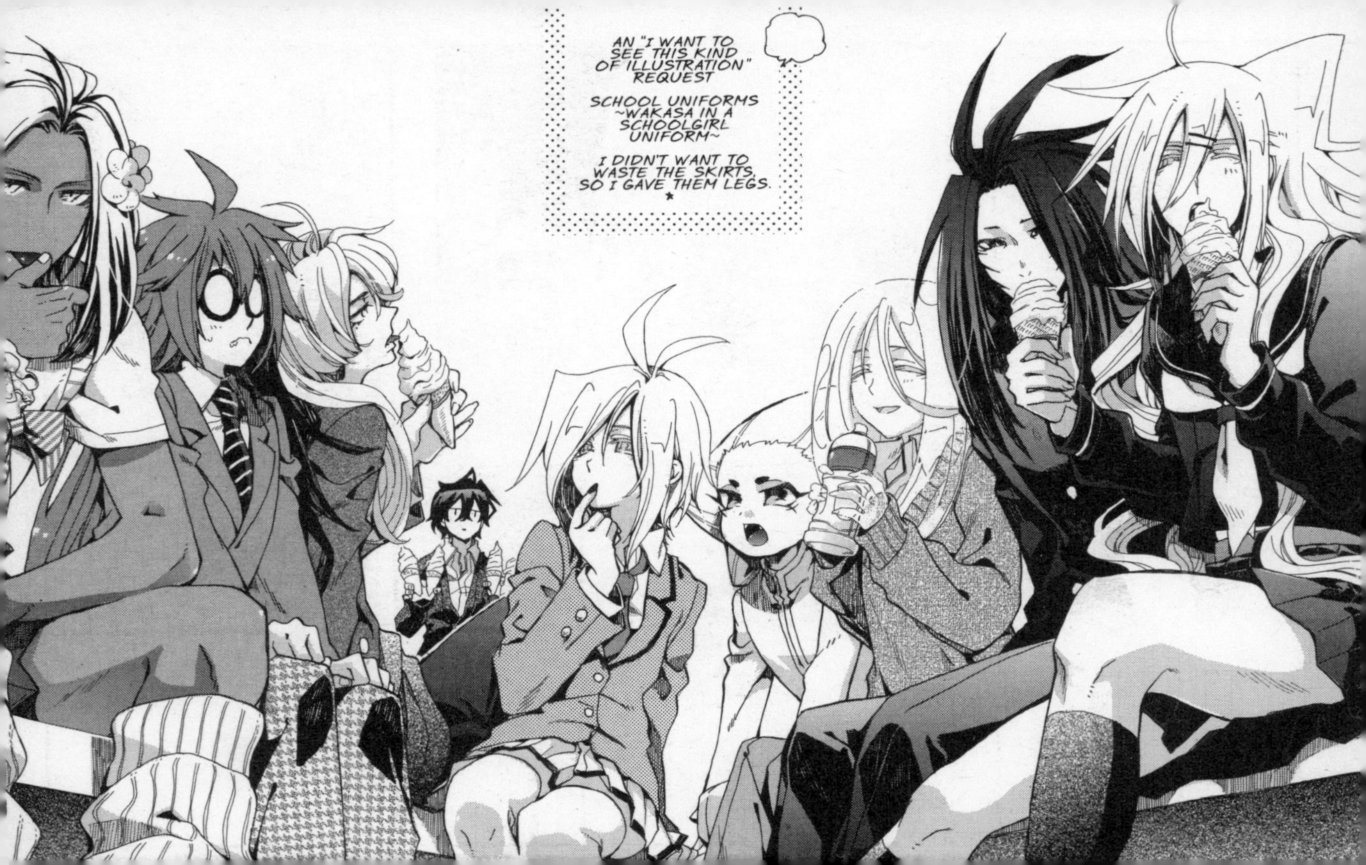
AN "I WANT TO SEE THIS KIND OF ILLUSTRATION" REQUEST
SCHOOL UNIFORMS ~WAKASA IN A SCHOOLGIRL UNIFORM~
I DIDN'T WANT TO WASTE THE SKIRTS, SO I GAVE THEM LEGS. ★

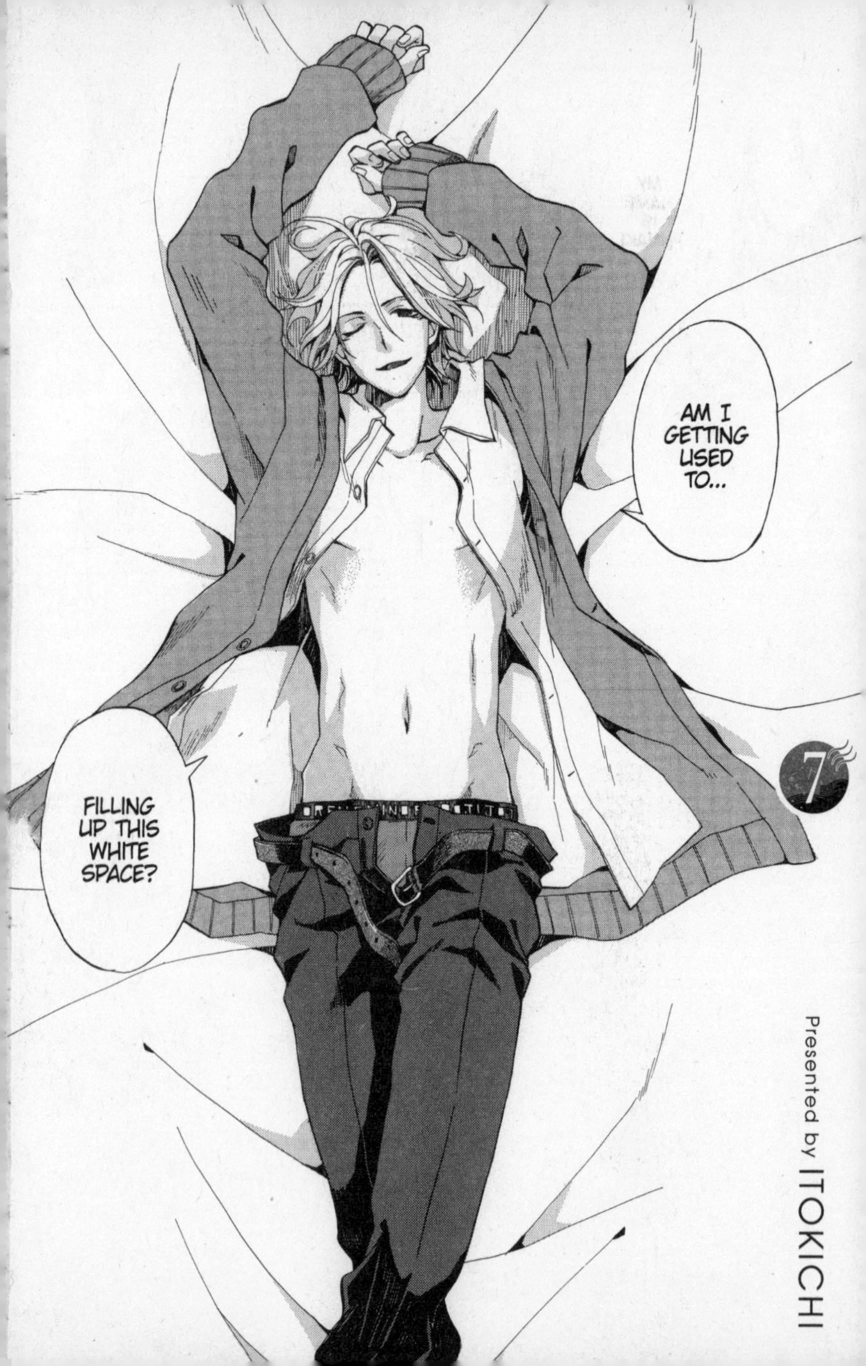
AM I GETTING USED TO...
FILLING UP THIS WHITE SPACE?
7
Presented by ITOKICHI